SCATTERSHOT

SCATTERSHOT

MY BIPOLAR FAMILY

A MEMOIR

DAVID LOVELACE

DUTTON

DUTTON
Published by Penguin Group (USA) Inc.
375 Hudson Street, New York, New York 10014, U.S.A.
Penguin Group (Canada), 90 Eglinton Avenue East, Suite 700, Toronto, Ontario M4P
2Y3, Canada (a division of Pearson Penguin Canada Inc.); Penguin Books Ltd, 80
Strand, London WC2R 0RL, England; Penguin Ireland, 25 St Stephen's Green, Dublin 2,
Ireland (a division of Penguin Books Ltd); Penguin Group (Australia), 250 Camberwell
Road, Camberwell, Victoria 3124, Australia (a division of Pearson Australia Group
Pty Ltd); Penguin Books India Pvt Ltd, 11 Community Centre, Panchsheel Park, New
Delhi–110 017, India; Penguin Group (NZ), 67 Apollo Drive, Rosedale, North Shore
0632, New Zealand (a division of Pearson New Zealand Ltd); Penguin Books (South
Africa) (Pty) Ltd, 24 Sturdee Avenue, Rosebank, Johannesburg 2196, South Africa

Penguin Books Ltd, Registered Offices: 80 Strand, London WC2R 0RL, England

Published by Dutton, a member of Penguin Group (USA) Inc.

First printing, September 2008
10 9 8 7 6 5 4 3 2 1

 REGISTERED TRADEMARK—MARCA REGISTRADA

LIBRARY OF CONGRESS CATALOGING-IN-PUBLICATION DATA
Lovelace, David.
    Scattershot: my bipolar family / David Lovelace.—1st ed.
        p. cm.
    ISBN 978-0-525-95078-3 (hardcover)
    1. Manic-depressive persons—Family relationships.   2. Manic-depressive illness—
Treatment.   I. Title.
    RC516.L68 2008
    616.89'5—dc22   2008013901

Printed in the United States of America

For Mary and Hunter

SCATTERSHOT

I opened the door, the kids tackled me, and my wife said, "You need to call your dad. He's been leaving messages for days." I dropped my pack, kissed them all, and sat down. "You need to call him now. I tried to reach you." Hunter pushed onto my lap.

"Why? What is it?"

"It's strange. He sounds pretty strange."

I knew what it was already. I should have seen it before I left town. I wanted to come home and tell stories, hear the kids talk, but instead I moved to the bedroom and locked the door. I lay facedown as the kids rattled the doorknob and called from the hall. "What did you bring back, Dad? What did you get us?" They began quarreling. I pulled a stuffed toy, some markers, and a pouch of fool's gold from my carry-on, opened the door, and passed out the gifts. I sat on the bed and tried to think it out slowly but I couldn't. It was pointless. I knew what it was and hit play.

"Hi, David, hello, Roberta. This is Dad Lovelace, Richard Lovelace. Mom is much better now. She's more herself. We've been praying and singing hymns. She enjoys that. Dad Lovelace." Not good. The "Dad Lovelace" thing did not sound good.

"Hello again, David and Roberta. Dad Lovelace again. I just

wanted to mention that there's really no reason for you to come down. Mom is much better, more herself. The family gathering was just a real shock to her system. I think she just needs to rest, so don't come down. It's not a good idea. Thanks, Richard Lovelace." The "Richard" thing was worse.

Before I left for Colorado, I had driven my folks back to Boston's North Shore to see family. I now acted as chauffeur. My mother was eighty-one that year and terrified of driving, has been since 1950. My father was only seventy-four, but suffering from night blindness. When I arrived at their apartment, my mother, Betty Lee, was far from well. She sat on the couch with her forehead clenched and her eyes screwed tight. Her jaw was slack and wet with saliva. I helped her out to their car and felt her thin arm with its hollow bones—just a bird's wing. She curled up in the backseat and fell asleep within minutes.

My father, usually reserved, practically bounced on the seat beside me. He talked nonstop, all the way east. Dad, a theologian, hadn't published in years, but he now carried two manuscripts and spent most of the ride describing them in great detail. It was a long two hours. My parents' car shuddered over sixty. The speedometer had worked loose somewhere in the dash and it fluttered and buzzed. Just past Sturbridge, he pulled out his second work, a memoir, and I winced. He read me his life so fast it was done before we got to our exit.

When we arrived my mother's condition shocked everyone and my father began assuring the family. He said Betty Lee was just adjusting to new medication. I mentioned the onset of Parkinson's but my father broke in. "Now, we're not sure it's Parkinson's. She has some Parkinsonian symptoms—that's all." But

Parkinson's is a progressive disease. It doesn't hit like a stroke. My father said he had all her doctors on the case.

"Including Bryant?" I asked.

"Including the shrink," he said.

The party proceeded while my mother sat on the couch, silent and pinched. Shadows moved through her face as my father squeezed her hand and whispered in her ear, acting as a sort of interpreter for the bright, laughing room. He spoke for her as well, answering questions and almost shielding her from the family's concern. He loves her very much but he was making me nervous. At dinner my father raised his hand in blessing, his ring and pinkie fingers folded down like a saint's. "As an ordained minister of the Presbyterian church, I ask our Lord God's blessing on this gathering. In the grace of Jesus Christ, his only begotten son, amen." My brother, Jonathan, shot me a glance and I shrugged. It was a strange blessing, even for a church historian.

A short time later Jonathan pulled me over by the cheesecake. "Dad's acting weird, Dave. I mean really weird."

"I know."

"He just growled at Jen. He started telling her how to raise our kids and when she started to defend herself he just growled."

"What do you mean, growled?" I asked skeptically. I typically run interference for my dad, and despite the night's odd behavior, I fell into form.

"I mean he growled."

"What? Like, you mean, grrrr?"

"Yeah, like a real dog. And he stared her down. I'm telling you, Dave, it was creepy."

"Okay, that's pretty damn weird," I admitted, and grabbed another beer. "He's weird, all right."

"It's none of his business how we raise our children. If we homeschool them or whatever. It pisses me off." He glared over at Dad. "It's more than weird, it's disrespectful. He doesn't respect Jen. She's almost in tears. It's like he hates her or something."

"No shit." I rarely see my brother angry. He doesn't share my temperament. I got high and cynical in high school; my brother played sports. He believes in fair play and gives everyone the benefit of the doubt. I glanced across the room. Dad was quiet, just whispering to Mom. "He wouldn't shut up the whole way down here, just kept talking. And you know what? He's got a memoir."

"A memoir. Really?" My brother smiled. "Are we in it?"

"No, not really, it's all about his head."

"None of the fishing trips? Nothing?"

"It's all theology—Jonathan Edwards and the Great Awakening. You know. I mean, sure, there's stuff on us, but not much. And now all of a sudden he's giving opinions on all of us." I laughed. "The whole family." My brother and I fell silent and studied our parents there, hunched up on the couch.

"God, it's sad."

"She looks awful," Jon said. "Really bad. She's aged ten years."

"Twenty."

"What do you think?"

"I don't know, Jon. You know how Mom gets," I said, echoing my father. "She's having a spell. As long as Dad lets the doctors figure it out, follows their orders, she'll pull through."

"Dad. Yeah, what about him?"

"I don't know. He closes ranks when Mom gets sick. Gets all

defensive." I pulled at my beer and shrugged. "I'll keep an eye on them," I promised. "Don't worry." Both my siblings consider me the favorite child, my father's golden boy, and it's true he listens best to me. Perhaps it's because I'm the eldest, or the loudest. It's not because I'm the wisest; I'm not. Nevertheless, because I have clout and because I live closest, I work the front lines. When it comes to my parents, I'm the first responder, the medic. I sometimes forget this.

I moved back into the party and tried to reassure the family about my mother, who had sunk into the couch, frightened, her eyes following me. "My mom's all right," I told my cousins. "She gets like this sometimes."

My father cut in. "Betty Lee is just having a little case of the whim-whams."

In our family "whim-wham" is code, a defanged reference to any number of moods and psychological disorders, be they depressive, manic, or schizoaffective. Back in the 1970s and '80s—when they were all straight depression—we called them "dark nights of the soul." St. John of the Cross's phrase ennobled our sickness, spiritualized it. We cut God out of it after the manic breaks started in 1986, the year my dad, brother, and I were all committed. Call it manic depression or by its new, polite name, bipolar disorder. Whichever you wish. We stick to our folklore and call it the whim-whams.

"Her whim-whams happen periodically and she always comes through. We're adjusting her medications. Betty Lee and I pray together every day and that really works wonders. She has wonderful doctors, wonderful—a neurologist for the Parkinsonian symptoms and a general doctor, Dr. Hill, that we just love."

"And Bryant, the shrink?" I asked pointedly. I know my parents' psychiatrist. He's mine as well and he's better than most. In my experience, a psychiatrist's most salient feature is brevity. The therapist's fate—the actual listening to patients—terrifies most psychiatrists. They clock their twelve-minute office visits with ruthless efficiency and write scripts in a flash. It takes longer to flush your radiator than it does to alter your brain chemistry. Before Bryant, I barely knew my psychiatrists; I knew the guys down at Jiffy Lube better.

"Bryant? Oh yes, of course."

"And what does Bryant say?" My father sat surrounded by suspicious relatives.

"I believe it's a combination of factors. The new—"

"What's Bryant believe?"

"Please, let me finish. The new drugs she's taking for the Parkinson's are interacting with the lithium in particular. All the church activities and her artwork. She's just exhausted." My mother wanted to illustrate children's books and she still paints small watercolors, sweet little cards with families like ours, two boys and a girl. She has a fondness for still life and she paints when she's well. As he spoke my father held her hands while she sat mutely beside him. Her expression was clouded, her eyes closed as if she were trying to remember herself. None of us bought my father's explanation. It was clear she hadn't painted in a long time. All of us feared the cycling return of my mom's paranoia, her hallucinatory despair.

"What about church?" my brother asked. "Has she been going? I mean before all of this."

"Yes, of course. She was attending a women's Bible study,

which she really enjoyed. I drive her every week or she gets rides." Rides, most likely. For the large part, my father's avoided church ever since he quit preaching. He says the music's too modern or the preaching's too basic, but it's really the people; there are too many people. Without those rides my mother would never see them, all the people she needs.

"So what does Bryant say?"

"The drugs. We're working together to get the right balance."

He had assured no one. My father is known to maintain a significant back stock of medications, many of them psychotropic. Trays of multicolored pills, generations of them, lay open throughout his apartment; he experiments with an almost alchemical zeal. These pills attest to his faith in technology and the clean workings of mechanized flesh, of the impersonal. For my father, salvation works in two spheres, the spiritual and the chemical. Both realms contain great and authoritative mysteries. The former requires prayer; the latter requires pills and then nothing at all—no family discussions, no fifty-minute sessions, no thought.

Ten years ago at my father's direction I poisoned my mother with lithium. My father's teaching duties had called him away and my mother was staying with me when her paranoia began. She seemed unsteady when Dad dropped her off but he assured me that her medication had been adjusted and would soon set her straight. Her psychiatrist increased her dosage and my father gave me detailed instructions. I did as I was told and she grew worse, much worse. Her psychiatrist would not return my phone calls. My mother lost the power of speech and wandered the house frightened and lost. Food dropped from her mouth. Finally, after days of trying, I spoke with her doctor. "Take her to the hospital" was all he would say. I asked if it was the lithium, if he had prescribed the new dose. "Take her to the hospital." He said that three times and hung up. I never spoke with him again. She spent four days in intensive care. Most of us blame the doctor, some my father. I blame myself—for following orders, for crushing the white pills into her applesauce when she began choking on water.

We left the party early. I held my mother and kept her from falling. She looked cold and frail, like a small animal. I threw my coat over her. I didn't want to talk and turned on the news. But Dad wanted to talk and he turned off the radio. He spoke rapidly on politics and the church, sometimes his boyhood. After an hour I tried the radio again; he switched it off without missing a beat. I was tired and sad and so I stopped listening. Outside Springfield, going seventy on the Mass Pike, a woman ran out in front of the car; she missed our bumper by inches. She disappeared before I hit the brake, out of the black and back into the darkness, just like that. The next day I called my father. He said Mom felt better. I asked to speak with her, but he said she was resting. And the next day I left for Colorado, ignoring the signs.

Now, a week later and back from the mountains, it all crashed into place as I lay on my bed and listened to his rambling messages, the kids laughing in the hall and calling me. Of course. Of course, I knew it. I stopped the messages; they just circled around, making me dizzy. I dialed my parents' apartment. Their phone was disconnected and I got up to go. Driving down to Northampton it all seemed so obvious: my father's new manuscripts—two books in two months, the long dinner when my father spoke openly, his new Web site, the newsletter, and now all of the calls.

Their apartment door was locked. I rapped at it hard with my knuckles. The lights went off. I banged on the door, called out. The lights went back on and my father, through the door, said, "Yes?"

"Dad, it's David."

"David Lovelace?"

"Yeah. David Lovelace. Can I come in?"

"No, I don't think that's a good idea."

"Why? What do you mean, not a good idea? Let me in."

His voice lowered. "No," he said slowly, deliberately, as if he were training a dog. "You will not come in. No, you will not. Your mother is resting." I tried the knob again and stepped back. There wasn't much to see from the window. I knocked again but he had stopped talking. There would be no negotiation. I walked past their building, a long row of modest two-story apartments, pushed through some bushes and onto the rear patios. The weather was wet and cold and I saw no one as I stepped from one small yard to the next. Then I saw my father through his sliding glass door. He sat in front of a dismembered phone, its wires and jacks stripped and spread out. The kitchen waste can overflowed next to him: smoked salmon wrappers, tins of tuna, mayonnaise jars, and newspapers. He saw me and reached for the lock but I beat him and jerked back the door.

He stood, towering over me. "You are not coming in. I forbid it." I pushed past him, into the smell of it, my father's madness: the tang of rotted food and the earthy, nauseating smell of vitamins. He backed off then and shrugged; his anger vanished at once. He smiled and spread out his hands. His shirttails were out and his clothes stained with food. "All right. All right. Maybe you're okay. Maybe it's best. You'll see it's okay, David Lovelace. It's best. Welcome." He sat down smiling and his eyes were sharper than knives and too bright to watch.

I sat down slowly, my back to the wall. "Where's Mom?"

"She's upstairs, resting. She's had a bad shock."

"What do you mean, a shock?"

"The family, Rockport. Seeing the family is always a shock."

"Not for her," I muttered to myself. "Dad, I got your calls. I tried to reach you. What's with the phone?" I asked, pointing at the wires, the gutted phone on the table.

He shook his head. "We're having a terrible time with the phones here, just terrible." He paused, calculated, and struck a casual pose. "So, what brings you down here?"

"I'm concerned about Mom. I'm gonna go up and see her."

My father stood. "Well, okay, if you must. She's really doing much better. She's much more herself. Try not to wake her." I moved through the living room, the scattered plastic pillboxes. My father had found a large book on Goya and had it propped up, open to the crucified Christ, with his holy bleeding head and his hand raised in blessing.

Upstairs, I couldn't wake my mother. She was lying on the floor in her nightgown. Her bed was stripped and someone had pushed foam rubber under her head and back. I thought she was dead. I dropped to my knees. I could hear my father moving slowly up the stairs. The air was fetid and it smelled of urine. I leaned close and heard her breathing, rapid and shallow. Her lower lip trembled; for a brief moment it seemed she would speak. Her thin eyelids fluttered slightly and I could see her eyeballs roll and drop beneath them. Then my father appeared in the doorway, smiling hopefully. "You see, David, much better."

I stood and moved back. I was badly frightened by him and felt myself shaking. "Dad, what's this green crap?" It was all over her, some of it wet and bright green, most dry and gray, like clay. Her hair was matted with the stuff. It ran from her mouth across her face and down her neck. The thin blanket she had was covered in it. I checked her breathing again, worried she had choked on it. "What is it?" I asked slowly. I tried not to scream.

"Oh. That's a soy protein product we've been using. Lots of B-twelve. You know that settles her nerves. It's a powder. You mix it with water. I feed it to her."

"I see. Okay. What's she doing on the floor?"

"She fell." My father blocked the door. I couldn't breathe and I felt like retching. I needed help and the phones were all fucked.

"Dad, I gotta go. I'll be back later, but right now I gotta go. I think Mom needs help."

My father smiled; he almost beamed. "Well, David. That makes sense. It's been good to see you. I'll let you know how she's coming along. We pray together every day." My father knew it was a series of tests now and he felt he had passed the first one, held it together. He hadn't raved and I was leaving the apartment. No one would take her away. No one would ask him to leave. They were inseparable.

I didn't have a phone so I drove straight to the cops. I regretted it immediately. The cop behind the Plexiglas made me sit and wait while he talked to his radio. He was younger than I am. This was a waste of time; I should have just called an ambulance. I paced until a shitty little speaker crackled.

"Sir?"

"My mother needs an ambulance. She's unconscious and my father is manic, is having a manic break." Should I say "crazy"? Did he even know what "manic" meant?

"Sir?"

"Crazy." There, I'd done it. Fuck. "My dad's fucking out of it. He's bipolar. My mother needs an ambulance."

"Watch your language, sir. The address?" I gave it to him. "All right, sir. Just have a seat. I'll send for a patrol car."

"I'll meet them back there."

I paced the parking lot; I should have called an ambulance straightaway. I knew the cops could make it worse, much worse, just by showing up. I remember seeing their lights through the windows when they came for me, and they lit the room red and flashed. I had hit the floor and crawled to the bathroom. I locked the door and looked for razors—just to scare them, I thought. When they came up the steps and rapped on the door, I stripped and ducked into the shower. My friends said, don't worry, Dave, don't worry, and then they let them inside. I could hear them all talking and I clapped my hands on my ears and started to sing. I slid down in the shower and sang.

I waited outside my father's apartment and remembered Woody Woodward, a local man who died up in Brattleboro. He was scared and so he found a church, interrupted the Sunday service, and asked for help. He spoke rapidly and incoherently. Woodward appeared delusional; he claimed the CIA was after him. He had a penknife and when the police came he held it up to his eye and pleaded for help. The cops shot him seven times, including once in the back and once as he lay on the carpet. Then they cuffed him. He died in surgery and both policemen were cleared of wrongdoing.

That's what can happen and that's how we think: seven shots and dying right there at the pulpit. We see how scared all the straights are—how primal that fear is—and we feed off that fear. We know how fast things go bad. One minute you're asking for sanctuary, the next facing guns.

I waited twenty minutes in the parking lot. I knew my father was watching. When the police pulled in I knew he was inside, pacing, making decisions. Fortunately, the police moved calmly. They listened closely and we planned our approach together. I kept saying my father was harmless. "He isn't dangerous," I said, with my mother dying upstairs.

I knocked on the door but my father was spooked and hiding. I led the cops through the bushes and wet patios, the brown oak leaves in drifts. My father sat by the broken phones and when the cop rapped on the glass he turned and smiled. He held his palms out and shrugged.

"Sir, open the door."

"Okay, okay. That would be fine but—"

"Please open the door, sir."

"All right, all right. This is just fine. Just give me a moment." My father stepped into the adjacent bathroom. He came out a few tense minutes later with his hair combed and his shirt tucked in, and he unlocked the door. I could see him throttle down against all the drama, the cops and the lights, against his worst fears: that his mind had burned down, that they'd bury his wife and lock him away. Now here they were, standing in his kitchen with guns and clubs, and somehow he smiled and spoke slowly, a professor again, a calm, reasonable man. One cop stayed with him and one came with me. My mother hadn't moved. The cop cursed slowly, under his breath. He knelt on one knee and felt for her pulse.

"What's all this green crap?" he asked, and I told him. For a moment my mother seemed like some tribal death head, smeared with ritual clay and locked in a trance. The cop gagged. "Open the window," he ordered, then radioed for the ambulance. I went downstairs and found my father explaining his prayers and his potions, the green soy dust all over his table.

"You see that," he said, pointing to an imprinted book bag. "That's the symbol of the Presbyterian church. I am an ordained minister in the Presbyterian church. The mainline Presbyterian church, not one of those split P's." My father leaned and picked up the bag. It was indeed a Presbyterian book bag, clearly emblazoned with a cross and large capital P. My father exhibited the bag's symbol with solemnity. The book bag had become a talisman for him and he rarely let it out of his sight.

I told my dad about the ambulance, that we were taking Betty Lee to the hospital. I knew my father understood the situation deep down, knew he couldn't duck it. Below his smile, his careful manners, beneath his delusions, he knew it was grave. He knew his wife was near death and that he was not right and that he had left her there dying. He knew the soy protein was bullshit, that he sang the hymns all alone. He knew that his chattered prayers were all bent and broken and still he prayed to God they would work. And they did, too, because I came to triage his mind and pick up my mother, because I knew what to do; I'd been on both sides. My father watched from his full-blown mania, from his paranoid seat at the right hand of God, as the disgusted EMTs stared at his smile and lifted my mother onto the gurney.

I love my father. I knew what he was attempting because I've done it at times, passed myself off as sane by sheer force of will. Like my father, I've seen the beautiful cartwheel of thoughts pitch past and crash and I've learned not to speak of them, to let them all go. I can stand inside a desperate circus and force my mind to slow, if only for a few moments. It is the hardest work I've ever known. And now I watched my father attempt it, try to gather a mind much deeper than mine, try to hold back a green interior ocean full of monsters and wonders. I watched as he reeled in each rocking moment, as he stood in her bedroom and loved her and smiled.

I left him alone in his apartment and drove up to the hospital. They taped oxygen tubes under my mother's nose, pushed a needle in her arm, and taped it for the glucose drip. They said she was severely dehydrated, that her blood was like sludge. They pulled some of it for a lithium level. I explained the green soy drink again. We talked about strokes. I mentioned her state at my cousin's in Rockport and I mentioned her lithium poisoning. Still, she was unconscious and a stroke seemed most likely. I walked with my mom and a nurse up to intensive care. There'd be an MRI in the morning. I sat a long time by her bed and it felt like a grave, but her eyelids still fluttered. I left her, called Roberta from the lobby and ran out of change. I went back to my dad.

It was long past midnight and he was awake. His bed was stripped, too. I suspect it hadn't been slept in for weeks. I told him that Mom was all right now and resting, that we would go over in the morning. I was exhausted. I asked for his car keys. He stood then, his smile tightened, and he spat out his words. "Absolutely not. I'm legally entitled to drive. We've been all through that."

"Dad, I can't let you drive."

"Oh, you can't, can you?" He rose up and snarled. "That's enough. That's more than enough. Get out now, David Lovelace." I threw up my hand and left without another word. Hell, he could light out for anywhere.

I slept hard and woke early at home. I called my brother to let him know it had busted wide open. He said he'd come on the weekend. I waited an hour, called my sister Peggy, and said Mom might be dying.

"She's still not conscious?"

"No. I mean I haven't been there today but it looks pretty bad."

"So, Dad just left her like that? On the floor?"

"Peg, he's out of his mind. You can't blame him. I mean maybe you can but that's not important right now. I've got to get him somewhere, into a hospital."

"Right," she said, and slipped into gear. She doesn't have it but she knows all about our disease. She knows the drill; she's a professional, a therapist with a practice out west. I needed her badly. "Get him to the psychiatrist—what's his name?"

"Bryant."

"Get him over to Bryant right away, like this morning. It's an emergency and he'll make room in his schedule. We need to get Dad safe and back on his meds today. He's a loose cannon right now. Bryant should give you the paperwork to commit Dad if he won't sign voluntarily."

"He probably won't, not after yesterday."

"Right. Make sure you get the form. Each state's different. I don't know what it's called out there, but Bryant will know. Okay? I'll book a flight but it might be a few days. I'll see. Now, call Bryant immediately and then keep me posted. Use my cell."

I booked an appointment and drove back to my father's. This time he let me in before I could knock. He was waiting for me, playing *Don Giovanni* loudly and pacing. His clothes were the same. Books and papers littered the floor. He held out his strangely limp, sweaty hand and I shook it. "Thanks, David, for coming. I'm so glad you did what you did. You know best." He smiled. "Everything's just marvelous here."

"Good."

"Listen, David, I did just as you suggested. I dumped Bank of America."

"You did what?"

"I went in a few days ago and closed my account. I got everything out of safe-deposit." He thought I'd be pleased. He'd heard my complaints about the mega-bank, how they turned me down for a loan. I realized he had taken my financial rant seriously.

"Where is it?"

"What?"

"I don't know, the stuff you had in your safe-deposit box. What was in the box?"

"Oh, our will, a few of Grandmère's rings, I think our life insurance policy. And the gold, of course."

"Gold?"

"British gold sovereigns."

"Sovereigns. How much?"

"Well, the markets fluctuate, of course. You know, Peter Grady got us to cash out all our stocks and buy gold. Remember Peter Grady? From church? A marvelous idea, just wonderful. Y2K?" He shrugged. "No problem at all. There's always gold, no matter what—"

"Dad, that was five years ago. Besides, it didn't even happen."

"What didn't happen?"

"Y2K."

"Yes, it did. Clearly it did. Just look at the date."

"Okay, okay. How much?"

"Sixty, seventy thousand if you want just a rough figure. If you'd like, we can look it up. I have today's paper." He had the whole month's papers in a pile by the welcome mat.

"Where?"

"It's in the basement."

"In the laundry room? The building's laundry room?"

"No, no," he reassured me, "next to it. It's in a yellow tackle box."

"Do you mind if I go get it?"

"Not at all, not at all."

The yellow tackle box was there all right, on the concrete floor next to my father's snow tires. I hauled it upstairs. I suggested we walk downtown to my bank. I assured my father it was local and benevolent, a good place for a safe deposit box. He shrugged and put on his coat. An aria finished as we stepped out the door. "Wonderful piece that," my father said. "Wonderful."

Sixty grand worth of gold is heavy. I worried the tackle box might snap open, its tiny hinges give out, so I held it under my arm, hoping my dad wouldn't change his mind, hoping I wouldn't end up chasing him around town with a plastic box full of gold.

The bank's atmosphere quieted my father somewhat. I sat with the tackle box on my lap and tried to offer as little information as possible. "You know," my father said, "gold is a much sounder investment these days than paper—bonds and such."

The manager fiddled with some keys on her desk. She wore one of those unfortunate business suits and her nails had been done up with tiny stars. "Oh, that may be so, sir. I get a number of questions about it."

"British sovereigns. That's the way to go. Here, I'll write that down for you."

"Dad, she doesn't need you to write it down."

My father's voice slowed, became emphatic. "I am writing it down." He finished and handed his note to the banker with a flourish. He smiled. "When the meltdown comes, your best bet is gold." You couldn't argue with that. I smiled at the manager. She moved through the forms, my father filled his box up with gold, and we escaped without incident.

Now, with the gold safely squirreled away, I considered my father and how best to help him. I got the car and we drove to the hospital. To visit Mom, I told him, and then go from there. My mother seemed unchanged—cleaned up, but no better. No one at the desk knew anything. My father leaned over her bed and whispered encouragement. He pulled her beat-up old Bible from his Presbyterian bag and read a psalm quietly, his face close to hers. He prayed for her. He loves her so much.

Next, I brought Dad to our psychiatrist. Bryant was efficient. He asked one simple question and let my father do the rest. "So, Richard, how are you doing?" At that my father rambled for five minutes, discussing medicine, interdenominational feuds, God, opera, his mother and mine. He modeled his Presbyterian book bag, holding the great P to his chest—a sort of crazed denominational superhero. Bryant finally cut in. "So, Richard, you would say you are—"

"Wonderful."

"Well. Quite frankly, Richard, you shouldn't be. Your wife's in the ICU; she may have had a stroke. You shouldn't be wonderful."

My father dropped his smile and took another tack. "Yes, yes, of course. I am quite concerned. I think it was the medicine you were giving her, frankly. But she's in good hands now. David Lovelace is here and things are moving along well."

"I'm afraid you're acting inappropriately. I understand religion is important to you, but you're using grandiose religious terms—"

"You're Irish Catholic," my father injected dismissively. "You're antireligious."

"Richard, you're delusional. You've given me every indication of a manic break." He pulled out the green pad. "I'm giving you a prescription for Seroquel. That should help you sleep. I've got some samples here somewhere." He rummaged in his file cabinet. Psychiatrists' cabinets may or may not contain files, but are regularly filled with brightly boxed samples: psychotropic candies, Wellbutrin pens, and Zoloft staplers.

Bryant found what he was looking for and gave me two boxes. He asked my father to wait outside. "I agree with you. Your father's full-blown. I suspected as much and he's just confirmed it. He left three increasingly incoherent messages on our machine last night."

"He loves answering machines."

"Yes, well. Are you all right?" he asked me. I nodded. "Your meds good? You'll need to keep it together. Stay in touch. Now, we should get him in right away. We'll try Northampton first. Can you get him to go with you, sign himself in?"

"I don't know."

"I'll call Cooley Dick and recommend hospitalization."

I told my father we'd head back to the hospital around dinnertime to check on Mom. No change. I took my dad to the snack bar and told him what I thought, what Bryant thought. I could see his thoughts race now, looking for an out. "Look. It's up to you, but the psych ward isn't bad here. You should consider spending a few days, just to get your meds straightened out, get some regular sleep." The last thing he wanted was sleep—he had too much to do—and there was no chance in hell he'd take Seroquel without supervision. Your average mood stabilizers— lithium, Depakote—are aspirin compared to antipsychotics like Seroquel. Seroquel is better than most, but any antipsychotic hits like a club to the head. They knock manic patients out of the trees. Twenty years ago doctors had given me the granddaddy of them all, Thorazine, and it hammered me. My muscles went rigid and my mind stopped dead and I lurched through the ward like Frankenstein's monster. I want to say I'd take it again if I needed it, but I fear that I wouldn't. I'd run.

I know my father considered it and he might have done it but for my mom. "Mom will be right downstairs," I said. "You'll be on the fifth floor and Mom on the third. You could visit." I knew there would be no visits. The fifth floor was a lockdown. This was the first of my lies. "Look, Dad, you're a little out of whack. That's all. You'll be out in a few days." Another lie. "You heard what Bryant said, you just need to slow down a bit so you can take care of Mom. She needs you." That much was true.

"Bryant is antireligion. He doesn't believe in the efficacy of prayer. He's friendly enough, sure"—my father's face twisted—"but he's not a Presbyterian. He's not even Protestant."

"Okay. Forget Bryant. He's a papist. I'm sorry I brought him up." It was strange. I was reasoning with Oliver Cromwell: milord, the blood-letter is not a heretic. "Listen," I said, "let's get you away from Bryant, get you hooked up with folks who under-stand." And so, Bryant's judgments were rendered null, just like that. He was my father's enemy now, perhaps all Christendom's, and I wouldn't mention him again. Dad would never take his drugs now.

"You know the drill, Dad. If you sign yourself in here, you can leave whenever you wish. But if you decide not to sign yourself in, well, then I'll have to do it. Then a whole bunch of bureaucracy gums up the works. Just sign in. For Mom's sake." I looked at him straight. I could smell his mind working fast, sparking. His eyes spun just like slots and I waited for the payoff.

"All right, David. If you think it best. Personally I think it's overkill. I'm perfectly fine."

"But you'll do it?"

"I guess."

I moved quickly now. We exited the hospital's main doors and walked around to the emergency entrance. A bit dramatic, I thought—provocative—but psychiatric admissions pass through those gates. Walking past the stacked ambulances, I prayed he wouldn't stop, wouldn't turn and ask questions. The ER was bright, a scratchy electric yellow that hurt my eyes. It was a limbo and I've waited here, too, waited for the wheelchair upstairs, the next ferry over the Styx. Over there, on the ward, they knock you down dead and hope you rise again sane on the third day or month. My father was jittery, mercurial; the triage nurse was harried and dismissive. She pushed us back on the list. In the ER a cut finger—a handful of stitches—takes precedence over our often fatal disease, despite the bad odds. One out of every four untreated bipolar individuals dies by suicide. Not there on the ER floor, mind you, but later, after they give up and leave. Suicide is simply the finishing touch, an end to slow death by depression. You can't blame them.

But my father stayed because I did, because I asked him not to leave. I did everything short of card tricks to keep him occupied, keep his paranoia at bay. A social worker finally took us in hand. She did not work for the hospital; she was not a psychiatric nurse. She worked for Safety Net, an independent, state-funded advocacy group. I had to get past her first, prove to her I was a good son, that my father was indeed mad. It was unfortunate that at this moment he looked remarkably sane, relaxed even, charming.

He was good, all right; he managed the act better than I ever did. But after a forty-five-minute chat with my father, the social worker took me aside. "I agree with you and Dr. Bryant. Your father could benefit from hospitalization. He's agreed to sign himself in, and that makes it so much easier. Unfortunately, there are no available beds on ward tonight. Could you come back tomorrow?"

I looked at her incredulously.

"You think I can get him back to commit himself again tomorrow? After two and half hours in the ER?"

"I don't know." Why did they wait to tell me? Were they just practicing? My father would have to wait a day for the next ferry.

When I got home Roberta pulled out her calendar and we scheduled the crisis. She told me not to worry about the children; she could make it home for Mary's bus and we'd get extra days at Hunter's preschool. "Get someone to cover the bookstore. Just concentrate on your parents and I'll do the rest."

Mary overheard us and came into the kitchen. "What about my play?" She was ten years old and had the lead. "Dress rehearsal's tomorrow."

"I've got to teach tomorrow afternoon," Roberta said. "I can't get out of that. You'll have to take her." Mary had her costume on, just a big sweater. She was Charlie Brown and had a date with a pumpkin.

"I'll take you, Mary. We'll just have to go a little early and pick up Papa. All right?"

"I guess so. Is he coming to rehearsal?"

"No, he has an appointment."

"Good," she said. "I need to practice first. Papa might get bored."

"Don't worry about that, darling." I glanced at Roberta. "That's the least of our worries. He's not coming. We just need to drop him off at the hospital. It won't take long." It seemed like a reasonable plan, not ideal, of course, but reasonable. It wouldn't take long—the paperwork was done. My father wasn't dangerous and if I worked it right he wouldn't be scary. It was okay for Mary to see this, to begin understanding this part of the family. How bad could it be?

Bad. It was another day, and so another round of forms was required, another psychiatric evaluation by a non-psychiatrist, another long wait. I had promised that today would be quick and told Mary that we could have ice cream afterward, but we'd already spent forty minutes in the waiting area. Now, waiting again in the small, bright examination room, my father and I tried out some small talk as Mary sat in the corner and whispered her lines. We pretended nothing was out of the ordinary, just another errand: pick up milk, drop off kids, commit Dad to asylum.

Finally, the door opened and a slight man in a white coat and holding a clipboard slipped inside. "Hi, I'm Mark," he said. That's it, just Mark. Not Dr. Mark, not even Mr. Mark. He was balding but had managed to coax a wispy gray ponytail back from his temples. He was Safety Net and he was letting his freak flag fly. He was on our side, defending us from doctors and other medical professionals. After another forty-five-minute interview, wherein my father lost his much-abused patience, brandished his Presbyterian book bag over his head, insisted Bryant was a heathen

Irishman, and repeatedly referred to me by my full, somewhat unfortunate given name—David Brainerd Lovelace—the interview concluded. I realized Mary had wandered off.

My father now refused to enter voluntarily, to commit himself. It was hard to blame him; I wanted out, too. Both the breadth of my father's knowledge and the force of his controlled mania seemed to diminish our friend Mark. He warbled like Joan Baez while my father belted Rossini. Mark seemed unsure as we stepped into the hallway. Where the hell did Mary go? I'd been too busy bottling my rage to notice. Mark put his hand on my shoulder, an attempt at compassion. "Well, I have good news. Your father seems okay. He's presently not a danger to himself or others. I cannot recommend that your father be involuntarily committed at this time."

I pushed back from him, stunned. "Okay? You think he's okay? My mother's upstairs in a coma. He left her on the floor for days. Tried to force-feed her some green, soylent product. He's off his meds. He's noncompliant. He's driving around. Last night he saw some infomercial and bought a three-thousand-dollar mattress."

"The incident with your mother was a few days ago now. He seems better."

"What the fuck?" I was close to losing it. "How the fuck do you know?" Nurses watched from their stations, agog. When she heard my voice from down the hall Mary returned, her hands and pockets full of candy corn raided from somewhere out back. I stepped into Mark's face and he backed away, held his clipboard out, and ducked slightly.

"How do you know he's off his meds?" he asked defensively. "Has he had a blood level?"

"A blood level? No, I've been too busy visiting my mother in the ICU and talking with not-even-doctors to arrange a fucking blood level." I'd lost it and Mark moved closer to the nurses. Mary stood riveted, popping her candy. "What? Are you trying to protect my father? Do you think I want to do this? Do you think this is fun? Do you think he's a victim, that I'm victimizing him?" I was loud now. I wanted to hit him.

"Mr. Lovelace, I understand you're upset, that this is upsetting." Mark looked sympathetic and nervous. His eyes grew large and moist. He was breathing rapidly. "We all want what's best for your father." I snorted. "We all want what's best for him." Mark gestured to the caring ER staff—three openmouthed nurses and two newly arrived and very large orderlies. "You have to understand. Your father needs an advocate. I'm his advocate. You know, they used to warehouse patients—"

"This isn't a fucking warehouse, it's a hospital and I want a doctor. His psychiatrist called and said to admit him."

"Yesterday, he called yesterday," Mark clarified.

I leaned in to the well-meaning Mark and grabbed his nametag. "You're a chickenshit, Mark. Do your fucking job. I'm not leaving until my father's locked up." I stepped back, disgusted. "I don't want to talk to Safety fucking Net anymore. I want a doctor." An orderly closed in behind me and I saw security approach fast down the hall. I stopped and smiled grimly.

Mary stood beside me. It was time for her play. "C'mon, Charlie Brown," I said softly, and pulled her close. I held her tight and turned toward the orderlies. They stared me down and I said under my breath, "You're not locking me up. You can't lock anyone up." I looked around at them all and back toward my father. He sat quietly in the bright examination room and smiled at my scene. "Goddammit," I said, and grabbed my daughter's hand, pulled her away from all this and marched toward the door. "C'mon, Dad!" I yelled over my shoulder, and I kicked their swinging door as hard as I could. It hit the wall loud, like a rifle crack.

I unlocked the truck and Mary climbed up quietly. She wouldn't look at me. Great, I thought, now my daughter needs therapy—already. Good grief. I saw my father moving slowly across the lot. "Sorry, darling," I said. "Sorry about all this." She just nodded and picked at her sweater. I held the door for my father and he stayed quiet as well. "I'm driving you home, Dad. I need to get Mary to rehearsal."

"Of course, of course," he said, and fell silent for most of the drive. I thought he was gloating until we got to his door. "What about Betty Lee? We didn't see Mom."

"I know, Dad, I—"

"She's all right, isn't she? She'll be all right?"

"Sure. Sure, Dad. Try to get some sleep and I'll see you tomorrow."

Back in the truck I apologized again. "Sorry, Mary. I had no idea it would be like that, take so long. Lousy way to spend the afternoon, huh?"

"Yeah, I guess." She pulled on Charlie Brown's sweater and smiled. "It was kind of funny, Dad."

"Funny." Nothing was funny. My father was out; he had won the first battle. I had no way to slow him or keep him safe.

"The way you yelled at that guy in there and when you

slammed the door. I've never seen you get mad like that. I thought it was funny."

"What about Papa? How did he seem?"

"Crazy, I guess. But okay. I mean he wasn't scary or anything." Then Mary opened her script and began practicing her role. She seemed fine; she was learning. My mother stayed with us once and fell sick. Mary was just a toddler, and she watched Grammy move through the house all heartsick and broken and unable to speak. She's seen my medicines. Five years ago I was manic and sat on our porch with her and her brother. Mary was seven and Hunter just three; I was forty-two and full-blown. She had some clay and we sat and made figures while my mind rushed away and I tried not to follow; I tried to stay home. My wife, Roberta, came home and rescued me just like the first time, twenty-two years ago. Roberta is quiet, strong. She knows the school calendar and remembers the mortgage. She leaves me notes in the morning. She says the kids will be fine, that they take after her side on this, my family's disease. They'll have, she said, the best of both worlds, and I want to believe her.

But I want to be ready. I've seen both my parents drown in the sickness. I've seen my brother sink down. I've denied my own madness and I've loved it almost to death. All my life I've heard my family blame each other, some devil, some church, genetics, and shrinks. We're ashamed and afraid of our minds. I want to believe my wife and not worry. I want to get strong and show my kids how. I want my family fearless and proud.

TWO

My parents met in 1954 at the Peniel Bible Conference, a small church camp in upstate New York. This camp shaped my parents' courtship, their marriage, and the rest of their lives—all of our lives, really. It's the closest my brother, sister, and I ever got to a hometown. Peniel sat at the base of Mount Cobble, best described as an oversized hill with a good view. The camp took its old-time religion straight from the tent revivals of the Great Depression and it looked it. Unaffiliated with any specific denomination, any real source of funds, the camp was built from the basics: sweat, rough lumber, God, and the Devil.

The dining hall was sheathed in wooden slats pulled from World War II ammunition crates. It was a long, utilitarian building with a massive stone fireplace set at one end and it smelled of wood smoke and oatmeal. The pine woods were full of cabins built from damp, greenish pine and dotted by red and white lichen. Each section, the boys' and the girls', had two outhouses. Our assembly field was the packed earth between the dining hall and the chapel, and it doubled as the playing field. Peniel had an underused baseball diamond in a place we called the Dustbowl.

The Channel, our swimming hole, was a cleared stretch of marsh full of soft mud and sharp grasses. There were redwing blackbirds and painted turtles, too, and there was no swimming on Sundays. The chapel was a simple pine building with a great bronze bell on its porch. This bell woke us, sent us to calisthenics, meetings (Bible study), meals, more meetings (prayer), and bed. Peniel washed my whole family in the blood of the Lamb—regularly—and that's something each of us carries in various ways. It's hard to forget.

My mother was born in 1925, the youngest of three children. Her father was a banker and the family lost almost everything in the Crash of 1929. He lost the rest five years later when his wife died. My grandfather continued; he kept his suits pressed and found work, but his sorrow went bitter and poisoned him. He began attending the fire-and-brimstone crusades and was saved by the infamous Billy Sunday, the preacher who rallied for Prohibition. "There isn't a man who votes for the saloon who doesn't deserve to have his boy die a drunkard," Sunday thundered. "He deserves to have his girl live out her life with a drunken husband." This made good, stern sense to my grandfather. He renounced the Devil and set about raising his children, my mother, Betty Lee, her sister, Rose, and her brother, Frank, in a dark world full of sinners. My grandfather ruled his house absolutely, with righteousness and a hard hand, and my mother, the youngest, served him from breakfast to bedtime. He remarried but his new wife resented the children. Their stepmother berated them all for years and then she just left.

My mom was the youngest and seemed to suffer in her childhood the most. She was nine when her mother died. At sixteen, her brother, Frank, took charge of the family's happiness. He staged my mother's dearest memories with magic, vaudeville acts, and art. He called her "Midget" and she was his magician's assistant. He scoured the city for costumes and wigs and had his younger sisters up on his backyard stage every day after school. Rose dressed my mother; she turned her baby sister into princesses and cowgirls and fairies. The three of them pretended together; they acted out other people's stories, happy ones. Frank and Rose are the heroes of her happiest memories. Mom is the one who still carries her father's heartbreak. She was his favorite, and all of her love is stitched down by worry.

My dad was born in Hollywood, where his father fixed scripts for Twentieth Century Fox and drank. When he smashed my grandmother's Rolls Royce she initiated divorce proceedings immediately. As soon as the court allowed she moved my six-year-old father to Albuquerque, New Mexico, where she burned every letter, photograph, and press clipping concerned with the man. If my grandmother could have extracted her ex-husband's DNA from her son, she would have done so immediately. She never spoke of Hunter Lovelace again, not even with my father. She told him Japanese submarines were the reason they left California. An attack, she said, was imminent.

My father grew up a virtual orphan on the high New Mexican desert. By the time he turned nine he discovered books could rescue him and let him leave his autocratic mother far behind.

The farther the better, and for my father that meant spaceships. Back then, before the Bomb, science still conjured a utopian future. The classic science fiction of the era took this on faith, built its castles in the air and sometimes destroyed them. My father never quite outgrew these stories. He let go of the hardware, sure, but he never let go of the vision, his hope for a shining city on a hill.

Gus Armstrong, my father's only high school friend, dragged him out of the books and into the desert. They caught Gila monsters and hunted, jumping ducks from irrigation ditches along the Rio Grande. They found a case of dynamite down in an old mineshaft and they spent weeks blowing boulders from cliffs. They spied on a Hopi snake dance and afterward caught two of the rattlesnakes and brought them back to town. The rattlers' fangs had been ripped out for the dance. My grandmother tolerated them until new fangs appeared.

In the summer of 1948, just before my father went east, Gus Armstrong decided to round out my father's preparatory education with a trip to a brothel he knew in Juarez. Driving south, the boys entertained themselves with a twenty-two-caliber pistol, shooting road signs and groundhogs from the car window. A groundhog ducked; my father pulled back the pistol and slipped the gun's hammer. Bang. Silence ensued and then Gus asked calmly, "Richard. Did you just shoot a hole in my Buick?"

"No, Gus," my father answered, just as slow and deliberate. "I did not. I shot a hole in my leg." Gus pulled over, fashioned a sort of tourniquet, and they turned back home.

"I guess that trip just wasn't God's will," my father remarked to me years later. The doctors left the slug in my father, just above his right knee, and when I was a boy I'd ask to see the bullet all the time. The bullet is still lodged right there in his muscle, like a piece of God's will, coppery green and buried in flesh. Shortly after the aborted trip to Juarez, my father limped into Yale on crutches, a gun-shot atheist.

In 1943 Frank encouraged my mother to enroll at the Pratt Institute in New York City. He had become a successful photographer and supported his worried kid sister with money and love. My mother hoped to illustrate children's books and she worked extremely hard, repaying Frank with her happy watercolors: the girls all in pigtails, their brothers with slingshots, calico aprons for Mom, and for Dad a pipe and the paper. But her normal undergraduate concerns began building and mutating. She stopped worrying about grades but feared for her soul. She worked harder and harder to stay with her painting, to keep her paranoia contained.

She finally broke at the end of her senior year, just prior to project deadlines and exams. She had been studying and painting for days. She was jacked up on coffee and had stopped sleeping, just pushing herself. And then late one night she looked up from her paintings, the blue skies and children, and she saw a wicked figure, a demon hunched in the corner of her room, watching. She snapped and heard voices; the creature just stayed in the corner, waiting. Her close friend and roommate, Margaret, sought help. By the next day she was labeled schizophrenic and put away. Her diagnosis didn't change for forty years.

It was 1949 and psychiatrists diagnosed almost all delusional

illness as schizophrenia—"shattered mind." Nervous break-
downs were one thing, but with hallucinations it was pretty
damn hopeless. They didn't have antipsychotic drugs. They didn't
have Thorazine, Stelazine, Trilafon, Zyprexa, and the rest. All
they had was electroshock. They'd been using it for eight or nine
years when my mother got sick. The treatment wasn't yet perfected, but it was a fairly simple procedure. Electrodes are placed
on either side of the patient's head. An electric stimulus is applied, causing seizure and convulsions lasting fifteen seconds or
so. Patients may experience short-term memory loss but no evidence of brain damage has been linked to proper dosages. They
had established the proper doses by the time my mother got sick.
Now it's called ECT and technicians use muscle relaxants to
inhibit the full-scale convulsions. This removes physical dan-
gers such as the breaking or dislocation of bones. Sedatives are
administered to quell panic. ECT is often effective, especially
with chronic, drug-resistant depression. It seems to work for
some people—no one knows why exactly.

It seemed to work for my mom. She was there for quite a time
but her delusions did pass and before long she returned to her
painting. It remained unclear when my mother would be released but in those days, before all the medicines, a diagnosis of
schizophrenia usually meant long-term hospitalization and even
lifelong institutionalization. Eventually, one of the nurses noticed her artwork, the healing it had brought, and she began
advocating for her release. My mother's college roommate, Margaret, enlisted help from her church camp and Peniel brought
in its big guns. Miss Beers was the central leader and spiritual
guide of the camp. She was formidable, a veteran of the prewar

mission fields of Japan. Grover Wilcox was a fundamentalist preacher from Newark, a firebrand who turned his house into a church and combed the ghetto streets for souls to save. His sense of righteousness made him fearless and he hit like a freight train. Beers and Wilcox descended on the hospital like twin holy terrors and demanded my mother's release.

Wilcox brought my mother home to his house church, where his family gave her a room and a place at their table. My mother stayed afraid but Wilcox had built a mighty fortress and he kept her safe for a time. He kept my mother from slipping out of the world, even as he renounced it. He didn't approve of art, but he helped my mother graduate, finally, from Pratt. She took a job teaching art in Newark's elementary schools. Every morning my mother stood in front of kids from the projects, handed out scissors and glue, and tried to organize art. Art teachers are just a step removed from substitutes. Their motives are pure and their discipline vague. They make excellent time-honored targets and provide ammunition in the form of art supplies. And my mother, she was a hopeless disciplinarian. She raised me. Mom says teaching art in the Newark public schools was the most terrifying experience of her life. The next summer, when the pastor offered her a ride to Peniel she jumped at it. He packed up his family, thirty-odd church kids, a few lost souls, and my mother and headed upstate.

As for my father, he soon outgrew science fiction, pistols, and groundhogs. He majored in philosophy and music composition. He studied existentialism seriously enough to be terrified and found Schoenberg's twelve-tone scale appalling. He packed up his life and moved everything into his head. He often closed his eyes in concentration, as if hearing some silent, slow music. This slow music made driving dangerous and dating awkward; by his senior year my father had dug himself into a social and ideological hole. It wasn't long before an odd student named John Guray stepped into it.

Guray was prematurely bald, walked with a limp and a cane, and wrote light verse. He wore berets and had discovered psychoanalysis. Guray was made for psychoanalysis and began practicing his art on my father incessantly. He kept notes and made charts. He pondered my father's dreams. It was Guray who convinced my dad to travel west and find his father. In fact Guray went along for the ride, guiding my father and his subconscious across the country.

My dad had not seen or heard from his father until the day he and Guray tracked him down. They found him in Hollywood, working on a studio lot. "He was nice enough. Somewhat reserved," my father said to me recently. "He introduced us to some blond starlet. I think he wanted to make sure we weren't gay, that we showed some interest."

His father then introduced them to Cecil B. DeMille, and when my father asked, "How did you part the Red Sea, Mr. DeMille?" DeMille replied, "I didn't, son. God did." And that was it. That's all my father told me. That's all he knew of his father. A blond bombshell and Cecil B. DeMille stole the show.

Upon their return to New Haven, a crestfallen John Guray claimed the analysis and their relationship could go no further, that my father had experienced a great breakthrough. He then produced a bill for four thousand dollars. All my father got from plumbing his subconscious was a road trip and a ridiculous invoice. My father felt he really owed Guray—that's how lost he was. He looked for guidance in his books and found it in Thomas Merton's autobiography, *The Seven Storey Mountain.* Merton's story brought him to God. Yale's so-called New Critics, Cleanth Brooks among them, had given my father a well-lit, archetypically ordered universe, and now Merton's God would give it meaning. My father even considered monastic life in Merton's order.

About this time John Guray began sending my father handwritten bills that he marked "Overdue." My father avoided him and began attending church. Guray began attending church and suggested my father meet a minister acquaintance, Don Mostrom. Before long my father was attending a weekly Bible study run by Mostrom and some other theologically astute, serious men. A number of them spoke highly of the Peniel Bible Conference; a few were in leadership roles as members of Peniel's Prayer Council. They tore up John Guray's bills and began mentoring my father.

My dad had recently been fired from Berman Salvage & Scrap, where he had earned his way by scraping gold tracings from discarded spark plugs. He had few prospects. But he had a Yale philosophy degree, so he found a job teaching seventh graders at the Riverdale Country School. Like my mother, he found the experience unrewarding. He's referred to his pupils as "snarling, derisive children of affluence." He fled in a hail of spitwads and headed straight for Peniel—again, just like my mother. His career had stalled, perhaps, but he was now clear about what he wanted to do. He wanted to help build the Kingdom of God—that "shining city upon a hill" proclaimed by the Puritan leader John Winthrop. He went to Peniel because it was a big job and he was unsure where to begin. That was 1954, the summer he met my mother.

It's a wonder Peniel Bible Conference ever brought my parents together, a tribute to the biological imperative. Love is a great mystery, and nowhere more mysterious than at Bible camp. In my experience the place routinely smothered romance with spiritual angst and Bible study. We were taught that no matter how attractive we found fellow campers, we were all clothed in the Old Man or the Flesh, camp-speak for our corrupt, fallen natures. My father, of course, has a different view. I know my father believes they were set up. Why else, he argues, would they have made him assist in my mother's arts and crafts class? But in the end, it wasn't church history or Peniel's machinations that drew them together, it was my mother when she's well—her empathy, her ease and laughter with friends, and what my father calls her "cheery, elfin smile."

They were married in 1958, just after my father graduated from Westminster Seminary. My parents honeymooned in Lenox, Massachusetts, where Dad commenced Mom's education at the Tanglewood Music Festival. When they returned from Lenox, Grover Wilcox ordained my father as his assistant pastor. He moved in, and so my parents began their life together on the top floor of a house church in Newark, New Jersey. Wilcox was known for his legalism, a worldview held by the hardest of the hard core, the separatists of fundamentalism. Wilcox labeled anything secular—art, sports, politics right or left, beer—"of the World," a distraction from God. He disapproved of my father reading the *New York Times*. He threw out the arts section. His church piano was for hymns only—certain ones—and my father remembers playing a Beethoven sonata when Wilcox barged in. "What is that, Richard?" he yelled. "Scales?" Wilcox and other Peniel leaders took pride in their cultural isolation, in the blessed assurance of songs known by heart. My father was suspect; he worked on a whole different scale.

But the following summer Dad connected with Julian Alexander, a like-minded minister from Scotch Plains, New Jersey. They were washing dishes together in the camp kitchen when my father began complaining about Wilcox and legalism. "The elders at Mostrom's church drink beer all the time. And John Murray, at Westminster, the theologian, he drinks sherry." He threw a pot down in the sink. "Did you know, Julian, that Calvin's salary included forty gallons of wine annually? Or that Luther recommended drinking a beer before confronting the Devil?"

Alexander was himself an intellectual and allergic to legalism. He enjoyed my dad's mind and loved his idiosyncrasies. I believe he hired my father on as youth pastor just so he had someone with whom to discuss Luther, Calvin, and Kierkegaard. His church provided my parents a house, furniture, and a generous stipend. Freed from the Wilcox house church, my mother could wear her lipstick again and my father could listen to anything.

They were finally making their life together and things proceeded smoothly until I was born in 1960. It took my mother six months to recover. Her postpartum depression soon deepened into paranoia and delusion. It had been ten years since her last breakdown. She lay on the couch and suffered Old Testament fears and delusions—she was damned or maybe a prophet, Elijah perhaps—and all the while church ladies came with their casseroles and left with their gossip, their prayer concerns.

That summer, as my mother recovered, Dad carried me around camp in an unzipped plaid suitcase. I was swaddled in blankets, a sort of precious luggage. It was as if I'd been found in the rushes down by the channel, or perhaps baggage claim. If I returned to Peniel tomorrow—and it's still there—I'm sure some ancient camper would chuckle and say, "I remember that suitcase. Your father was a riot." My father has long been the camp's celebrated eccentric, a subject of lore and apocrypha.

My mother recovered over that summer and when we returned my parents discussed having another child. They consulted a psychiatrist, who advised against it in no uncertain terms. It could "aggravate my mother's schizophrenia and pass it on," he said. They ignored him and my mother gave birth to the sanest Lovelace in the bunch, my sister, Peggy. Again, my mother slipped into the black. I was just two years old but I remember her black eyes. I remember how frightened I was growing up, scared my mother would leave and never come back. Peggy says at age three she began worrying for our mother, afraid she would make Mom cry.

I didn't share that worry until later. By age three I had thrown church picnic chicken and coleslaw at deacons. Desperate, God-fearing adults had tethered me to trees. Bucktoothed, thin, and agitated, I resembled the young Jerry Lewis to my sister's

Judy Garland. She was a beautiful kid, crowned with brown curls. She possessed a quiet, reflective spirit and a holy terror for a brother. By all accounts, but especially by the accounts my sister still continues to share every Christmas, our sibling rivalry was intense and one-sided. I did get the most attention. Any kid who deploys airborne sprocket weapons built from smashed clocks, spikes breakfast cereals with stockpiled Tabasco sauce, and generally lays in wait for his saintly sister will get the most attention. My sister retreated to her room and read for the greater part of her childhood. She resents it to this day. Still, she was better off on the moors with Heathcliff than in the backyard with me.

My mother was happiest at Peniel, where she spent her summers painting still lifes and camp signs, and always painting Bible verses on banners. I remember helping my mother decorate the chapel with the armor of God. Together we cut the cardboard shapes: the helmet of salvation, the breastplate of righteousness, the sword and the shield of faith. Mom painted them silver and black and we hung them from the rafters. Peniel made clear to the children that we were at war. In the camp nursery—the Olive Yard—all of us sang, "We may never march in the infantry, ride in the cavalry, shoot the artillery, but we're in the Lord's army." As soldiers of Christ ours was a battle "not against flesh and blood, but against principalities, against the darkness of this world." I loved it. A holy war is the best kind of war a boy can have, full of demons and superheroes. Vietnam wasn't important when the Prince of Darkness himself hid under our bunks and threw darts from our woods.

Peniel was more think tank than camp. Its program was a veritable wailing wall of religious training and I spent each July and August ducking out from the tent. It didn't matter. By the time I was ten Grover Wilcox had my loud mouth testifying on the streets of Lake George, confessing sins before I had committed them and diagramming the Four Spiritual Laws on signboards with marker. Peniel's religion was hard to dodge, even twenty miles away. I suspect Peniel's founders, Miss Beers and Mrs. Mac, viewed recreation as a gateway to sin—exercise heats up the flesh and leads to temptation. They made no excuse for the camp's asceticism, its unrelenting schedule of chapel meetings. It was our evangelical heritage, stiffened through Prohibition and run straight through the Depression.

I remember my cabin challenging another set of boys to an eating contest in the dining hall. Before it was over the camp's cofounder and disciplinarian, Mr. Mac, hauled us up in front of the camp. We stood shamefaced as he glowered. And then, after a long silence, he began.

"Gluttony, campers, is one of the deadly sins. Gluttony makes a mockery of the gifts God brings us. Gluttony is wasteful. It is selfish. Now, these boys are no more sinful than the rest of us. They want to be good, mindful of God's blessings. But gluttony is an abomination to the Lord..." He continued straight through dessert.

Today's Republican megachurches have no problem with gluttony. Evangelical churches lure children to camp with imitation rock bands, Jet Skis, and parasailing. Peniel, with its outhouses, its stick-framed chapel and broken-spined hymnals, seems a poor country cousin, its children just a motley crew of preachers' kids and other unfortunates. It was hardscrabble but we made our own fun or we stole it. There were plenty of rules and we broke them. We swam on Sundays, stole canoes, and kissed girls. We ran away but never long enough, really, to leave.

It was fine, a boyhood surrounded by austere mystery, by dusty prayers, with the small mountain behind us and all the white pines, a place threshed and winnowed by prayer. We sang the old, muscular hymns I still love—"Lead on, O King Eternal"; "A Mighty Fortress"; "Power in the Blood"—and Sunday suppers were brimstone and honey, and it all made you hungry. There was no entertainment, no frippery. The camp got its name from an Old Testament story in which Jacob demands his god's blessing. He wrestles the angel all night for it, and at dawn the creature relents; it twists Jacob's hip, blesses him, and leaves. He called the place Peniel and that's what we learned there. We were crippled and blessed and taught to be thankful.

Every August, after leaving Peniel and before heading back to Scotch Plains, we visited my dad's mother in Woodstock. We never called her Grandma; we weren't allowed. As a young woman my grandmother had taken her inheritance to Europe, where she came of age and commenced a lifetime of seasonal grand tours. Although her means came from unwashed cowboys once removed, my grandmother adopted old money and the old world as her own. Shortly following my birth she actually willed herself French and insisted the family call her "Grandmère." She got her table manners from Marie Antoinette and enforced them with a cold imperial stare. She was a lifelong member of the John

Birch Society and supported Woodstock's Christian Science Reading Room. She had sent her food back to kitchens and dressed down their chefs all across the Western world.

My mother, of course, was terrified by the time we hit Albany. By the Catskills the grooming had begun in earnest. She picked at our clothes and plastered our hair with her spit. "Now, David," she'd say, "remember to stay at the table until she lets you go. She will excuse you." My sister and I sat in the backseat holding our infant brother and happily fending off our mother's fluttering hands. We were off to see the matriarch, her meadow and the trout stream, but my mother continued to fret. Our station wagon filled with hairspray and fear. "Richard," my mother would say, "you should polish your shoes. I didn't have a chance to wash the children's outfits. Please don't bring up money with your mother."

My father, oblivious to my mother's growing panic, usually responded by turning up the radio and commenting, "Now, listen to this. This is a beautiful movement; listen to how the horn comes in." He would look up in the rearview mirror and say, "David, do you know what horn that is?"

"French," I'd answer. They were always French and he'd nod approvingly. He never asked our mother or Peggy what horn it was, he always asked me.

It was 1967 and we'd pass through Woodstock and ogle the hippies, turn left at the Bear restaurant and then down her long drive, past the ruined well, the leaning stone post with its BEWARE OF DOG sign. Grandmère was terrified of hippies. When we arrived, just after she assessed and welcomed us, she asked, "How was it in town? Were they out on the green?"

"Yeah. Tons of 'em!" I answered enthusiastically.

"Yes. Well." She turned from us and to her son. "The town, Richard, is in a state of siege, nothing less."

"It's lively, all right," he agreed.

"Well, the place looks beautiful," my mother said hopefully. "Your lilacs are lovely."

"Yes, aren't they?" Grandmère allowed, and looked back to my father. "It's nice to see all of you."

"So, Mother," my father asked. "How's the mildew this year?" Grandmère was obsessed with the hippies, my father with the mold. And with good reason; Grandmère's house was famous for its virulent strains. A river ran through it—literally. Groundwater sluiced down the shale mountain behind her and it flowed straight through her stone crypt of a basement. All the water smelled of sulfur; her rooms smelled of rotten eggs and Chanel No. 5. Mold attacked the house from below but Grandmère had a solution of sorts. She painted the interiors teal green, a color we called "Catskill Mold." She painted everything that color, the oak beams arching above our heads, the fieldstone fireplace, the furniture. She imported the massive teal-green curtains to hold back the north light. She installed green carpets. Her living room was a perfumed grotto, a wet place at the bottom of the sea.

But water saved Grandmère's house as well. The house overlooked a gently sloping meadow with apple trees and a trout stream flowing along its far side against birches. Years ago, someone had built a large stone pool in its path and the brook flowed through its wooden slat gates. It had begun to collapse before I was born, and over the years it gradually filled with silt until the stream broke down its bank and swept around the old ruin. The pool drowned in mud and wildflowers and tadpoles. My sister and I would greet Grandmère, cut loose, and run down to the water. Dad waved and said, "David, hey, David. Try to spot some trout."

Then my father always brought in the bags and stood in the kitchen with my mother and Grandmère, where he'd announce: "I need to run downtown. I can see the allergy situation is bad this year." He'd leave Mom and my infant brother alone in the house with Grandmère and dash back to the car. After two or three hours my father always returned with two dozen night crawler worms, a stack of lurid science fiction paperbacks, and a stockpile of allergy medications. He doped himself up on anti-histamines and disappeared into his books and his space travel, alone again in the New Mexican desert.

"In our family," Norman Maclean famously wrote, "there was no clear line between religion and fly fishing." Norman's father, also a Presbyterian minister, taught him the counts of a fly cast. "He certainly believed," Maclean wrote, "that God could count and that only by picking up his rhythms were we able to regain power and beauty." It was different for my family. In Woodstock, just after dinner my father and I would take our Styrofoam cup of worms and our rods and walk down through the meadow. When we were close Dad would crouch down and we'd whisper and thread the thick night crawlers onto the hooks. We'd crawl closer and flip the baits over the grassy bank and my father would count to twenty. If nothing happened we'd leave the worms drowning and go watch television. In the morning I'd run down and pull out a trout, dead and all twisted up with the line. In fact, it wasn't really fishing, it was trapping, and an ignoble introduction to something I love. Discipline and patience are hard-won in my family. Years later, after Grandmère was gone, I lived in her house until I learned fly casting, how to fish all her streams. I came home to teach my father and brother and together we fished through the Catskills' own legends: the Esopus and Willowemock and Beaverkill.

When I was nine, Peggy and I brought a cassette tape we had made especially for Grandmère on Dad's new machine. After dinner we begged Grandmère to turn down William F. Buckley—the man somehow dominated her television—and listen to us, to the new tape we had made. "Well," Grandmère said. "If we must. We shall wait until the next commercial." Peggy and I squirmed while Bill Buckley listed our gains in Southeast Asia. It was a long list but finally Grandmère turned the sound off and my father popped the cassette into his portable recorder.

"HI, GRANDMÈRE. THIS IS DAVID," it said. "I'M GOING TO READ YOU SOME RECORDS. WORLD RECORDS FROM THE GUINNESS BOOK."

"Hi, Grandmère, this is Peggy. I want to say a poem that—"

"THE WORLD'S FATTEST MAN WEIGHS FIVE HUNDRED SIXTY-TWO POUNDS TEN OUNCES STRIPPED NAKED. A MONSTER PIG WAS KILLED BY AN ELEVEN-YEAR-OLD PHILL-I-PINO BOY IN 1962 AND IS CONSIDERED THE WORLD'S LARGEST SWINE. THE WORLD'S MOST—hey, cut it out, Peg, I'm reading. THE WORLD'S MOST PRO-LIF-FIC MOTHER WAS RUSSIAN. NADIA BUKansky or something GAVE BIRTH—stop it, c'mon, stop it—TO SIXTY-NINE CHILDREN FROM 1725 TO 1765. THE MOST HOT DOGS CONSUMED IN . . ."

Grandmère's smile, normally frozen, had calcified. She was clutching the arms of an antique chair, her eyes fixed on my mortified mother. Just under my tinny voice you could hear my sister crying. Dad and I thought it was great. Everyone just loved it.

Grandmère said a quick thank-you and lapsed into silence, watching William F. Buckley talk on the screen. My father picked up his science fiction and my mother picked up Jonathan. Grandmère finally broke her silence. "It was quiet here," she said. "Just the real artists before that communist boy moved in up the road." It all went to hell, my grandmother maintained, when Bob Dylan came in 1965. "You know his manager, that Jewish man, what's his name? Grossman. He owns property in Bearsville. Just over the stream."

"Oh, really," my father said. He held his book on his lap and kept reading.

"Richard, I was speaking to Henry Maust yesterday." The Mausts were Grandmère's only Woodstock friends. "Henry came home yesterday and found a number of naked hippies just lying on the lower field. Just lying there. Imagine, Richard." The red menace and flower children kept Grandmère on her toes. When she drove us to town in her Cadillac, she had us lock all the doors. "Put your hands in. I'm rolling up the windows." We were pushing twenty miles an hour. "Hilda Maust said a hippie on a bicycle actually reached into her car. Imagine," I couldn't imagine. I couldn't believe a hippie tried to grope Hilda Maust. There were far more interesting things to do in Woodstock than grope Hilda Maust. The town was full of psychedelia and head shops. Even the hardware store was a head shop. I loved it.

Our last mornings in Woodstock had ritual. My father and I would clean the last brace of brown trout. My mother had finished packing by eight a.m. and lay on the green couch in a state of nervous collapse while Grandmère fried the trout in bacon fat, filling her kitchen with sweet smoke. After the trout and English muffins Grandmère would give us all stiff little hugs and we left. Grandmère would soon leave herself, decamp to her winter lodging at the Women's Republican Club in New York City.

My father always slowed at the base of Grandmère's long gravel drive; he'd honk and we'd shout, "Good-bye, Grandmère," and then, finally, relax. Mom and Dad would start laughing again; Peggy and I could get back to our quarrels and jokes. Despite all the forced manners, the endless wait to be excused from her table, I never wanted to leave my grandmother's. I loved its ruined slate pool, the meadow, the trout with their red spots circled by orange, their brown sides sliding into buttery yellows. The Catskills are old mountains, worn down and haunted; Woodstock was an old artists' colony shot through with new colors. Scotch Plains, New Jersey, stood in stark contrast to all this, a flat patch of white suburbia, my father's church full of middle-management parents and bored kids.

I know my father struggled as much as I did. It was hard to just blend into the normalcy of a suburban pastorate, especially at the helm of a youth group. His occasional sermons often confused the congregation with concerns they viewed as tangential to the gospel, things like poetry, music, and film. My father was aloof and cerebral and lacked many of the basic ministerial tools, social skills like facial recognition. Dad was terrible with names. He once buried a body without knowing its gender, fudging the pronouns. When he looked out over the faithful, I'm convinced Dad simply had no idea who most of these people were or what they were doing in his church.

Nevertheless, he grew close with Willow Grove's pastor, Julian Alexander, and before long they were staging all manner of unlikely cultural events. The church youth group performed my father's adaptation of *Waiting for Godot*. Julian and my father presented a series of dramatic readings, including *No Exit* and *Franny and Zooey*. My dad's flock of teenagers grew both in numbers and enthusiasm. My father and his group began dismantling preconceptions, the distinctions between high culture and low. "They got me into the Beatles," my father told me, "and I got them into Schumann." Eventually, my father embraced the artistic bloom of the '60s and in doing so inflamed Willow Grove's cultural anxieties. He quoted Bob Dylan in sermons. The church mothers didn't know what to do.

Christ taught his followers to be "in the world but not of it." My father emphasized the former and, moreover, he argued for total immersion, and it wasn't all Bach. He took me to see *A Clockwork Orange* and *Deliverance* when I was twelve. The good Presbyterians of Willow Grove still remember when their church sign announced:

> **Sunday Services 9 & 11 am**
> **This Sunday: God's Eternal Grace**
> **Next Sunday: Rosemary's Baby**

The deacons protested and Julian asked us over to dinner. After grace and the passing of pot roast, Reverend Alexander allowed that the sign had spiked interest. "We've been getting calls, Richard. Are you aware that the film is a horror film? An R-rated horror film?"

"Yes. Have you seen it?"

"Certainly not. I understand it involves Satan."

"Absolutely. It is Satanic," my father enthusiastically concurred. He helped himself to seconds. "It emphasizes how counterfeit spiritualities promise heaven without a real Christ."

"Look, Richard. I'm not sure I can help you if you go through with this. I'm not convinced a sermon on *Rosemary's Baby* is a good idea." Julian chuckled in spite of himself. "You know, they might riot."

"Julian, I would not recommend this film without a good reason, without a real message."

Julian remained skeptical. "That's all well and good, Richard. But I don't think it—" A thought struck him. He put down his water glass. "Richard, you don't plan to show the film, do you? I cannot allow it. We don't have a projector." He winced. "Do we?"

"No, no. Of course not." My father laughed. "It's a good movie—I loved it—but I'm not going to show it. It's just a sermon illustration, that's all it is."

Julian smiled in spite of himself. "A pornographic sermon illustration?"

"The film is about modern witchcraft. There's some sexual magic, I suppose—offscreen. It's not pornographic. I wouldn't recommend it if it didn't have redeeming social values."

"Such as?"

"Such as witchcraft is bad news."

Julian relented and the Rosemary sermon was a huge success. People poured in that Sunday to see what rough beast was lurching toward them. It was standing-room-only and my father made them stand in a church a little bit larger, a little more open to the world. Excepting the witches, of course; they had to stand outside.

Meanwhile I ranged with a band of neighborhood boys through frog ponds and vacant lots. We were all seven, eight, or nine, busy testing the boundaries of backyards and parents and school. I was the minister's kid; I pushed harder than the rest because I had much more to push—all the weight of my sin, my father's congregation, and all the heavenly host. I couldn't listen anymore. My kindergarten teacher dragged me by my ear to the office. By second grade I was sneaking out after dark to soap cars and egg houses. I stole copies of *Mad* magazine. When we went to the circus I convinced my parents to buy me a real leather whip. I terrorized church picnics and flunked out of Sunday school. I was not a bad child, simply my father's. It's kid stuff, but ministers' children must run amok. They maintain the cosmic balance.

One Saturday morning, the neighborhood bully, a large dim-witted boy named Eric, began taunting my band of friends. My whip had been confiscated by then but I still had my slingshot. Eric said I was a lousy shot, that I couldn't hit a barn, and then the rock hit his forehead. He stood there, stunned, until blood covered his face. Everyone scattered. I ran home, hid in my closet, and cried for twenty minutes until I heard Eric's mother arrive. I crept into the hall and listened.

"Your son," began Eric's mother, "is out of control. My boy could have very easily lost his eye."

"I'm terribly sorry. I'm sure David didn't mean to hit him."

"He didn't, did he? Where did he get that slingshot, that weapon?"

"I'm afraid I bought it for him. After he lost his whip." Mom suspects she's guilty of everything and confesses at every opportunity.

"Does his father know this? Does the church know about your son?"

"Yes, I'm afraid so."

"You will punish him. He can't just roam the streets with weapons." I heard a chair scrape and ran for my room. "I'll be leaving now, Mrs. Lovelace—"

"Please, Betty Lee."

"I hope your son understands what he's done."

She left and I crept down to the kitchen. My mother sat very still and I thought she would cry. I crawled up into her lap and she kissed my streaked face, pushed back my hair, and just held me.

By now my father was attending Princeton, working toward his doctorate in church history. Julian and he had long since agreed that my father's strengths lay with academia. He couldn't run a church. He was, as my dad puts it, "administratively incompetent." In 1968 he published his thesis as *The American Pietism of Cotton Mather.* I remember his doctoral thesis in piles—three-by-four note cards stacked on the cold linoleum of his church basement office. And I remember standing with my fa-

ther in the church office, helping as he mimeographed and col-
lated late into the night, meeting his doctoral deadline by the
hour.

It was clear to the deacons that my father possessed negligible
management skills and found discipline tedious. But it was his
eccentricities, the ones Willow Grove's teenagers found so cool,
that alarmed the church as a whole. It was widely rumored my
father closed his eyes in prayer while driving the church kids to
camp. He let the teenagers listen to "Sympathy for the Devil."
He rode around on a Japanese motorcycle far too small for his
frame and, worse, he regularly perched me on the bike's gas
tank, stuck a peewee football helmet on my head, and cruised
the streets. By the end of summer the church officially forbade
dangerous spectacles involving six-year-olds. They put my dad
on a short leash.

It wasn't simple culture shock. Beyond the ridiculously small
motorcycle, the rock and roll, the salacious sermons, and Mahler
blasting from his church office, my father had one other con-
suming interest, one that clinched his suspect identity at the
church: snakes. Mostly snakes, and also some lizards. He had
never kicked the reptile-hunting habits of his desert boyhood.
Claiming he was allergic to any common, domesticated pet, he
spent large sums on reptiles. He began haunting exotic pet stores
in the city, rank basements lit only by heat lamps and run by
unshaven snake enthusiasts with names like Sal or Jerry.

If my father had left his pets to their reptilian stupors, safe in
their terrarium homes, his collection would have remained no
more than an eccentric's hobby, harmless. Instead, he insisted on
taking one or two of the animals to his church office daily,

barricading the door with his thesis draft, jacking the thermostat up to eighty, and blasting his music. He flaunted the snakes. The habits of the hognose, in particular, provided my father with colorful sermon illustrations and he spent an inordinate amount of pulpit time exculpating common, garden-variety snakes from the sins of Eden's symbolic dark serpent.

As my father completed his doctorate, a general and inevitable consensus formed. My father was, in a word, ill-suited for the ministry. My mother was unstable, a poor choice. A growing chorus of alarmed parishioners brought a wide range of Lovelace anecdotes to the church deacons. Their youth pastor had allied with the scourge, the unwashed, the counterculture. Church members wanted my father dismissed. At the deacons' meeting, a phalanx of balding, relatively unimaginative midlevel managers found my father deeply strange but all agreed he was doctrinally sound and appreciated his affinity with the church teenagers. My father's eccentricities were duly noted and discussions ensued, but no disciplinary action was taken.

Their mood darkened considerably, however, when Willow Grove's cleaning woman quit abruptly after encountering a small alligator snapping at her from the church organ's keyboard. An emergency meeting was called; my father reclaimed the vicious little reptile from the deacons and promised to leave him at home with the rest. He listened to their dire warnings with equanimity as his loathsome pet scratched and hissed from the cardboard box on his lap. By now my father had perfected his classic deacon meeting defense. He simply wandered off in his head, rhapsodic, detached from any parish concerns.

He wasn't worried. Princeton would award his doctorate in

church history that spring. He would send out his impressive credentials and just wait for the right teaching position to open. He was a ministerial lame duck; he was on his way out. Now he could devote his time to Brahms and his reptiles, take more father-son trips to the Jersey shore to catch sea robins and blow-fish. It was a great relief to all involved.

Meanwhile my mother had her trials, shy and thrust into the role of a minister's wife, God's hostess. She bravely bought Tupperware, chatted awkwardly through Jell-O mold suppers, and kept me in Band-Aids. My sister retreated and my father was busy. I needed an accomplice and so I spent my entire seventh year praying nightly for a brother. When Jonathan finally showed I took all the credit. It was the power of prayer. I just kept at it till God relented.

I forgot what my prayers would cost. Mom lay on our couch in New Jersey, holding my infant brother, unable to speak, afraid for her mind and her soul. My mother soon drifted into paranoia and then deeper into delusion. She was damned and everyone damned her. When the churchwomen began arriving with food, began holding her baby, my mother's fear grew worse. They had plotted to take her family, to poison her, to carry out Satan's terrible will. I watched her each morning as she lay on that brown couch. She haunted the room. And then my mother was gone and we couldn't go see her. My father smiled and said Mom was just resting but I knew better. I knew she was crazy. Mom's mind, my father said, had begun skipping and just needed a knock, a bounce back into its groove. But I knew things. I had heard things. I knew what had happened before I was born. They took her away. They locked her up. She lost the power of speech and she growled like a dog. When I was seven a nightmare lodged in my chest and never left. Alone late at night I saw my mother snarling and snapping. On some level, I think, my siblings and I felt responsible for the sickness that followed our births. My mother's postpartum delusions threw shadows over my family's world. She broke into black rooms we never could enter. My father began to shield my mother from the outside, from trouble and finances, from parties and friends—even from us. I spent my childhood afraid for my mother, afraid I would lose her to hospitals, to all the whispered secrets. It became my lifelong fear—our family madness, my mother barking, my mother convulsed.

THREE

In 1968 my father was named professor of church history at Conwell Seminary, a small evangelical school outside Philadelphia. Conwell soon merged with another conservative school and we all moved to Hamilton, Massachusetts. We didn't really belong in Hamilton. In fact, my father's employer didn't belong in Hamilton. Theologians do not mix well at the hunt club. On Boston's North Shore matters of religion were settled properly ages ago. God chose sides and the hunt club won. Sunday mornings are set aside for polo games and horse trials, not church. The Catholics had already fled the place, leaving a large, empty campus above town, and, in a sort of religious lateral pass, they sold it to us.

Dad went on ahead to Hamilton and Mom stayed behind with us and packed. She seemed fine then, fully recovered from Jonathan's birth. He was almost two, my sister seven, and I was nine years old. Dad brought his mother house shopping and Grandmère put a down payment on a low-slung, damp house surrounded by oaks and scrub saplings. He found it in Hamilton's scruffy outback, where ranch homes with mulch-pile lawns were hidden away in the woods like the servants' quarters. Dad wired the house for sound, set up his snake room full of heat lamps, unpacked his typewriter, and sent for us. Grandmère loved Hamilton. She believed there was hope for us yet.

In any third grade the new kid always gets it in the neck. And in New England, the new kid is new until two or three generations stack up in the town graveyard. I was pilloried at the bus stop and shunned at school. The heir to a major banking concern beat the tar out of me by the lockers. The children of law firms gathered to taunt me. My fistfights all degenerated into inconclusive heaps; they won me no allies. I hated school and every afternoon I ran home, dumped my books by the door, and headed for the woods. Just across our street was a series of bridle paths that went for miles, through marshes, thickets, and streams, until reaching the rolling estates closer to town.

Before long I tired of aimless walks and begged for a BB gun. I snuck along the bridle paths and took ambivalent shots at squirrels and songbirds. I fancied myself a poacher of the king's deer when I carried that gun, and incredibly, the cream of Hamilton society played along with me. On one gray November afternoon, miles from home, I heard what sounded like a pack of wild dogs barking and baying. There must have been dozens. I held my popgun tightly as the noise got closer, and then it arrived. The hounds tore around the corner and came straight at me. They were mad, the whole slobbering, yelping lot of them were mad and charging full tilt. I slipped behind an oak tree and looked for a limb. The dogs didn't slow, their tongues lashing and eyes rolling as they passed, chasing something, not me.

I heard a horn and then it made sense—at least in a limited, theatrical way. It was the aptly named Myopia Hunt Club, my new neighbors. I dropped the gun and kicked leaves over it just as the first horse and rider came into view. Another dozen or so rounded the bend, resplendent and ridiculous in brass buttons, red swallowtail jackets, and boots. The man in the top hat blew his horn again and the entire spectacle rode past swiftly and awkwardly.

None of the riders acknowledged or even made eye contact with me, a scruffy, modern American boy who had wandered into their game. Myopia has guarded their club's mix of near-sighted tradition and horses since 1882. Nevertheless, by the time I arrived lax zoning and thoughtless development had degraded both fox and Brahmin habitats. The club had stooped to dragging fox scent through the lower class of Hamilton neighborhoods. It was embarrassing for all of us, my poaching deer that didn't exist and the whole gang of them, costumed by P. G. Wodehouse and chasing a nonexistent fox.

I was overjoyed. I had found people—grown-ups—who were stranger than us, stranger than my family. Next time maybe I'd get caught and they could place me in their imaginary stocks down in front of their English-like club. I was heartened and redoubled my hunting efforts.

My father flourished at Gordon-Conwell and hit his stride as a church historian. His doctoral thesis, *The American Pietism of Cotton Mather*, was now in print and well regarded. Academia, even evangelical academia, gave my father's eccentricities license and he was respected by the school's faculty. The social graces required of ministers are not expected of professors. The students loved his lecturing style and his classes filled immediately. He was forgetful and distracted and they loved him for it. He couldn't remember their names but he knew his stuff cold.

My father argued that Cotton Mather, of Salem witch trial fame, had laid the foundations for modern evangelicalism. Dad asked his readers to look past the trial, but I put it front and center. Mather played a pivotal role, arguing for the court's admission of "spectral evidence": dreams, visions, and nightmares. Years later he defended the trials in his work *Wonders of the Invisible World*. In short, Mather legitimized hallucination in the New World; he brought hysteria into the courtroom. I'm no church historian but I am a Lovelace. I've heard my mother speak of demons and my father of angels. I've watched my family's religion conspire with our brain disease to conjure spectral evidence and trumpet it.

Mather's world proved too dark for my father, and he soon jumped a generation and focused on Jonathan Edwards and the Great Awakening. Edwards's sermons sparked a wildfire revival that spread through the colonies and across the Atlantic. He had it all: rock and roll fame, brimstone, and poetry. Edwards was a theologian's action hero, America's answer to Luther, and he became my father's intellectual touchstone. My brother was named for Edwards, and I was named for his missionary friend, David Brainerd. These two preachers stand at the opposite poles of my family's religion and give witness to its ongoing cycle of redemptive ecstasy and damning guilt.

Edwards claimed that true grace was evidenced by a supernatural illumination of the soul. Further, he argued that as "visible saints" his congregation should expect the bodily effects and feverish symptoms of salvation. Before long he had his congregants swooning in the aisles, crying and convulsing. Neighboring preachers denounced the church as hysterical, even possessed. Ultimately, Edwards conceded that some of these signs were suspect, but not before he had raised the psychological bar: the evangelical rush, the high as conversion's sure sign. I tried to catch this ecstatic proof all through my youth. All of us did.

I've never received this blessed assurance, but I've found its complement. I found what David Brainerd suffered at the faith's other pole: the sickness of the soul, the self-loathing that marks a true pilgrim's progress. Brainerd renounced the colonial world and lived in self-imposed exile. He lived, he said, in a "hideous and howling wilderness." Brainerd complained ceaselessly of "vapoury disorders," of distraction and despair. At the end of his life, he retreated to Edwards's spare room, finished up his sad notes, and died. He said he was unworthy of love, foul and sinful. His heart, he wrote, was a cage of unclean birds. My sister, Margaret Lee, has never seen this place. She's the only one of us who isn't bipolar, the only one of us named for a loved one rather than a Puritan.

When he wasn't lecturing, my father preferred to write at home in the living room. He would hole up with symphonies blasting and a constrictor draped around his shoulders. The three of us children were altogether too young for my father's distracted, intellectual disciplines. Even my mother lacked the critical tools necessary to share in my father's cerebral world. I'd lose myself in the woods, and my sister lost herself in books. My mother put flowers and vases on her kitchen table and worked on her paintings while Dad hunkered down in a low uphol-stered chair, hunched over his typewriter and insulated from the family by a wall of classical music. There was always music in the living room. Finally he ran speaker wires out to the kitchen and our dinners were swamped in Brahms and Bartók. My father would sit at the head of the table and hum, his eyes closed as his right hand hovered with the strings. He ate be-tween movements.

"Who can tell me the composer of this piece?" he'd ask, and my sister and I vied for his approval. My mother never guessed. Once she had me pull the wires out of the speakers.

"Now listen to this. This passage gives it away. Who wrote it?"

"Mozart." My guess was always Mozart with a Beethoven fallback. The occasional choral work had to be Bach.

"No, no. Here's a hint. *Afternoon of a Faun.*"

"What's a fawn?" my sister asked.

"Bambi's a fawn," I said. "Duh."

"Okay then, it's Beethoven," my sister said confidently. "It has to be Beethoven."

"What's Beethoven have to do with fawns?" I challenged.

My sister faltered. "Okay," she said. "Okay, Bach."

My father smiled broadly. "Wrong. You're both wrong. It's Debussy!"

Of course, Debussy.

But my father had other records, records the Willow Grove kids had given him. He didn't have much rock and roll but he had Dylan's *Highway 61 Revisited.* I listened to it over and over and memorized its lines, especially: "God said to Abraham kill me a son / Abe said man you must be putting me on / God said no Abe said what / God said you can do what you want Abe but / The next time you see me coming you better run." Dad had his Debussy and I had my "Desolation Row."

Some nights, when he was sick of Puritans, my father bundled me up and we went fishing. It was always just my Dad and I. Jonathan was too young and my father rarely invited my mother or Peggy. My father cited their complete and utter lack of interest and I think deep down he welcomed it. After all, they were girls. But Dad and I, we always fished.

We returned again and again to Salem Willows, a broken-down amusement park beside smokestacks and the harbor. It smelled of fried food, cigarettes, and drunks. At night—it was always at night—we would walk out on the long, dark pier, twenty feet above the water. Thirty-five years ago, before all the draggers clear-cut the ocean, my father and I could regularly catch twelve-pound cod on cut clams and jigs just out from shore. When the fish hit I lowered our rusted Coleman lantern just about down to the water and lashed the line. The cod flashed white in the bright green water and I'd hold the rod while my father dropped a nasty fist of grappling hooks. I'd horse the fish toward Dad and he would wait for the moment, yank and haul the fish up hand over hand. When we stood on that pier, I couldn't have cared less for the sad merry-go-round behind us, its seasick music and moldering horses. I didn't need cotton candy, spinning lights, and rides. And I don't think Dad needed Debussy. We were happy just standing in the dark with some hooks and a box of slippery, translucent clams for bait, waiting for fish.

Waiting for ducks was an entirely different matter. I remember sitting in duck blinds all through dark November afternoons, scanning the horizon for anything other than seagulls. "Seagulls are protected," my father explained, to my great disappointment. "We can't shoot seagulls." We used a small skiff to navigate through the salt marshes and, if necessary, retrieve ducks. I wanted a dog, of course, a retriever, but my father pleaded allergies and said the snakes were enough. We didn't really need the dog; we rarely hit ducks. Instead, we sat and watched our rather sad group of plastic decoys bob out in front of our hovel while I listened to my father talk about jumping ducks along the Rio Grande of his youth: whole rafts of them, he'd say. I don't remember bringing home edible ducks, but the family feasted on sea duck occasionally, a kind of feathered herring. I was too young for a gun and just played with the duck call. My father had a twelve-gauge monster of a Browning, a goose gun if there ever was one. It was an automatic and it jammed every time.

Although our duck hunts never lived up to their promise, I loved the idea of hunting. Anything. I spent more and more time on the bridle paths killing small innocent things with my BB gun: chickadees, nuthatches, large beetles. I knew it was wrong but I kept score. I played for keeps. I longed to poach larger game from Myopia's forest but stags were scarce, as were pheasants and partridge. This left squirrel. It was clear I needed more gun.

"Dad," I said, "it's perfectly fine to shoot squirrels. There's a season and everything."

"I don't know, David. It just seems cruel."

"People eat them all the time, Dad. Really."

"I've never seen anyone eat a squirrel. Maybe in Appalachia."

"Dad, there's tons and tons of squirrels out there. A few less wouldn't matter." My father resisted the idea, but I kept at it. I found recipes.

The Browning was useless on ducks but we knocked down a half dozen gray squirrels in no time. Hitting squirrels with a twelve-gauge shotgun is as easy as it is pointless, and although the gun's kickback knocked me into the leaves repeatedly, I quickly mastered the skill. I could squirrel hunt and trout trap like a professional. My father and I had left legal concerns such as trespass, gun law, and license vague, so when we heard the shouting my first instinct was to run but my father stood his ground. It was Mr. Mosley, our neighbor. His son, Dick, beat me regularly down at the bus stop.

"What the hell do you think you're doing?" Mosley asked.

I dropped the squirrels and my father said, "Oh. Hello, Mr., Mr.—"

"Mosley."

"Right, Mosley. Mr. Mosley. I'm Richard Lovelace and this is—"

"I know who you are. I want to know why you're out here killing squirrels with a damn shotgun." My father stared at him blankly. What could he say? That we needed the food? That squirrels were overrunning our lawn? Killing our livestock?

"Listen, Lovelace. This is no way to teach a boy. Take him to the dump and shoot rats if you have to. Go ahead. But if you kill another goddamn squirrel with a shotgun around my house I'll have you arrested. Understand?" My father nodded silently and Mosley stalked off, back through the woods. I picked up the dead squirrels by their tails and ran for home; Dad caught up with me on the back porch. He gave me some pointers on gutting and skinning the poor things, put his gun away, and went back to his typing. I threw the innards, the heads, and the feet into the woods.

My mother had not been apprised of the hunt but was unconcerned when I came into the kitchen and slung a sack full of dressed squirrel into her sink. She was standing over the kitchen table, fretting over her calligraphy. "Hi, dear," she said, and looked over. "Oh, David. That's a good pillowcase, dear. I could have given you an old one. What's in there?"

"Mom, I'm making up a surprise for dinner," I told her. "I need onions and carrots." I pulled the recipe from my back pocket. "Let's see. I need chicken stock. Do we have any chicken stock? I'm making a stew."

"All right, dear, use bouillion—those cubes up in the cabinet. Just look at that pillowcase." It was filthy and spots of blood had soaked through the flowered cotton fabric.

"I'll wash it. I promise." I peeked in at the sadly diminished squirrels. Bits of thread and fuzz stuck to their shiny, sinewy bodies. "Never mind, Mom. Just don't worry about dinner." I pushed her out of the kitchen.

By this time my mother had seen just about everything. She wasn't worried about my surprise; she'd find out soon enough. Mom had enough concerns. She dressed us, got us on the bus, cooked our meals, and washed our clothes. She periodically

wrested the checkbook from my father and pleaded for bud-
getary management. She kept our family presentable, even with
snakes in her spare room and dead squirrels on her stove. And
yet, banished from her kitchen, she just stood in the hall at a loss.
There was nowhere for her to go. The front of the house with its
sonic-boom speakers and Dad was off-limits, their bedroom was
dark and small, and the family room smelled of snakes.

Dinner was horrible, of course, a shocking, watery mess with
the rodents floating up out of the boil. My sister began crying
immediately. I myself was racked by guilt and nausea but recognized I must eat squirrel or admit to wanton slaughter. My
mother made toast. Only my father tucked in with gusto. "Not
bad," he said. "Not bad. Better than eating frogs."

Mom cleared the table and made me promise to throw the left-
overs, my entire stew, into the woods after family devotions. Every
evening, my father shut down his music, read a passage from the
New Testament or Psalms, and asked our opinions. I always had
opinions and Dad always followed them with his own, longer and
more coherent, commentary. After that came the prayer.

"Does anyone have something they would like to thank God
for? Any prayer requests?"

My mother spoke up. "We need to rake the leaves, Richard.
I'm worried about the leaves. It will snow before we know it." No
one wanted to pray about the leaves, not again. God couldn't do
anything about the leaves; our house was in the middle of the
woods—what lawn we had was moss. Raking was a Sisyphean
task my mother asked us to perform every autumn, an offering
to the neighbors.

"Betty Lee, we are aware of the leaf situation and have been for some time. We will put that before the Lord. Are there any other requests?"

"Peggy won't let me watch *The Three Stooges*. She says it's stupid."

"She's correct." My sister beamed. "Watch the Marx Brothers. Does anyone have concerns other than the leaves and *The Three Stooges*? Does anyone have anything to be thankful for?"

"Squirrels," my sister said softly. "I want to pray for the squirrels."

Then we held hands, my father prayed for spiritual awakening to sweep the globe, and we were dismissed. Generally, I'd go back to the television, my sister to her novel, and Mom to the sink. On Friday or Saturday nights we'd go down to the basement and play poker. My father liked what he called "classical poker," five-card stud, and he would roll his eyes when I called one-eyed jacks or suicide kings wild. We all enjoyed playing, even my mother, who had been raised to believe cards were sinful. We had done our best to make the basement into a family room. We glued colorful carpet remnants to the linoleum floor and the walls, a patchwork of shag rectangles and tightly woven squares. But the basement would flood every spring and the scraps would lift up, and the snake cages always needed cleaning.

The squirrels exacted their revenge the next spring. My sister and I convinced my parents to take the requisite trip to Disney World. My father bought a pop-up camper and loaded it with fishing gear. We hooked it to the back of our station wagon and together with the rest of the East Coast we headed south to

Orlando. We forgot Jonathan at a gas station in South Carolina. It took us some time to reach an exit and effect a U-turn. When we returned, horror-stricken, Jonathan was just sitting on the curb with his special blanket, calmly sucking his thumb. He wasn't worried; he'd made the necessary Lovelace adjustments already. When we got to Florida my sister contracted sun poisoning, I was bitten by a barracuda, and my screaming brother was forcibly removed from Captain Nemo's submarine. Back home, my father parked the camper in the backyard and we all did our best to forget. The squirrels shredded the pop-up, just totaled it. My father paid cash to a passing backhoe operator and he dug an enormous hole in our backyard and buried it. That was our last family vacation. We never went farther than Peniel again.

Dad's snake habit was becoming a problem, undeniably. Upon moving to Hamilton, no longer regulated by life in a parsonage, my father's affair with reptiles reached crisis proportions. An entire room of our small ranch house was dedicated to terrariums, heat lamps, rodent foodstuffs, and the like. It was a humid cave of a room, reeking of mouse fear and snake droppings. It smelled fermented and nutty, like burned cheese and acorns. The snakes drove my mother to despair. My father simply refused to consider their removal. He seemed incapable of even smelling them.

We owned a reticulated python of considerable size named Ringo; a boa named Boris; an anaconda; any number of indigenous snakes; two alligator-like caimans, Wally and Jinx; and Igor, who hung baleful and motionless on our living room curtain. It was Igor, not Camus, who taught me life could very well prove meaningless. Lettuce was his only comfort. Generally, Igor was removed from the curtain and sequestered with the other reptiles only when company was expected. He was forgotten on occasion. Once, to my mother's horror, he joined the faculty wives' prayer group.

If Igor hinted at the immutable, absurd nature of the universe, the caimans argued for its undying malevolence. It was Jinx who commandeered Willow Grove's organ and threatened my father's ministry. Now the beasts glared up at us from my old bassinet. They never slept. We force-fed them using bits of raw meat pushed down their beastly throats with pencil erasers. At every opportunity they sank their needle teeth into our hands and held on until we swung them over our heads and tore them free. The relationship proved so bloody awful that their eventual death and dismemberment by Woodstock raccoons was viewed as a blessing, the best for all concerned. I should emphasize, there is no reason to entrap, purchase, or possess a pair of caimans. They don't keep each other company, they don't wait for you to get off the bus, and they don't play fetch.

As for the snakes, I was my father's willing accomplice. I gave up hunting the king's squirrels and joined my father, who spent his leisure hours stalking the local snake population. We drove slowly through the surrounding neighborhoods in the early evenings, watching for garter, corn, and hognose snakes sunning themselves on the blacktop, pulling the last heat of the day from the road. Down by the bridle paths, we found an old white door lying in weeds, peeling and pulling apart with the rain. It was the perfect snake trap, providing a dark lair of soft earth covered by a warm solar collecting roof. We visited the door regularly and I snatched any number of garter snakes from under it, including a pregnant one that bore twenty-one squiggling babies back in my room. Once I lifted the door and found a young milk snake; its orange, brown, and white patterns made it a jewel, as beautiful as a brook trout.

The summer I turned twelve my dad dragged home a sorry-looking fiberglass hull. Ipswich Marine said it sank out behind Crane's beach when the bilge pump crapped out. Second time. They pulled the boat out of the channel. "She just filled up with rainwater," they assured my father. "Twice. It's nothing structural. No holes. It's just the bilge pump. We'll put in a new one." They said all the owner wanted was salvage costs. The Coast Guard had called the boat a "navigational hazard." My father called it a stripped-down, no-nonsense fishing machine. It was a 1965 Cathedral Trihull.

The boat, my father, and I spent considerable time at Ipswich Marine. The mechanics liked my father; they called him the Professor. "It's like this, Professor. All you've got is a hull. That's it. Just a hull. But it's bulletproof. When she has an engine she'll plow through anything, four-foot seas, rips, sandbars. She's a fishing machine, Professor, you're right. She sure is." They sold us an ancient and rectangular outboard, spray-painted and mounted it. The boat got new steering and wiring harnesses. We named her *Strider* and commenced plowing through four-foot seas, rips, and sandbars.

We fished weekends and after school, day or night, early spring through the first snow, most often with weather permitting but most notably not. We fished the mouth of the Merrimack River primarily. The Merrimack powered New England's shift from the small farms to massive brick workhouses and it pushes past the great textile mills of Lawrence and Lowell, past miles of brick, stone, and broken glass, all of it shuttered now, bricked-up and silent. The river drains all this. It floods the mud flats just past Newburyport and then roars out to the Atlantic through a pair of massive granite jetties, a great engineered channel. The ocean's ingoing tide pushes up huge standing waves at the mouth and its outgoing pulls wicked rips. We plied it at night in a two-time loser of a bulletproof hull with a tired, spray-painted engine. Confused seas and questionable piloting plagued the *Strider,* but we came back because along with everything else, the river dumps out an enormous amount of bait—herring, alewives, crabs, worms, silversides, and sand eels. Mackerel moved through; striped bass, bluefish and sharks, even five-hundred-pound tuna patrol here. And back then there were cod, actual codfish.

Launching and loading the *Strider* was not the most danger-ous phase of operations but it was the most humiliating. Misfor-tune at sea, for that matter stupidity at sea, is a private matter. At sea no one is watching when you, say, let the anchor line's bitter end slide overboard (we did that), run aground (we always did that), run out of gas (yes), or fall overboard (see below). Death at sea is considered heroic—even ennobling—quite unlike, say, forgetting to set the station wagon's parking brake on a ramp while it's attached to a three-thousand-pound boat, or drilling a hole in the hull while mounting a deck chair, or forgetting the boat's drain plug prior to launching.

We pushed our luck and the nearby Coast Guard station's

patience, and one night the worst almost happened. It was in the fall and my father was alone at the mouth hoping for codfish. He set anchor in a hard running tide and the *Strider* swung round fast. The engine's prop caught the anchor line and held its stern down into the current. The river poured past the engine and swamped the boat almost immediately. Dad grabbed a knife and leaned over the transom; he fell into the water and cut the boat free. He pulled himself up onto the half-sunken boat and it spun past the jetties. The engine was underwater, its batteries dead. He said he prayed for all of us, that we'd be all right. Out past the jetties the boat slowly drifted out of the current. The tide turned. My father found an oar we had stashed, stood in the water, and paddled for Salisbury Beach. Hours later he walked up and banged on a door. They gave him rum, scavenged an anchor, and made our boat fast against the incoming tide.

Twenty years later I sold the boat to an old friend for pocket change and didn't see it for years until I stumbled across it in Rockport. It was up on stanchions behind some tourist shops on Bearskin Neck. Five or six kids were scraping away at its hull and I asked them how they ended up with it. "Me and my brother found it out past Salvages," one said. "Just floating, banging against the rocks. No one claimed it. The number's expired." His story seemed unlikely but maybe it was true. I couldn't ask my friend; he was gone. Long ago I decided to believe it, that the *Strider* kept floating without us.

Back home in Hamilton, undrowned and admired by his colleagues, my father began a new book that became the central work of his life. Using Edwards's writings as a template, my father hoped to shape the next Great Awakening. It had already begun, Dad believed, within the counterculture. By 1968 the media brought wild tales of Jesus Freaks and their movement to my father back east. Gone were the blue-eyed, pastel images of Christ from Sunday school; his profile began resembling Che Guevara's. It was a strange, paradoxical movement—the marriage of hippie rebellion and fundamentalist religion—and for a season the press could not get enough, nor could my father.

My father believed Peniel should get into this act and so he arranged a field trip. Twelve skeptical church folk boarded a van bound for Love In, a Jesus commune in Freeville, New York. It was a massive barnlike structure, embellished by the requisite stained glass, hippie towers, and flags. Dad had made arrangements with the so-called freaks for lunch but we stood tightly grouped in their driveway like frightened birds. A few tense moments passed, and then a bell like Peniel's rang and the fabled Jesus People emerged from the pines. My father's great hope for the church approached in overalls, bandanas, and hair. A tall, smiling man said, "Brothers, sisters, welcome," and my father allowed himself to be hugged. "Are you from, from…"

"Peniel Bible Conference."

"Yes. Peniel." All of us stood quite still. "Welcome."

My father stepped forward. "All of us are very excited about what you are doing here. Living together."

"Thank you." The man threw an arm over Dad's shoulder. He had straw or something in his beard. "My name is Ed. Please, everyone, come and eat with us."

He led us into a large dining area outfitted with picnic tables and packed with believers. "Everyone, everyone," Ed intoned, "we have visitors here for lunch. These brothers and sisters are from Peniel Bible Conference." Ed ushered us to the front of a buffet line and we helped ourselves to lentils. We returned and sat in uncomfortable silence until a group prayer welled up around us, a marathon grace involving hand waving, swaying, and shouts. There were murmurs in an unknown language comprised of the letters L, M, and N. It was tongues! They were speaking in tongues, the language of angels! I was thrilled. And also the angelic young women weren't wearing bras! I was thirteen years old and surrounded by women without bras waving their arms around. Their eyes were blissfully clamped shut. They were oblivious to my wide-eyed prayers. God, I was thankful. I saw my dad smile as well. He had his first chapter: "Jonathan Edwards and the Jesus Movement."

My father believed in an artistic and spiritual renaissance that would flush all the mediocrity out of his church: the shallow self-help books, its awful attempts at musical relevance, its pathological fear of art and outsiders. He welcomed the curiosity and rebellion he found in the youth movements and wanted to chart a way out of what he called "dead orthodoxy." He wanted to find the sublime. Instead, the Jesus People became the worst kind of latter-day Puritans, isolated and judgmental. Dad's new culturally hip church filled with believers in book-burning apocalypse, in rapture and flight from the world. They stopped listening and, sadly, my father stopped speaking. Eventually, my father, whose mind had welcomed so many artists and thinkers, locked out his tone-deaf peers. Dad learned to love his music in silence.

He was most present, at least for me, on the ocean and duck marsh. My father wouldn't give me a shotgun; I was too young. He wouldn't allow a pet retriever and so when we shot ducks we lost them. But we rarely hit ducks. In short, waterfowl hunting was cold, boring, and pointless. But when my father asked me to go, I jumped. I loved to be with him. We hunted on the salt marshes behind Plum Island. The Merrimack River lies to the island's north, the Ipswich River to its south, and it's cut from the mainland by the Parker River and acres of salt marsh. The island is protected as a bird sanctuary, an essential stopover of the Atlantic Flyway. The salt marshes are essential as well but they're not protected, a gauntlet. My father and I figured we could bag our limit of ducks there easily. Bang, bang, bang. Dad had an aluminum skiff and we loaded it with decoys and ammunition. We put in a few miles inland on the Parker River. It was November and cold and the sky was a white blank. Aluminum skiffs are loud: they clang and ring at every wave and footfall. Ours was dented and old; it popped rivets and sprung leaks every time. It wasn't worth much but the engine was good.

The marsh looked all the same to me but Dad marked a point where the grass and black mud jutted into the river and turned. There was an empty duck blind; my father nosed toward it and I plopped the decoys down in a nice-looking, sociable group. We drifted down with the river for a few minutes and then Dad gunned the engine quickly and cut it. He tilted it up and we slid onto the bank. We never got ducks but this time we would; I knew it. This was the Parker River National Wildlife Refuge, a sure bet for dead ducks. It was low tide. Dad and I dragged the skiff up through the crushed mussel shells and soft muck until it got hard. Dad picked up his shotgun and we climbed up over the bank. It was a good walk to the blind but the silver boat was best stashed at a distance. The damp ground sucked at our boots and the hollow spartina grass popped.

We saw two ducks and they saw us as well. I hadn't complained but I was cold and I wanted to go home. By dusk we both wanted to go home but the boat had already left. It was almost high tide and the river was slapping against the spot where we had left it. I hadn't thrown the anchor, nor had my father.

"Well," my father said with remarkable equanimity, "it can't have gone far. It would have hung up on something." He didn't even curse. And so we started downstream, hopping ditches and slogging through mud—keeping busy. I knew my feet were wet but I couldn't feel them. There was no point in crying. Just before dark my father said, "All right, David. I think we should forget about the boat and get to the highest hump we can find. The tide's still coming." I knew I would cry and he looked at me and smiled. "It's not coming that far up, don't worry. We'll see someone. I've got three shells here and I'll use them to signal." When it was pitch dark and all I could hear was the salt water moving on the marsh, my father said, "I think we should pray. Let's pray for your mother to call the Coast Guard."

It worked—not right away, but it worked. She grew concerned and reported us missing around ten p.m. By then I was hypothermic. My father had me stand and walk in circles, stomping my feet. He sang the old hymns from Peniel and had me sing along. He knew all the verses, each more somber than the last. I was delirious and the songs turned from triumphant assurance. I heard lost graveyard sounds. At eleven p.m. the Coast Guard found our skiff capsized off Crane's Beach, the engine dangling by its fuel line. After that they called out a helicopter. We could see its searchlight sweep back and forth over the river moving up from the sea. When it got close Dad lifted his shotgun and blasted three times. A boat was radioed. I was hustled aboard and wrapped in blankets. They wanted to take me to a hospital but Dad and I refused. It made the local papers: HAMILTON MAN MAROONED WITH SON. "'We sang hymns and prayed to keep warm,' Lovelace said."

The next day my sixth grade gym teacher lined us all up and then he said, "Hey, Lovelace. I heard you got stuck on a marsh." I nodded and looked at the floor. "Heard you sang hymns." He smiled and chewed at his gum. "How'd that work, huh?" The kids all stared and some of them laughed. I didn't speak. I wanted to know why I had to pray all the time, why I had to sing. I wanted to know why the world kept floating off, whose mistake that was, and why my family felt so alone. I began to realize that our beautiful ocean could drown us. That we shot animals dead or put them in cages. That my mother could drift and that my father lost boats. That my father's God said to Abraham, kill me a son.

FOUR

In 1974 Dad transferred the reptiles, my mother sprayed dis-infectant, and my grandfather moved into the snake room. Mom's father had spent the last decade working the family cir-cuit. He'd spend six months with my aunt Rose, long enough to confirm all his long-standing paternal judgments and begin shouting. Rose would get on the phone and plead with her brother, Frank, who would host Grandpa until his anger refocused, gath-ered momentum, and turned on his family. Then Frank called Mom and it was our turn. It was emotional tag team, except Mom never called on her siblings. She never shook off Grandpa's dis-dain but assumed he had cause and that cause was her fault. She saw herself through his eyes: her shortcomings as a daughter, a wife, and a mother, the disappointing family she'd made.

There was no grace period with Grandpa, no honeymoon month spoiling his youngest grandchild, telling us stories, or feigning interest in snakes. Instead, he immediately began rak-ing leaves—obsessively raking leaves—and shooting dark glances at the men of the household. Whenever I looked out a window Grandpa was there, muttering angrily and wrestling a tarp filled with wet leaves, seasons upon seasons of them. I was fourteen that fall and I was awkward and sullen. Above all I was lazy. I spent my afternoons watching reruns and expended what energy I possessed in odd, useless projects. I drank Moxie and collected the cans. I lined the walls of my room with my empty orange cans. I caught pregnant snakes and named all their babies. I didn't do homework and I never ever raked.

"Richard," my mother said one night as we gathered for dinner, "look at Grandpa out there. I'm worried for him."

"Who?"

"Grandpa. Right there under the window. In the shrubs. He's been raking for weeks."

"He has?"

"Yes. And none of us are helping." My mother gave Grandpa a little wave from the kitchen window and mouthed the word "dinner." "Look, he's not coming in. He's shaking his head." It was true. Grandpa had redoubled his efforts. He had a stiff mustache and a gray crew cut and jabbed his work gloves at the tarp like a boxer. He waved Mom off and started dragging his tarp toward the woods.

"He's going to kill himself," I said. "He shouldn't be doing that."

"Who asked him to?" my father asked. "We live in the woods. We don't need the leaves raked." My mother sat slowly. She stopped arguing and twisted her hands until they dropped in a hard little ball. Grandpa wouldn't stop, the ugly brown leaves wouldn't stop, and Dad wouldn't start. I wouldn't start either, no way. Grandpa was none of my concern.

Mom stopped talking. She stared at her empty plate and forgot about food. She moved into her worry, stepped further and further from our bright kitchen. My mother saw darkness so often in daylight that we stopped paying her heed. My father counted on Peggy to hold Mom's hand, to keep her from falling while he typed. I watched television with my seven-year-old brother. I wore headphones. She'd have been on her own in the dark if it hadn't been for Peggy.

"You know," I said, "Grandpa said I was planning to kill him. He said I was trying to poison him."

"Let's have dinner!" Jonathan shouted. My mother rose.

Dad smiled. "Oh, you're kidding, right? He said you were going to kill him?"

"Yup. That's what he said. I came in from school yesterday and he started shouting at me. He said, 'Don't think you're getting away with it, Buster. I'm watching you.' Stuff like that."

"Poison!" my brother screamed gleefully. "What poison?" Peggy sat quietly and my mother busied herself at the stove.

My father was fascinated. "He really said that?" I nodded. "Wow. What did you say?"

"I said I wasn't planning to kill him. What do you think? He's crazy, that's all. I just pushed past him and went upstairs." I looked past my father to the window and watched Grandpa scrape at the yard.

Dad chuckled and shook his head. My mother quietly set a platter of chicken on the table. She set the cauliflower and cheese sauce down. "I'll just make him up a plate," she said in a whisper, gathered the food, and wrapped it in foil. Then Mom sat and waited for grace.

Grandpa had transformed the snake room into a comfortable den and hid there when he wasn't outside raking leaves into guilt.

He still ate our suspect food, but he ate most of it alone in his den. It wasn't difficult to avoid Grandpa, but one afternoon he ambushed me. He hopped out of the kitchen and stood at the top of the stairs. "I know what you're up to, boy. You can't fool me." He held a can of Moxie in one hand and a broom in the other.

"What, Grandpa?" I stopped on the stairs, well out of his reach, and smiled mockingly. "What have you got on me?"

"You're on drugs, boy. I know it. I can prove it." He held up the orange can and shook it at me. "Right here."

"What do you mean, Grandpa? What do you mean, 'right here'?"

"It says it right here, on the can. You're on acid. I knew it."

"Acid."

"That's right." He smiled triumphantly. "Carbonic acid. This Moxie's full of it."

"That's what makes soda fizz," I said dismissively, and climbed toward him. "It's just soda, Grandpa. Christ."

"Watch your mouth, David." He took up the doorway and refused to move. "Don't you take the Lord's name in vain." I kept moving up and tried to duck past him but Grandpa jabbed his broom into my neck. I stumbled back, fell, and slid down the stairs. "Jesus," I cursed at the floor. I got up and shook out my arms as he glowered above me. "I mean, goddammit, Grandpa." I turned before he could shout, walked through the garage and back into the woods. Dad sent Grandpa back to Rose.

The first year I got hit with depression it seemed warranted, reasonable. My depression wasn't clinical; it wasn't grave; it was just natural. I had hormones. I'd read *The Catcher in the Rye*. Besides, it was 1975 and the music was terrible, just entirely wrong. My classmates and I inherited very little from our older brothers and sisters: no sense of purpose, no hippie dream, just dirt weed and old records. There were no antiwar marches—there was hardly even a war—no Woodstock, no tragic overdoses, nothing. There sure as hell wasn't any free love. We were ten years late. We'd been swindled and my classmates were oblivious. I shunned them, and so I spent most of my time sewing patches on blue jeans and listening to Neil Young records. I had round glasses and brown hair down to my shoulders, where it curled up with an unfortunate sort of bounce. I was voted "Most Earthy" in my class and dragged to *Saturday Night Fever* in overalls. I wanted a cultural watershed, and when President Carter reinstated draft registration I ran down to the post office looking for something to burn.

I had three friends in Hamilton and all of us were cultural misfits. Our fathers taught at Gordon Conwell, an isolated hothouse of midwestern evangelicalism. My friends and I were regarded as a sort of invasive species at school. All of us had washed out socially early in the first grueling rounds of puberty, and so there was a certain Darwinian inevitability to our friendship. We had been raised by theologians and thrown to the wolves, to the beautiful daughters of bankers and their lacrosse captain boyfriends. William Beck was the only one of us without evangelical ties, but after he stood in front of our class and announced his papal ambitions he too was shunned. "I intend to be Pope," read the opening of his career essay, "I will live in the Vatican." After that we took him in; he was one of us. We sat in our parents' basements with black lights and posters. We talked about Jesus, the moral problem of breasts, and what went wrong with Paul McCartney and Wings.

Hamilton's parties, football, and polo games couldn't hold us; they wouldn't have us. Local church youth groups were an obvious choice, the last social outpost. They had to take us in, but they didn't. Finally, we found a church out of town where no one knew us. West Peabody Congregational welcomed us with open arms. That church was filled with lapsed Peabody girls and religious fervor. Our retreats featured nonstop French kisses and prayer requests. I got baptized (again) in a cold Maine lake just to impress the girls. I was shameless. I mimicked the kid beside me when he spoke in tongues. I belonged.

I didn't belong in school. My chemistry teacher returned my midyear exam and shook his head. "I don't know how you did this, David. But you have flunked flunking." My wood shop teacher placed my project, a deformed little pencil box, on the center of a bench and smashed it with a three-pound sledge. I was in my third year of algebra. I skipped out of gym and had numerous fistfights with a pair of ill-tempered brothers, identical twins. It was all terribly confusing. Only my English teacher and her *Scarlet Letter* made sense. She had long dark hair, was partial to miniskirts, and possessed a tremendous set of black leather boots. She gave me a copy of Keith Jarrett's *Köln Concert* and I was sure that I loved her. I spent passionate moments alone with the record and afterward lay spent and weak with shame. I am worse than Arthur Dimmesdale, I thought. I should be made to wear a great scarlet M for my sins.

Meanwhile, my father's book, *The Dynamics of Spiritual Life*, had been published to good—if largely evangelical—reviews. It had made quite a splash, in fact, and my father's calendar filled with speaking dates and side projects. He spoke against the church's isolation from the greater world, and especially the world of art. He promoted cultural awareness, an appreciation of anything fine—high, low, sacred, and secular. He put "Howl" on his required reading lists. "Quite simply, this poem is about loss—loss of purpose, loss of mind, loss of God." Students complained it was obscene and my father glowered. "Of course it's obscene."

He began dragging our stereo up to the seminary once or twice a semester. His music lectures were soon packed; they drew crowds of earnest seminarians, skeptical colleagues, and random onlookers. I went. He started lectures with Bach and then broke the cultural ice with some Simon and Garfunkel:

> And the people bowed and prayed / To the neon god they made / And the sign flashed out its warning / In the words that it was forming / And the sign said the words of the prophets / Are written on the subway walls / And tenement halls / And whispered in the sounds of silence.

My dad hit stop and looked up from the tape deck. "Okay. How about that? The neon God." He stopped and scanned his puzzled audience. "Don't you see what's going on here? Culturally? This isn't just pop. 'Hello, Darkness my old friend.' That's not Frank

Sinatra. You wouldn't hear Frank Sinatra singing about false prophets, people writing songs that voices never share."

My father was big on the Beatles. He liked Joni Mitchell, Leonard Cohen, and Dylan but avoided the Stones and was downright scared of the Doors. And then he discovered a strange new hybrid, Christian rock. He stacked our living room with vinyl, some of it good, most of it poorly produced and mediocre. He championed the decent musicians and befriended a number of them. He even produced a record or two. My friends and I took up the cause. We believed one musician in particular, Larry Norman, was the ultimate outsider. He was our model rebel: too Christian for rock and roll, too rock and roll for the church. He met with my father once in the living room and my brother and I spied through the door. He was due to perform and dressed at our house. After he left we looked in the shower. I found a few wisps of his long blond hair and we saved them. We were, undoubtedly, in an alternate universe.

My mother blamed coffee and Satan for her anxieties. She always had a jar of instant decaf and drank cup after thin cup of the stuff. She took her vitamin B pills and sat with her brushes and paints, and every three or four years her worries curdled into paranoia. She was sure the neighbors were reading our mail. The mail carrier let them. They knew we hadn't paid the phone bill. The bank knew and Dad was hiding the checkbook. Or Grandmère would call. All Grandmère had to do was call and leave a message for Richard. That was enough. The seminary trustees planned to fire Dad because of the snakes, because of the records.

My father reassured my mother every morning and he prayed with her dutifully. But when we arrived home from school he often called Peggy into the living room. "See what you can do for Mom. All right? She needs you; she's getting the whim-whams."

"But, Dad, I don't know what I can do for her. Why don't you take her out? Or call some of her friends and invite them to dinner. How about David? Why doesn't he do something?"

"That might be too much of a shock. No. You just go talk with her."

My sister always did. She dragged all her childhood guilt into the kitchen and sat holding Mom's hand. She did this for years until her guilt turned to anger. Why didn't Dad do something? It was Dad's fault and he did nothing but control Mom and keep her from friends. As for me, I stayed downstairs by the snakes, watching television with my kid brother.

My first depression found me watching television. I got farther and farther away and lost with Gilligan until one day I stopped understanding. I couldn't follow situation comedy, its plots, mishaps, or jokes. I found *The Brady Bunch* incomprehensible. Its laugh track made me weep. When I spoke I heard my words unravel into just sounds. Nothing was in sequence and my thoughts blinked off one by one. I could see them. I was scared that my little brother could see. I was like Mom. Jonathan avoided me now, I could tell. I could see him in sepia, those brown heartbroken shades where dead people pose. I saw us all now in sepia. I stopped washing my hair and brushing my teeth. It was pointless. If I did it I'd have to do it again. I saw my mom. I knew the way she stuttered in the kitchen, the way she turned from us and dropped into some hell. The muscles in my face let go. Alone in the bathroom I made a smile in the mirror and it strangled my eyes. I saw my mom.

I found tears on my face. I shuttered my room, refused meals, and gave in to my stupor. I now know the symptoms of clinical depression well: changes in brain chemistry, a quantifiable loss in electrical brain activity, speech and thought slowed to a crawl, delusions, in short a complete exhaustion of the mind. All I knew then was the mark. I was marked for it, for madness, just like my mother. I waited for the hallucinations, watched for them. I lay in bed and stared into nothing at all. My heart was a nest of unclean birds—just like my namesake's. I stopped attending school. I couldn't dress myself. The hours lasted days and every hour I sat and considered my suicide. I wanted to drown. I wanted to take the boat out past Dry Salvages, five, maybe six miles past, and then gun it, hit the throttle and jump. But I knew I'd never do it and that knowledge disgusted me. I was just a kid and lacked the courage. I was a fucking coward. Suicide was a big decision and I couldn't even choose my socks. I despised my socks; their smell made me sick.

I couldn't even stand up and no one could help me. In fact, there wasn't much anyone could do for me back then—just take away the razors and watch me. There weren't many drugs. Today they feed suicides antidepressants, stoke the poor suffering kids with chemical courage. They help most of the time but sometimes, rarely, the medicines hasten tragedy. Sometimes they work just halfway, just enough to get them to jump.

I couldn't sleep and day was identical to night, just shadows sliding across blue bedroom walls. My friends visited once, spoke at me, and left. I told my mother to turn them away after that. I didn't speak the same language as they did. I couldn't even feel the same emotions. Mom brought me food and took it back to the kitchen. She opened the curtains and made me sit up. I could hear her talking to Dad in the kitchen and I knew she blamed herself for my sickness. My father knocked.

"David. Hey, David, are you awake in there? Can I come in?" I was awake. I was always awake. You never sleep; you just lie down and beg to.

"David?" He came in and sat at the foot of my bed. He asked how I was feeling.

"Tired. I'm just tired. I'm trying to sleep."

"I just came in to try and cheer you up." I stared at him. He smiled and tapped at my knee. "You know, Mom and I were just saying how nice it's been to have you around. I mean you're hardly ever here anymore, out running around with your friends doing . . . well, who knows what you're doing."

"Yeah."

"Look, what I'm trying to say is that we like you this way. I mean you're more thoughtful, more sensitive. You're not blaring bad music through the house." It was a calculated jab and he hoped for a response, but I couldn't respond. I just stared at my blankets and my father continued reluctantly. "Don't get me wrong, David. I don't mean to belittle what you're going through. I think it's extremely difficult. St. John of the Cross called it a 'dark night of the soul.' This is normal. This is Satan testing you. He's tempting you just like he tempted Jesus in the desert. You're in the Slough of Despond. Once you pass through this, you'll be a stronger Christian."

"Slough?"

"Bunyan. *Pilgrim's Progress.*" He stood and moved to the door. "I'm proud of you."

When I felt stronger I made myself leave the house. Later that winter, I was hiding in the seminary library, curled into a carrel with my head in my hands. Someone said, "Excuse me." I knew no one at the seminary; that's why I was there. They couldn't be speaking to me. "Um. Excuse me," a man said again. "Are you David Lovelace?"

I turned my head and squinted up at him. "Yeah. So?" Two well-scrubbed seminarians beamed down at me.

"Are you, um…are you having a dark night of the soul? I mean, excuse me, but your father, Dr. Lovelace, says you're having a dark night of the soul."

"He does."

"Yes. You know, St. John of the Cross."

"I know St. John of the Cross. I know the dark night of the soul. Yes."

"What's it like?"

"Oh, come on," I said. "Fuck off. Please? Just fuck off." I got up and stumbled past them. Evidently my father had been bragging about my depression, about his son, St. John of the Cross.

By early spring I began improving. The Sanka and vitamin B my mother pushed started kicking in, I guess. I went back to school and let everyone whisper, and I whispered, too. My voice frightened me; it sounded like cancer. I avoided my friends and I sat at our family dinner table under duress.

One night my father had big news. "Guess who's coming to dinner next week? Chuck Colson!"

"Chuck Colson." I looked down at my plate. "Wow."

It seems Chuck Colson, Nixon's own hatchet man, had experienced a jailhouse conversion, read my father's book, and started up his own Bible study with some of the old gang. My father had been flying down to DC regularly and mentoring a select group of Watergate conspirators. Revival makes for strange bedfellows, and Chuck Colson and my father had become fast friends. Wow. I couldn't wait.

When Colson arrived I wore my patched jeans and I pulled out my ponytail and dragged hair across my face. Dad introduced us and I shook his hand silently. At the table Dad chatted with Colson while my mother flitted nervously and served up the steaks. My father kept trying to pull me into the conversation.

"Well, you know, David and I are great fishermen. We love the ocean." Colson thought that was grand. I just stared at him.

"David's been considering Wheaton College. The one in Illinois. Evangelical." A fine choice, said Colson. I didn't eat anything. The smell of food still made me nauseous; I hadn't eaten in days. I just moved my silverware while the hatchet man sawed at his meat. Dad leaned closer to the big man. "Confidentially," he said, "David's been having a bit of the dark night of the soul." I excused myself from the table.

Apparently my family and friends could not understand me and it was quite clear I would never appreciate St. John. I just got angrier and angrier until I punched at the walls and got up and left. I ran through the woods. I quit church. I looked at my mother, saw her eyes all clouded with cataract fear, and I knew that my death would return. We'd been dealt a raw deal, Mom and I. She was stuck with her hand but I figured on folding.

I went back to church one last time, back to West Peabody. I wasn't sure but I was sick of the praying and all the old answers. My godly parents had been fruitful; they had multiplied and had commenced my religious training at once. It's like this: when you're a preacher's kid, eternal life is a done deal by the time you are baptized—all you have left is mortified flesh. It seemed such a cheat and so I raised hell. It was a matter, I think, of cosmic balance. So, of course, I came back to church to raise hell, to blow my goddamn dark night all to pieces.

I skipped out of youth group and wandered the church halls. I pushed into the pastor's office. He was upstairs in the sanctuary, meeting with the deacons, or elders, or some bullshit mission committee. There was nothing of interest on his desk; the office was neat. I didn't know what I wanted but I soon found it: a fire extinguisher, chemical, type II. I pulled the pin and squeezed the trigger just a bit. A tiny, noxious dust cloud appeared. I squeezed again and once more, ringing the preacher's desk with small, perfect clouds of sulfurous yellow. A light, postapocalyptic dust was falling. It was lovely, I thought, and then the cylinder kicked back into my chest and opened up like a flamethrower. I ran for the door holding the thing while its hose thrashed at my arm. "Fuck!" I screamed down the hall, "Fuck!" and ran through the church hollering with the thing and with the smoke alarms screaming. I got to a side door and pitched the extinguisher out on the pavement, where it spun like a huge broken bottle rocket. The deacons were standing out front because inside was hell. I told the firemen I didn't know why it happened. The thing just went off. Boom.

Anger pushed me back into the world but it was the fishing that freed me—Ipswich Bay. By now I had floated over most of it and run aground on the rest. It was something about drifting, just standing alone on the currents, that made me grateful again. The flat line of horizon stayed quiet and the fishing pulled me close. It was a different, more serious prayer and it saved me. It was the spring run of mackerel—shoals of small tinker mackerel moving beneath me, quickly, just under the surface. I jigged up five at a time on a long line of small, silvery hooks. I live-lined the smallest, pushing a large hook through its lips and flipping it back, watching it flash down. I wanted the big fish, the first migrating stripers or bluefish. Deep down I wanted what the old man caught and lost to the sea. I love waiting for the hit, the living, thrashing hit from the blank green. I love what pushes silversides up in a spray, what swings the gulls down and leaves the boat bloody and feeds us.

I recovered, but my room was stale with my sickness. I had maybe sixty-five dollars. I was a broke preacher's kid with wanderlust and so I turned to the mission field. It offered the best opportunity for a boy with my talents and connections, and before long I was mass-mailing frightening little cards asking for tithes. My awkward yearbook photo gawked above the bold caption: "Please Help Me Witness for CHRIST with Teen Missions!" A small write-up followed, describing the mission project, the construction of a Christian orphanage outside Manaus, Brazil. Finally, in bold letters below my pitch, Teen Missions' trademarked call to action ordered, "Go Lay a Brick for God!" I could lay bricks; how hard could it be? I had been called to Manaus and I shamelessly hit up every relative and every Peniel preacher I could find.

In truth, all I'd been called to was a chance to get out of the country, all expenses paid. As for the gospel, that was a bit more complicated. I had lost it somewhere in that dark night but I knew it cold. I could deliver the Good News at a moment's notice. If asked by a Brazilian with average English skills, I could explain the basics. If necessary I even could discuss the mysteries of the triune God or the problem of evil. Lack of belief could not dissuade me from the mission field. Besides, I still liked Jesus. I now practiced a sort of benign pothead agnosticism counterbalanced with sporadic contempt. In short, I was seventeen. I was bipolar, seventeen, and ready to cycle. I no longer wanted to save the world. I wanted to see the world, sure, but mostly I wanted to meet exotic girls and convince them I'd seen it. I cut my hair, signed the Teen Missions doctrinal statement, and caught a bus for the Lord's Boot Camp in Merritt Island, Florida.

Prior to shipping out, teenagers from all over the country received training at the Lord's Boot Camp. We lodged in mildewed tents where nocturnal armadillos crawled under the canvas and our backs, seeking body heat. Reveille came through a loudspeaker system just before dawn; we got some grub at the mess hall and then commenced the laying on of brick. Lecture subjects alternated between Jesus's infinite love and my unacceptable behavior. It was a nightmare. What the hell had I been thinking? I must have been sick.

One morning at break I was playing my harmonica when a Lord's Boot Camp staffer walked up. He squinted at me. He had a crew cut. "What's the name of that song, son?"

I shrugged. "I don't know. It's not really a song."

"Yes it is, son. It's a song. Is that a Christian song?" Non-Christian songs were forbidden at the Lord's Boot Camp.

I rolled my eyes. "Right, right," I said. "It's called 'Jesus Loves Me Blues.'" I was given work detail and lost my harmonica. I lost my copy of *Walden*—No Secular Humanism. I lost the girlfriend I'd met on the bus down—No Pairing Off. I even lost my shorts—No Immodest Dress. And so, stripped of my sins, I flew to Manaus with twenty other brainwashed workers. At seventeen I found myself one thousand miles up the Amazon, stacking misshapen bricks and sleeping in a hammock alongside fundamentalists. I should have joined the fucking army.

The first week we ate canned chicken and gravy over reconstituted potatoes. By the second week we settled for gravy with reconstituted potatoes. Soon after the gravy changed from a meaty brown to tan to a sort of milky gray color and resembled soupy reconstituted potatoes. We had lots of green Jell-O. We ate green Jell-O until the bitter end. We lived in a compound hacked from the forest—a baked dirt exercise yard beside a

rudimentary kitchen and a thatched area with benches and tables. There were tin cups and Kool-Aid. I now understand how
Jim Jones did it, how he achieved his dark ends.

By the third week I and two other missionary youths began
sneaking down to the river at night to fish. We built small fires
and ate small fish that had fangs. We smoked cigarettes bummed
from workers we met in the forest clearcuts, broken-looking men
with machetes who stood beside billowing brushfires. We bought
a turkey from a man who lived in a stick hut a mile or so downstream. It had one eye and was sickly. We fed it our baked oatmeal and fully intended to kill it and eat it when the time came.
The mortar and bricks ate into my infected hands. I knew I
could get sick there, that I couldn't hide there, that I had run
straight into my darkness. I stayed up and waited for Colonel
Kurtz.

Six days a week we ate salt tablets and malaria pills and
slaved relentlessly in the clearing. It felt more like a swamp in
the heat. We carried bricks, mixed mortar, cleared brush, and
cut the tin roofing. I dug an outhouse pit through ten inches of
rainforest loam and six feet of sand. Nevertheless we kept up appearances; the missionaries taught us how. Every day after lunch
we spent one blessed hour in the shade and we learned. The
men's course was entitled God's Gentleman. I learned how to
shave—never against the grain; this causes pimples—and how to
part my hair. In *The God's Gentleman Workbook* I found line drawings of various head and face shapes, with suggested hair parts. I
have a thin face, and the authors suggested I should part my hair
in the middle. The workbook was filled with cautions. There
was a picture of a long-haired man with a black X across his face.

Beards were advised only when confronted with weak chins or other, more serious disfigurements. The girls' workbook, *From Grubby to Grace*, was kept away from the boys but my fellow gentlemen and I surmised that it dealt with more intimate matters. I still possess my *God's Gentleman Workbook*. I brought it back from Brazil and placed it in a box in my mother's attic, along with a blow dart and a lacquered candy dish carved from a root. But I'm a backslider, I confess. I shave against the grain and I renounced combs years ago.

On Sundays we would eat a special baked reconstituted oatmeal with raisin sauce and then board the missionary's van and head toward the city to evangelize. It was shameful. I talked about a savior I didn't know to destitute strangers without English. I had lost twenty pounds. I'd broken my front tooth. Someone had stepped on my eyeglasses and one lens was Scotch tape. I needed phrase books for town; I needed phrase books for camp. In Manaus, only the fleeting glimpse of the ubiquitous, thin-tied Mormon missionaries could cheer me. Evidently, a circle lower than Teen Missions existed, haunted by pairs of dark-suited young men from Utah, cruising the cities of the world like Buddy Holly's sanctified ghosts.

Toward the end, when our building was close to completion, we were driven to a leper colony about twenty kilometers outside Manaus, a desolate outpost of concrete and tin buildings built on a series of dusty, deforested hills. Everything had been burned long ago. We met the sorriest-looking people I had ever seen, their faces bandaged, fingers and ears eaten away, some with open sores. I remember how they stood off from us and pointed, laughing. A tired uniformed woman coerced them into the damp chapel, where we commenced singing songs in English. But we had practiced singing "Jesus Loves Me" in Portuguese for the occasion. It was a big hit. In fact, the lepers laughed and clapped and joked with one another throughout that suffering afternoon. The sun outside stayed hard and bright as we stood in the small, dark room with our eyes cast to the floor. I had nothing for these people. I heard ghosts again and I thought I'd be lucky just to get home. My friends and I never ate the turkey but returned it to the man in the forest. He thanked us and then he got out a machete and killed it right there while we stood beside his smoky hut, queasy and mute witnesses for Christ.

We had flown into Manaus from the city of Belem, on the delta coast. For our return, Teen Missions had booked a twelve-day, one-thousand-mile boat trip down the Amazon. We were all tremendously excited until we saw the riverboat, a rusty steel barge with its upper deck half-fitted with sloppy welds. It could have been the boat Werner Herzog pushed over a mountain while shooting *Fitzcarraldo*, his film based on the rubber barons and their fabled Manaus opera house. It certainly looked like it had been pushed over a mountain by Werner Herzog.

The Brazilian crew and passengers kept to the lower deck. Some slept in cabins, some in hammocks hung from the rails. Our group had the upper deck, where we stood watching brown water slide past the dull green mangroves and vines. The Amazonian rain forest isn't all toucans and shamans. It's more than that. For me it was the drone and skip of an old diesel engine, an endless swamped tangle that pushed back toward low clouds and rain and then white towers and sun. Sometimes the river seemed as wide and slow as a lake and we steamed down it day and night.

The third day out, the captain blasted a whistle and our boat sidled up to a clearing, where there was a small thatched building and a pier made of sticks. A handful of Indians appeared, ragged and shoeless, some with straw hats. The crew threw over the lines and within minutes the clearing teemed with people laughing and shouting, Indians selling baskets of dried fish, passengers embarking with filthy woven bags or disembarking with planking or chickens or children. A battered red pickup careened out from the trees and swung toward the pier. Half a cow hung from the tailgate. The deck hands grabbed the cow by its two legs and dragged it down the stick pier. They hoisted the meat aboard with some difficulty and winched it up over center deck, second class, where it hung for days while the flies and the galley cook worked like piranhas. Up in first class we ate it for a solid week, in stews.

I slept under the sky in my hammock. It was August, and the Perseid meteor showers rained down into the forest as the stars climbed up from the trees. It was all god, I was sure of it: the Southern Cross above us, the butchered cow below. It was god haunting the sad dust of equatorial opera houses, god in the malarial rivers and leper colonies, in all of this terrible beauty. All the old words like "savior" and "faith" seemed broken now. All of it was broken and I most of all. I didn't have long. I figured it was a matter of months.

FIVE

The morning after I returned from Brazil my mother began force-feeding me. She was painting again and watercolors lay on the kitchen table every morning with fresh flowers, calligraphy, and scripture. She'd clear them away every evening and apologize. She hadn't believed in her art since college. Peggy was still reading; I spent days with my brother and the television. The house was either silent or filled with Dad's music. Not much had changed.

I was twenty pounds underweight and had a broken tooth, a serious intestinal complaint, and no plan. College loomed. I had some options, some acceptances, but I could not decide. I was sliding back toward despair and my mind was slowing down. I couldn't even plan the afternoon. The first week of August my father interrupted one of my stuttering reveries and called me into the living room. "Listen," he said. "Let's clear this up. It's not necessary to have career goals. You'll figure that out once you get to college. Remember, David, careers aren't important. What's important is your calling, your vocation—how you will help build the Kingdom of God."

"Well, that's good," I mumbled. "I'm glad I don't have to

worry about getting a job." I was getting uncomfortable even before Dad mentioned St. John, but when he brought in the Devil I rushed from the room.

I tried to take the long view, I really did. I knew Dad's spiritual approach was traditional and time-tested. Humans have spent thousands of years studying the soul and less than thirty studying neuroscience. Until quite recently, the world blamed mental illness on devils—black bile and devils. In my family it was never the bile. All questions remained religious questions, questions that my father channeled through seventeenth-century Puritan divines. According to Dad, God and Satan are having a long, drawn-out game of capture the soul and we are all up for grabs. I seemed to be the only one losing.

I shook off Dad's Puritans. It wasn't too hard; England did it in 1620. A year after they left for their new world, a depressed mathematician named Robert Burton published the world's largest compendium of depression. He called the Puritans a "mad, giddy company of Precisians" and explained that they doubted of "their Election, how they shall know it, by what signs … [and] with such nice points, torture themselves, that they are almost mad." Burton stressed bile over demons, "obsession over possession." His tome became wildly popular and created a royal court glutted with moody, world-weary posers. Burton wrote it, he said, to keep busy and called it *The Anatomy of Melancholy, What it is, With all the Kinds, Causes, Symptomes, Prognostickes, and Several Cures of it. In Three Maine Partitions with their several Sections, Members, and Subsections Philosophically, Medicinally, Historically, opened & cut up.* For starters he named the Head Melancholy, the Body Melancholy, and the Bowel Melancholy or "windie melancholy." The subclassifications followed: Jealous Melancholy, Hypochondri-acal Melancholy, Solitary, Romantic, Religious, and so on. Burton might have saved his ink. In my family it was always Religious Melancholy, twenty-four-seven. There weren't any others. The spirit ruled the mind and the mind ruled the brain.

Everyone knows the only cure for Religious Melancholy is more religious training—prayer, certainly, but mostly more religious training. I was in a tough spot. For months my father had been praying and pushing me toward a midwestern, evangelical school: Wheaton College. I no longer had the strength to push back. I couldn't confront my family about our God. I couldn't announce my desertion. That would mean leaving the evangelical trenches, a rush into no-man's-land, straight toward the guns and barbed wire. Instead I crawled out of the faith in secret and soon I was tangled. I knew if I struggled I'd reveal my godless position and so I came home from Brazil and played dead and hung on the wires. I hoped that when night fell my family would crawl through my blackness, cut me down, and carry me home.

My father flew me out to Wheaton College. He bought a leather-bound Bible, inscribed it to me, and left. Wheaton was awful. I soon discovered that I much preferred wasting away in an equatorial white-slave work camp run by religious fanatics over wasting away in a well-stocked cafeteria as classmates argued for the Pope's eternal damnation. Every class session opened with devotional prayers. I remember bowing solemnly over my pickled, partially dissected fetal pig. We had all signed a pledge not to curse, drink, gamble, have sex—especially homosexual sex—or dance. We could not listen to jazz. It was eerie, as if some sort of cultural virus had swept through the place, had left us all standing and smiling and hollowed out from the world. Theologians will discuss the problem of evil forever but I'm more interested in the problem of goodness, why piety so often breeds zombies.

I guess I was called to tour the new building on campus, the Billy Graham Center. It was there I realized that the jig was up and I could no longer pass as evangelical. Upon entering I was ushered through the Rotunda of Witnesses and then on to a sort of wax museum history of evangelicalism. The tour ended in a small, well-lighted place, a room made of mirrors, blue sky, and clouds. From a walkway arched over mirrors I witnessed myself hovering in midair. Bach chorales rose from cheap, hidden speakers—the very sound of rapture, full of wow and flutter. At eighteen I found myself trapped in a phony Heaven, staring at myself. Nothing had prepared me for this, not church, not drugs, nothing. It focuses the mind, floating in Heaven, staring at oneself. I bolted and never returned.

If God couldn't cure my religious melancholy I figured it must not be religious. And it wasn't black bile, I knew that. The stuff doesn't exist—God maybe, but not black bile. As for doctors, I sure as hell wasn't schizophrenic, and if I was headed there, I didn't want to know. No way was I going to a doctor. I just had bad moods. All I needed was some fun, a lot of fun, and that meant Colorado and skis.

My Volkswagen blew its seals at twelve thousand feet,

somewhere inside the Eisenhower Tunnel, the very top of a pass blasted through a mountain peak. I didn't care. I just coasted six miles down and into my promised land. I pushed my car into a gas station lot, scavenged what I needed, and starting walking. It was three in the morning and the snow shone blue and lunar and the air tasted like steel. I walked through the night toward Breckinridge, toward the mountains, my cure.

The cure didn't take. I was determined, I did everything right, but it just didn't take. I landed a job at a local lodge, a modest, ramshackle place that gave me a room. I worked at a shop called Spurs and sold cowboy hats and phony snakeskin boots to tourists. I quit when the mountain opened and got a job teaching four-year-olds how to ski. Mostly they stood in the snow and cried, but I had my season pass. That was fun. I fell for a blond, blue-eyed girl with a turned-up nose and a closet full of tight sweaters. She was Lana Turner on skis. Her bedroom was like some delirious untethered satellite and I'd leave in the morning sleepless and dazed. That was really fun. I had what amounted to it all in a ski town: a beautiful girlfriend and a ski pass. But it wasn't enough. It would never be enough. I didn't need fun. I just needed a doctor.

At age twenty, I had only experienced half the disease— depression—and an accurate diagnosis was unlikely. Instead I spent years believing that my agitation and unhappiness were my fault, and my periodic depressions simply confirmed my self-loathing. Increasingly, fear and anxiety made my decisions. I found stopgap solutions and sad little hideouts. It would have taken a full-blown crisis to pull me out my trenches. I didn't want this disease. I had no intention of stepping out to meet it.

Denial wasn't difficult, not yet. No one in my family had experienced mania. My father and brother weren't sick at all. My mother suffered from depression, she could get delusional, but her quiet paranoia always passed. On average bipolar disease—aka manic depression—hits patients in their late teens and twenties. My father held out into his fifties. Classically, the disease hits in adolescence, as it did with me, and it most often descends like black death. My father, brother, and I had six years before the shit hit the fan.

Simply put, bipolar disease results from the inability of the brain to regulate emotion. Manic-depressives are mercurial and experience their highs and lows intensely. The illness is often called a mood disease but this term obscures its deadly nature. Bipolar disorder is a brain disease. No doubt it can be exacerbated by lousy childhoods, whiskey, and stupidity, but it is biological in origin. Psychoanalysis, abstinence, and education can't hurt, but they cannot cure this sickness. Many sufferers do not experience the disorder's more extreme, psychotic symptoms, but the disease is chronic and life-threatening, the most lethal form of mental illness. Left untreated, one out of every five manic-depressives commits suicide. Considering the average onset age for bipolar disease, it's no accident that suicide is the second leading cause of death among college students.

Depression is a painfully slow, crushing death. Mania is the other extreme, a wild roller coaster run off its tracks, an eight ball of coke cut with speed. It's fun and it's frightening as hell. Some patients—bipolar type I—experience both extremes; others—bipolar type II—suffer depression almost exclusively. But the "mixed state," the mercurial churning of both high and low, is the most dangerous, the most deadly. Suicide too often results from the impulsive nature and physical speed of psychotic mania coupled with depression's paranoid self-loathing.

Patients who move between the two poles many times within the course of a year are called "rapid cyclers." A milder form of the disease, in which mood fluctuates but pulls back from extremes, is called cyclothymic disorder—bipolar lite. Properly understood and managed this form of the illness can prove extremely creative and productive. I've nibbled at the edges of hypomania all my life and I know I've benefited from it. It's hypomania, that precious, semilucid phase before mania, that is so seductive. It's brilliant—a quicksilver state charged with poetry, charisma, and sex. I believe it is possible to touch it and love it and leave. I believe it's a gift. But then I imagine cocaine addicts feel much the same way.

I'm more suited to counting angels dancing on a pinhead than to amateur discussions of neuroscience, and so I'll be brief. The brain communicates with electric signals. Neurons package chemical information into neurotransmitters and then fire them off to other neurons across spaces called synaptic clefts. If all goes well, the intended neuron—the receptor—catches the message, processes it, and then gets rid of it, gets ready for another. Most often the cell that sent the message gets it back to repackage; this is called reuptake. All this hums right along, with various neurons turning off or on, slowing and speeding, as needed. There

are a great many chemical circuits in the brain, but two neurotransmitters are of special interest to the bipolar: serotonin
and dopamine. These produce pleasure—they're lovely. But if
the brain can't regulate their movement, if they pool up or drain
down, there's trouble.

There are two categories of drugs presently used to treat
manic-depressives: mood stabilizers such as lithium, and antidepressants. Mood stabilizers do just that: they build an emotional
ceiling and floor, keep patients from going off the deep end.
Lithium is used both to regain equilibrium and to prevent future
episodes. It works at both ends but is best as a ceiling against
mania. Scientists now think it affects enzymes involved in the
processing of information within the neurons. I don't know how
it works and I suspect no one really does.

The new generation of antidepressants, including Prozac,
Zoloft, and others, is called SSRIs—selective serotonin reuptake
inhibitors. They help you feel better by keeping your serotonin
out there. I don't know how they work but I do know they can
work too well; they can push a depressed bipolar patient right
through the roof. They are a dangerous godsend.

I couldn't stay in Breckinridge; melancholy doesn't mix with hot
tubs and ski slopes. I cashed out my fun when the mountain closed,
broke it off with my girlfriend, and drifted back east. I moved in
with my family one last time and found carpentry work, framing
houses on the North Shore. I hung rafters in the bright sunlight,
stood in pine sawdust, and measured and cut. For a while the work
fixed me. I banked my money and applied to Colorado College.

In all likelihood, it was the last summer my family would live together, and no one acknowledged it. My father was alone and hard at it, stripped down to his boxers and undershirt and hunched at his typewriter. His outlook began darkening. The great cultural shifts of the '60s ground out and evangelical culture was never redeemed. His colleagues had circled the wagons. Jonathan and my mother were quiet that summer; Jonathan turned thirteen and found basketball, and my mother seemed well. She was painting. Peggy planned on attending Wheaton in the fall. Her news filled me with quiet rage. It was as if some insidious blue-eyed caste system preordained my family to evangelicalism. It seemed none of us could escape, but I bought a motorcycle and tried.

I rode west on the small roads past the upstate vineyards, the Finger Lakes, and on through Pennsylvania. I skirted the rust belt and left the East all behind. I traveled the small roads across Nebraska, Route 20 and Route 2, through tiny one-blink towns like Broken Bow and Valentine. The wind spilled the light yellow and the Sand Hills went rolling just like Ipswich Bay. If I couldn't be happy, stay simple and fun, if some soul sickness had me, I'd gamble for beauty like this. When I bought that motorcycle I bought the romance of sadness; I wanted to stay lost on the moors. Technically I was just headed to college, but still, I pushed it. I ran out of gas and money on Colorado's desolate eastern plains, about one hundred miles from school. I hitched to a truck stop and sold my new plaid shirt for three bucks' worth of gas. I got to Colorado College after midnight, unrolled my sleeping bag on the football field, and fell asleep, a melancholy poet, a broke, tired, and extremely happy melancholy poet. I could finally study what I loved and not have to pray about it.

I was twenty-two when I slept on that football field. I'd never heard the term "bipolar." Manic depression was a Jimi Hendrix song. Mom was just slightly schizophrenic; that's what I heard. That's what the hospital called her in 1949. But she wasn't; she was manic depressive. They could have done better. After all, the German psychiatrist Emil Kraepelin had written the book on manic depression fifty years earlier. His seminal textbook revolutionized the understanding of mental illnesses. Kraepelin posited the "manic-depressive synthesis": the two extremes were components of the same disease. He described it as a circular, periodic disease and differentiated it from schizophrenia, a far worse, degenerative condition. Kraepelin's detailed description took over two hundred pages but his suggested treatments only took five: bed rest, restraints, cold baths, and morphine.

Fifty years later the American psychiatrists labeled nearly all severe cases schizophrenic, including my mother. In a sense they had given up. Medicine had been dissecting the brains of schizophrenics and manic-depressives for decades and had found nothing abnormal, no cause. Slide after slide of "diseased" brain tissue showed no difference from healthy brains. Nothing seemed broken. Science had isolated the microorganisms that caused syphilitic madness; Alzheimer had found his tangles of cellular brain debris; and psychiatrists knew about hormones and thyroid dysfunction. But they could find no biological basis for manic depression or schizophrenia, and the radical advances of neuroscience were decades away. Psychiatry took another path and followed Freud. Schizophrenia and manic depression were diseases of the mind, they said, not of the brain.

Psychoanalysis was all the rage in 1949. German psychiatry had been disgraced by Nazism for its complicity in Hitler's savage eugenics. Postwar psychiatrists dismissed Kraepelin's earlier work, considered his categories too obsessive, too German. Unfortunately schizophrenics did not respond to the new talk therapy; neither did the manic-depressives. Nothing could be done so psychiatrists lumped them together and shipped them off to state hospitals and custodial care: bed rest, restraints, cold baths, morphine, and electroshock.

Lithium could have helped. It was out there. The ancient Greeks wrote of its healing powers. It had been used as a sedative as far back as the 1870s, but the salt proved difficult to patent and thereby profit from, and its use died out. But lithium still claimed some vague therapeutic value in the public's mind. Back when Coke had cocaine, 7Up was called "Lithiated Lemon-Lime Soda," but it took an Australian researcher named John Cade to rediscover the efficacy of lithium therapy. He proved it in 1949, the year my mother was committed. He didn't buy the psychoanalytic thesis and felt sure that the causes of manic depression could be found not in biography but in biology. He began studying the urine samples of manic-depressives, looking for a toxin common to all. He isolated their uric acid and tried injecting it into guinea pigs. Why not? It was awkward, for one thing; uric acid is not terribly soluble in water and the doses were lumpy. He added some lithium to increase solubility and began shooting the guinea pigs full of lithium urate. He switched to lithium carbonate and the poor little pigs calmed down, way down. They even sat still for their daily urine shots. Cade speculated that lithium might work on raving lunatics and he found a few desperate cases. After two weeks on lithium, a man who had raved for five years quieted. He stayed at the hospital but soon returned to his old job. Similar results were observed with other manic patients and a large test group proved its effect. Cade published his findings: "Lithium Salts in the Treatment of Psychotic Excitement." He didn't know how it worked; he just knew that it did. Scientists still aren't sure how it works. But lithium proved a magic bullet against mood disorders. Psychiatry was off to the races.

Though not quite. Psychoanalysts still called the shots in America and they remained skeptical of drug therapies. And then came the table salt fiasco. While Cade was shooting up guinea pigs, lithium was introduced as a salt substitute and American cardiac patients filled their shakers with the stuff. Some dropped dead, and this is how doctors first learned of lithium's low-dose toxicity. After that it took psychiatry twenty years to convince the Food and Drug Administration of the drug's value. It was finally approved for use in 1970, and it saved my family sixteen years later.

When I got to Colorado College I knew nothing about psychiatric medicines, had no inkling I could benefit from them. I studied street drugs in college, not legal medicines. Colorado College is a small, very private liberal arts school, idyllic, really, and the perfect place for learning. The college organized class schedules under the "block plan," wherein students took one intensive course at a time. One month it was Joyce, the next Nabokov. The system was perfectly calibrated to the attention spans of manic-depressive poets and drug-addled youths. And Grandmère paid tuition, room, and board.

I was suddenly, even understandably happy—nothing manic about it. I was the happiest I'd ever been. The English department loved me and I loved them dearly. I edited the school's literary magazine, brilliantly, for two dazzling weeks. I should have been content and hardworking; I should have edited the lit magazine for more than two weeks, but I was nervous and flighty, afraid of my mind. And the school housed me with all the other transfers, all the other brilliant washouts. We had all the best drugs and I used them like medicine but considered them fun, recreational. It worked great for a while, the best medicine I could buy without seeing a shrink, without confronting my sickness. Pot was a party mask I pulled over my symptoms. Besides, all the good antidepressants hadn't been invented yet.

Colorado College opened its welcoming, laissez-faire arms and I found that my drug of choice was acceptable, not a problem. As soon as class ended I made the campus rounds, smoking strong, sticky weed with various friends. My afternoons were slow, lovely. I unraveled quietly and it was the quiet I craved. I lay on the grass and read chapters of *Ulysses* and they made sense for ten to twelve minutes. I couldn't sit still without pot. It was a mild hallucinogen back then—before hydroponics and super strains—and it brought me the dreamy, sedative calm that I needed. It slowed my skittery mind.

Nevertheless I was a self-medicating fuckup. I just smoked, drank, and snorted whatever turned up. I was young, smart, and squandering my grandmother's money. Some kids get drunk and smash up Dad's car; I did drugs and smashed up my mind. I fucked up my own self-medication. I took whatever turned up. Maybe I was getting sicker, maybe my steering was shot, but it was my decision. I held the wheel and floored it. I hit the ditch and flew through the trees.

I wasn't alone; manic-depressives like their drugs. Street drugs are not chosen randomly; addictions don't just happen. For many of us, drugs provided a coping method of sorts. Some never get over their first loves. Studies show that 40 percent of the bipolar population is alcoholic. Only 7 percent of the general population needs that drink. Alcohol blunts agitation. It makes depression more interesting. Cocaine is very popular with manic-depressives; I loved it. A few lines can tap into that fast mind, that euphoric bravado that marks the first, beautiful stage of a manic break, hypomania. Manic-depressives use coke to augment or jumpstart their highs. The cocaine deals high and fast with dopamine and mimics mania quite well; its crash is a mini depression. Cocaine is bipolar disease in powder form, convenient and fast. Crack's even faster. Ecstasy dumps massive amounts of serotonin and dopamine straight into the system and damages the cells where it's stored in swaths. Permanently. It destroys future happiness. And the psychedelics—LSD, peyote, mushrooms—they can trigger manic breaks, blow a latent disease sky-high.

My friend Thomas was brilliant, a psych major with swagger and an elegant death wish. He would vanish for weeks at a time and then reappear mysteriously bearing cocaine and cognac. Our conversations ranged widely and rapidly—from poetry and religion straight through to psychology and getting more drugs. I had my requisite and seminal psychedelic experience with Thomas, when we ate mushrooms one morning in New Mexico.

We had driven down to Bandelier National Monument, a canyon full of Anasazi petroglyphs and cliff dwellings, a sort of psychedelic field trip. No one knows much about the people the Navajo called Anasazi, "the ancient ones." They were gone before the Navajo arrived. The trip site was genius, all Thomas. I lost Thomas early on, ran past him as he fell for a cactus. I lost my shoes and my shirt as well. It was hot and I was running up and down the canyon floor. A tour group arrived and stared at me. The canyon was getting busy so I walked a mile or so and found a series of sketchy ladders climbing up to a dwelling. I spent the afternoon sitting on what I hoped was a stone altar, quietly watching over the desert. I could see miles. I watched a hawk wheeling and assumed he was looking for me. Call it delusional, synthetic, or decadent, whatever, that shining sky was heartbroke and beautiful. I'd see it again if I could. But I can't. Besides, I know now that psychedelics are just shortcuts. They're not as good as the real thing, as madness. They're not even close.

I signed up for Melville, for a four-week seminar on *Moby-Dick*. Our class would meet in Chicago, at the Newberry Library, and study its impressive collection of Melville manuscripts and trinkets. There were twelve of us. The college had arranged our housing in a kind of academic flophouse with rooms by the week. I first read *Moby-Dick* in high school and I believed every word. I still do. The evangelicals call this inerrancy; I call it art.

Everyone else flew; I took a Greyhound. It started snowing pretty hard somewhere in Nebraska and the bus slowed to a crawl. I had nothing to read. So I ate just a bit, just a small cap of a mushroom. Just to take the edge off the trip. A short time later the bus turned sideways and the driver yelled to get down and I looked out the window and down to a ditch. There was screaming. The driver steered into the slide and recovered while I just sat thinking. A woman was weeping but I knew dying in Nebraska on a bus in a ditch would not happen. It was a hallucination, and you just ride out hallucinations. Still, with time moving so slow it took forever for the driver and God to work that out.

My next near-death wasn't as random; I felt I deserved it. I even approved its aesthetic. It was a slow descent down into the bowels of the Newberry, into the vault of the Melville Room. Down there, under all that great library's books, I knew it was true what he wrote: "To grope down into the bottom of the sea after them: to have one's hands among the unspeakable foundations, ribs, and very pelvis of the world; this is a fearful thing." I felt flushed, claustrophobic in that close little room squeezed between metal shelves. I got dizzy, speedy, and scared. It seemed crazy. I was just a kid and the book was just a novel. Relax.

Of course I loved the class, meeting for hours every morning to discuss the cosmos—the beautiful, appalling whiteness of the Whale. My classmates were sharp and beautiful, and Dan Tynan, our professor turned friend, revered the work. I cannot imagine a better adventure. I tried to stay happy and smart but I had struck a match on that bus while I pushed through the white Nebraskan prairie. In eating just that small bit of a fungus I started a fire that would burn down my mind. The experts call what happened to me "kindling"—a perfect, poetic term. It's the brain's "escalating response to a repetitive stimulus," as Drs. Jameson and Goodwin explained in their seminal text *Manic-Depressive Illness*. This escalation reaches a point at which the mind continues to flare long after the match burns out.

For me, the disturbance continued for months. Just a bit of that mushroom, a crumb, dropped the floor out from under me. I barely got high but I plunged into Melville's bottomless sea by way of Alice's rabbit hole. I went down fast, way down below the Melville Room. I was among bones, the ribs and pelvis of the world. My thoughts broke and tumbled in my head, the same dead pieces falling over and over again in the spin. I was drowning, quite literally, in my own mind and I went quietly and excruciatingly mad. My consciousness clouded into a feverish, sleepless dreamscape; I held on to what I had and by dumb luck I had Melville. He gave me what language I had and was right when he wrote, "The whale-fishery furnishes an asylum of many romantic, melancholy, and absent-minded young men, disgusted with the carking cares of earth." While I could still read I wandered that asylum. I still have that copy of *Moby-Dick*, its pages bent and stained, scribbled with illegible notes. I've waved it through hospitals like a talisman. My wife looks concerned every time I pick it up.

Before Chicago and Melville I believed in beneficence, in the unwavering beauty of the world. I was broke but undoubtedly coddled, unworried about home or love, and I was young, unacquainted with death. I believed in a sort of Deadhead transcendence, a pantheistic mellow, and I ate mushrooms to find it. In Melville's parlance, I clung to the masthead, one hundred fifty feet in the air. I can't say he didn't warn me. "Close your eyes in this mystic reverie," he wrote, "and you'll fall with a half-throttled shriek and drown in a summer sea."

Melville lets his orphan, Ishmael, swing open "the great floodgates of the wonder-world," where he sees the god-horror whale, the "grand hooded phantom," Moby Dick. "It was the whiteness of the whale," says Ishmael, "that above all things appalled me." It was the white of holiness and death shrouds and angels, the white of the shark, of corpse lips and absence and God. I drowned with all my stoned head transcendence and everyone, everything bled to this white, this monstrous ghost-bodied blank.

By the second week of class I stopped coming and hid in my flophouse room. My sleeping bag lay on an old blue-ticked mattress with a gray pillow, no case. I had a lamp, a hot plate on a battered white stove, and a small empty fridge. I pulled the shades and locked the door. I stopped bathing. My body disgusted me. I stopped eating and felt my thoughts slow, lurching to what felt like a halt in a matter of days. My thoughts were broken, actually broken. Neurologists demonstrate this, the crash in brain activity, loss of memory, inability to speak. If I dreamed I woke with a start, my heart banging, and so I stopped sleeping. My tongue was slow, uncoordinated. I bit it when I spoke. My new friends were all concerned. They visited me often and their visits were horrible. I sat up for them and was nauseated. I just wanted them to go away. I could not speak their language. Worse, I could not feel or understand their emotions. I was dead.

For one week in Chicago I had been the life of the tea party, everybody's friend, and then I was gone, a ghost with a withered smile. I only spoke with suicide. Suicide understood me, never would judge. I considered all the options. The little oven I had—its size just perfect for my head—was electric but I knew I had knives. I knew I could jump out the window, eleven floors, the simplest solution. I wanted the oven, though, no mess, no scene. The electric oven became my excuse because I was weak. I knew I couldn't do it. I knew I'd fuck it up. I couldn't even sit up. Who was I kidding? I didn't have the courage. I had to do it, it wasn't my choice. Suicide never is; it's just not volitional. It's just a tool and sometimes we are forced to use it.

Someone knocked at the door, kept knocking and knocking. Finally I dressed and opened the door and the light pushed me back. It was Dan, my professor, and I didn't let him in, just kept my hand to the doorknob and squinted.

"David, how are you?" I shook my head and stared at his shoes. "The class, all of us have missed you. It hasn't been the same." I didn't move, didn't look up. "We're having a big dinner tonight, the last day of the class, and you have to come. All of us want you to come." I couldn't let him in and I hated myself for it. I hated myself for fucking up. For worrying my friends. For becoming a ghoul and wrecking their party. Why should they have to deal with me? They were dead wrong. I wasn't worth their pity.

Dan stood at the door, perplexed. He didn't want to cause pain. "Look, David, look. Don't worry. You don't have to come down. But I'm going to send some food up. I want you to eat." This time I nodded. "And you know, David. You have an extension now. Don't worry about Melville right now. I'll get your paper sometime later. It's not important. All right?" I said okay and turned back toward my bed. My tongue tasted like sand. I didn't want fucking food.

The afternoon moved past. The brown light pooled behind the shades and leaked away slowly. Sylvia Plath. How long does it take to die with an oven? How long with your thighs pushed against the door? Or do you close up the door, crane your neck? I should do it, get out of the way. If I jumped would it be graceful? How would I fall? How long? Could it feel good, like sleeping? And then another knock on the door. A woman's voice. Oh, how would it look if she came and found me? A scream and blue lights. Cops. My family, my mother.

"What?" I called from the bed, lying on my side toward the stained plaster wall. "What?" I was hoarse.

"David, let me in. It's Sarah. I have food."

"Leave it." I was so stupid and mean, such a mess she couldn't see me.

"David," she teased, "now don't make me break in here."

I saw her standing there, perfect, blond, sorority sister. Cute as hell and utterly different from me, from this. I'd flirted with her through the first week, through "Loomings" and Queequeg. I can't see her, I thought, not like this, all wound in my sheets. "Hi, Sarah. I'm sorry, just leave it, I'm sorry."

"I won't just leave it."

So I stood slowly, naked and sick. I pulled up the sheet and covered my sickness and stood by the door. "All right, Sarah. All right." I cracked open the door and she was shining. I took the tin-foiled plate and she stopped the door with her foot.

"I'll see you later, David. I'm coming to check."

"No. Please." My old mind knew I should love this, anticipate this, her coming to me. But that was gone, I knew it, and this cold, sharp piece of knowledge cut at my chest. I took Sarah's food and leaned over the stove. I ate chicken. I ate at a thigh till I saw the bone, the small veins, and I spat at the sink. I ate rice. My jaw felt like a cramp in the chewing. I bit the side of my cheek again and again, shredded it. There was cake. I couldn't even look at the cake.

I sat on the bed. I wanted to call Sarah and tell her not to come, but I couldn't. I couldn't even do that, let alone stick my head in the oven. Sarah was wrong. She could get hurt, I could hurt her. She wouldn't come, she was just being nice. She won't. It's just pity, like you pity small animals that twitch on the road. I don't need a fucking night nurse. I need this to stop. This horseshit body all pasty and white, my filthy cock and idiot stare. It was wrong of me to eat their food, to mumble, to go to their party. They shouldn't have asked me. They shouldn't have had to. I'm a sinner. Okay? Okay, so I said it. Sinner. Flesh. I'm gar-bage, and Christ, if he ever existed, would spit in my face and I'd fucking clock him. No no no not that I'm sorry forgive me all that. Go ahead. Cast out my demons, go ahead try. I'm Legion. The door has a lock. It locks. I should be dead—dead dead. Nothing after, no stupid Heaven. If there is a fucking God and he cares he will leave us all dead. He'll slit open my belly and suck out my soul. Leave it dead on his cloud or some shit.

I moved across the room like an arthritic and checked the locks on the door. I knew I could keep her out, that I would, but I moved toward the bathroom, toward the shower. I scrubbed my white stomach raw and scraped at my groin. I smelled of soap and rot and went back to the mattress to wait. Sarah came and I just let her. I was wrapped in my sheet and she moved to the window and let up the blind. She was beautiful by that window, painted with light like a Vermeer. She turned and looked at me and I had to watch her face. I could not look away but I thought that I should. She undressed and all the time she looked in my bee-stung eyes.

I laid my mind in her breasts and she smelled of sunlight. I curled up against her belly, my leg caught over her soft, perfect hip. Her breath was the only air in that undersea room and she saved me from drowning. She whispered but all I heard was her breathing, and her hair fell down across my eyes and I slept. The following day the Melville seminar ended. I returned to Colorado and Sarah went elsewhere. I never saw her again.

I limped back to campus and barricaded my door. Thomas came by to cheer me up, carrying his cocaine and Remy. I asked him to leave. I didn't want his medicine. It got so bad I knew I would die, I was dying. I hadn't slept or eaten in weeks.

I called the school's health center and made an appointment, knowing the therapist would hate me, think me spoiled or faking or screwed up on drugs. I worried. I chose my appointment clothes days ahead of time, swapped out my shirts, counted the hours, and knew I couldn't go.

I arrived at the student health center and stood quietly at the reception desk. A woman stepped out of a room, glanced at the schedule, and asked, "And are you David?" I nodded. "Well, David, I'm terribly sorry. I need to go to my office downtown. Something's come up suddenly. I'm afraid you'll have to reschedule."

And that's how it happened, the rest of my life. A scheduling flap, an apology, and a linchpin pulls out. I could have gotten some medicine, some idea that this wasn't my fault. Maybe my father's God could have stepped aside long enough for me to discover my illness and steady my hand. No chance. The therapist hated me, that's all. I was just a spoiled kid who fell down with his drugs and scraped his knee. She was right, I decided. She was right not to waste her time on me. I couldn't even pick myself up off the ground. I could never go back to that office. I went back to my room and sweated it out like some junkie. Spring came and I crawled home.

I was almost better. My brain or my soul had purged its bad chemistry and righted itself. I went back to the North Shore for some carpentry work, for my mom and Ipswich Bay, but the other ocean hit when I got home—the same sour air, the corpse light, the dark crush when I walked in the door. I found my father in bed. I almost smelled lilies in the brown light. It was two in the afternoon.

"He's all right, darling," my mother said. "He'll get up later. He's just resting." He wasn't. It's nothing like rest. I wouldn't see him that day. I knew where he was, and he wasn't with us. Days later I caught him at the bathroom door, hunched in his boxer shorts, his eyes like smoke. I waved as he opened the door. I wanted to stop him, grab at his arm, and see if together the two of us could stop ourselves from drowning.

SIX

My father and I were like drunken sailors. I staggered the decks while my dad lay passed out in his bunk. Before long I took to my room and began sliding down. I hid for over a week until my brother barged in and shook me. "Dave, you got to get up. You got to do something. Don't just lie around. Please." He looked like he might cry. I sat up. "Dad's been lying in his bed for a year. He's been lying there since I was a sophomore. He doesn't even try." He walked to my window and snapped up the shade.

I squinted and said, "I know, Jon. I know all about it. It's awful."

"You don't know. You haven't been here. Mom can't handle it. Get up, Dave. Please."

"All right," I said. "All right, I will, but I can't talk right now. I just can't." I turned to the wall and pulled my knees up. I closed my eyes. Jon pulled the door shut. I was a fuckup and my brother was an orphan. Jon was adrift and I couldn't help him. Peggy lived in Chicago and Mom did everything now. She woke Jon for school; she fed him breakfast. She picked him up from his games and from practice and fed him again. Mom managed because there was no one else left, just this frail little bird with her two hollow shells.

Dad had taken a paid leave of absence from the seminary and they were kind enough to call it a sabbatical. Mom fielded all the calls from his students. She went to Dad's office and found their old, ungraded term papers. She explained to his colleagues and to the trustees that he was sick. "We don't really know. He's just exhausted," she said, but she knew. She knew how it was. My father was fading. He had joined in her sickness and so he was lost to her now, lost to all of us. Mom took a job as a home health aide, her first job in thirty years. She spent her days bathing the old, sick, and dying, then she came home and cooked dinners her husband refused. She went to bed alone with him, wrapped herself in his stale sheets, and prayed.

My father stopped listening to music: all he needed was the machine hum of his dehumidifier—white noise in a black room. He couldn't bear to hear us move through the house. He used an old coffee pot for his bedpan now and never came out until the house had gone dark. He thawed frozen shrimp in our sink and ate them with crackers. He watched television, drank wine, and hid his empty bottles in the garage. He abandoned our mother, that's how we saw it, and my siblings and I wanted to scream. I wanted to stand up, kick Dad out of bed, and show him how it was done. My rage pushed me out of my room. I didn't know shrinks or medicines or therapists. I just got angry and walked for hours through the woods.

I sat down and wrote my Melville paper and I took Ishmael's advice: "Whenever I find myself growing grim about the mouth...whenever my hypos get such an upper hand of me, that it requires a strong moral principle to prevent me from deliberately stepping into the street, and methodically knocking people's hats off—then, I account it high time to get to sea as soon as I can." I went back to Colorado and left them all there.

I finished school but my confidence was shot. My depression hadn't been conquered or even considered. It had just ebbed away, leaked out from my body. I was terrified, really frightened that it would come back and never leave, like my father's. I stopped making plans for the future, stopped considering grad school and academia. I couldn't teach. I couldn't stand in front of others; I'd break down and lose it. I relied on my cynicism to keep myself white and the rest of it black because it was the gray that really scared me, the twilight. I didn't want to see where I was going. I didn't want to look down and see where I was, and cocaine helped me with that. For a quarter gram I edited and typed my friends' papers. For a half I composed them. I had settled for some brittle glaze of happiness, just a little boy clutching his candy.

I graduated and drifted back to the North Shore. I had no plans; I just wanted to live in Gloucester, fish, and stay close to the bay. I found my mother just where I'd left her, alone in her kitchen. The table was blank, no color, no brushes, nothing. She was happy to see me but her eyes soon fell to the floor. I sat down at her table—tired from the motorcycle, sunburned, and utterly stoned. The living room was shut and Dad's papers were covered with dust. For two years my father had hidden in his bedroom and his shade now frightened the family. My brother's boyhood was damaged and now he was sick. His disease came on just like mine, with suicide thoughts in the spring. He was sixteen, same as I had been, just like clockwork. My mother ran out of words. Down the hall to the left lay her husband's shadow, to the right was her son's. I was scared, more frightened than angry. My father was dead and he spooked me. His depression had killed him, was killing my brother, and I thought I might catch it. I could smell the infection in Hamilton, in the stale, yellow air of the bathroom, the kitchen, and the hallways.

I knocked on my father's door. I opened it and stepped into the dark. "Dad. Dad, it's David," I whispered. "I'm home."

He rolled toward me, cleared his throat, and said, "Dave. It's you, you're back. Good. It's good to have you back. If you'll wait just a minute I'll—"

"It's okay, Dad. Don't get up. You don't have to get up now. I'll see you later." I backed up and closed his door softly.

My mother made pork chops. I pulled my brother from his room and sat him down at the table. I knew he was glad I'd come home, believed that somehow I'd help. He pushed at his food silently. My mother and I spoke about Peggy—out in grad school, Chicago, for social work. She was okay; she was fine; that's nice, I should call her. When it was over my brother exhaled and stood up. He stood still when I hugged him. He was sweaty and rank. I kissed my mother good night. Everyone was in bed by nine o'clock and I couldn't sleep. This disease was contagious. My brother had proved it.

I needed a place to live and I knew who to ask: William, my high school friend with the papal fixation. He had remade himself into a sort of fast-talking Brahmin and his real estate machinations were becoming legendary. Starting in college, he had maneuvered his way into a string of magnificent North Shore homes: beach houses, old captain's houses, mansions built upon seawalls. I'd return each Christmas and attend William's parties, lavish events thrown on bad credit in the elegant homes of strangers. All of them were winter rentals, each one as lovely and transient as his stories. He read Latin on occasion, knew the rules of polo, pretended to enjoy lacrosse, and bored his dates bragging of nonexistent stock portfolios. He'd given up on the Vatican; he wanted Gatsby's place now. He looked me in the eye and claimed he had gone to Phillips Andover, not our public high school. Our conversations grew increasingly short and confusing and our friendship waned. But William remained a genial, somewhat surreal host and he continued to find beautiful, inexpensive rentals.

I called him at his mother's. "David. How nice to hear from you," he said officiously. "Goodness. It's been some time. What can I do for you?"

"Do for me?"

"Yes."

"William, how are you?"

"I'm well, thank you. And you?"

"Good. I'm good." Bad grammar appalled him. "I'm back on the North Shore for the winter and I need a place to live. Do you have anything?"

"I see. Well, David, it's fortunate you've called. I'm negotiating an agreement right now for a house up in Gloucester. Turn of the century, stone construction, granite. It has a tennis court and a number of outbuildings: a barn, an old forge. There's a stone tower."

"A stone tower. You're kidding me, right?"

"I can assure you," he huffed, "that I am not. I will need some housemates and you're welcome to apply. Rent should be reasonable. As I say, I'm presently negotiating."

"I'm in."

"David, I—"

"I'm in, William. Cut the shtick, okay?" I knew I was inconvenient for William, a witness to his plebian past, but I charged past his defenses.

There was a pause and then William's clipped response: "Fine. Very well. I'll arrange a tour and ring back. Now, I'm quite busy at the moment, so if you don't mind."

"Sure, William. Whatever. I'll talk to you later." I hung up and smiled. I couldn't trust him, of course, I knew that, but William made me feel honest, upright, and sane.

Any misgivings vanished when I saw the house. It was set on a hill above the Annisquam River and the forest behind stretched across the heart of Cape Ann from Gloucester to Rockport. I found the stone tower back in the woods beside a small pond. It was maybe fourteen feet across and two stories high. Two goats grazed beside it. The tower was overgrown with thick vines and served no apparent purpose. It was a poet's tower. Perfect.

I walked back to the main house and found William and the landlord speaking on the front lawn. "David. Let me introduce Mrs. Morrison. She's the owner."

She thrust her hand at me. It was covered with dirt. "I've been gardening," she explained. "Call me Pat." I liked her immediately.

"David's a developer and he—"

"No, I'm not, William. I'm just a carpenter. I'm working in

Charlestown right now." I heard a loud, piercing squawk and another, and I started. We all looked up at an enormous green and red macaw perched twenty feet above us.

"Aw, goddammit," Pat said, and called her husband. "Norris! Hey, Norris. Get the ladder. The goddamn parrot's stuck in the tree again. Norris!"

"Help. Help me. Help," the parrot screeched.

"My son Tiger taught him to say that. That's Sebastian. He's a royal pain in the ass and he's filthy. My husband smuggled him back from somewhere. He was a pilot." William and I met more of Pat's family, various adult children. Pat pointed out a llama stabled under the tower. "His name's Butch. Don't get too close," she laughed. "Damn thing spat in Norris's eye once. We had to take him to the hospital."

Pat saw through William immediately and just rolled her eyes. Looking back, I know Pat saw William just as I did. He was a character, a self-deluded character, perhaps, but amusing. "Well, boys, the house is yours. I like you well enough. No big parties. Norris has all the paperwork and he'll take your money. You can move in after Labor Day. Something like that." Pat welcomed me into her house and before long I loved her and wanted her to adopt me. Her family was like mine, I thought, without the religion, the depression, and the ranch house.

I called Nathan Sargent in Breckenridge, told him about the place, and convinced him to move east. He was my closest and most levelheaded friend and I needed to shift the household's balance toward sanity. Besides, Nathan was a carpenter, a good one, and I had work for him. Frankly, I begged Nathan to come. I needed his help. I had landed a contracting job and was in over my head. A college friend named Dalton had moved east for law school, bought a property, and tracked me down. Boston's condo market was booming and properties were flipping right and left. Carpenters were scarce and unemployed English majors with tools could name their own price. I named mine and it was way too low. "It will be fun, Dave. Relaxed," Dalton said. "I'm living on the second floor. We'll convert the third floor first. I'll help."

The building was an asphalt-shingled three-decker in Charlestown, Massachusetts. It looked sallow from the street and out back it had more of an air shaft than a yard. Its linoleum was curled and its roof was shot. All of its lead-painted surfaces were begrimed with exhaust and neglect. Nevertheless my law student friend had high hopes. He saw exposed brick and period trim with a deck off the back and lots of houseplants. He wanted gas lamps and Back Bay Henry James, and he planned to make a killing. He outlined his vision over bong hits upstairs.

We wandered the building while I made up numbers and then Dalton summoned resolve. "Come on, Dave, let me introduce you to Mrs. Rourke. She lives on the first." He turned at the landing. "Listen, don't worry about her. We'll try to keep her happy until she leaves." Dalton knocked at her door and she invited us in. She was pleasant, in her late sixties and a widow. Her apartment was filled with religious icons and cats. She offered us tea.

The following week Mrs. Rourke met me on the front stoop. "Here, let me get the door for you, dear," she said as I struggled inside with a table saw. "What a big tool. I hope that won't be too loud." She couldn't stay, that much was clear. I hadn't even set up my workbench and there it was, all laid out. It was going to get loud and very apparent that I had come to evict her.

Nathan and I took sledges and crowbars and gutted the upstairs apartment. We cut through the plaster; insulation poured out like cancer, bits of brown shredded newspaper and dust clouds. We filled garbage bags with the stuff and left them in corners for weeks until they punctured and spilled out again. We pitched the trashed lumber out the back windows. We hacked at the walls until coffee break, when we sat on the stairs, our faces like chalk with our mouths little pink rings left by the dust masks. About the third week I asked Nathan how to read blueprints, what the smaller lines and some of the symbols meant. I bluffed with electricians and lost sleep over plumbers. I was failing badly and I knew it. I had never worked as a lead carpenter, let alone contracted a job. My original cost estimates were laughable, fictions written by a lapsed English major. I kept the crumpled lumberyard receipts in a battered red Sawzall box and became increasingly reluctant to add them together.

Dust and noise rained down upon Mrs. Rourke and by Christmas she no longer called me "dear." We were making that woman's life a living hell. We heard curses and mutterings when we passed by her door. She had sharp fingernails and an odor of cats followed her. Mrs. Rourke frightened us. She caught me once and asked me in for coffee. I sat nervously on her fur-covered couch and she brought me a cup. "I wish you could meet my son, Danny. He's a cop over in Chelsea." She smiled. "He should come by soon. He should see all of this. All the work you have done." She narrowed her eyes. "My other son's dead. A good boy, too. Went to mass. Died of lung cancer." She coughed. "He got it from plaster dust. You know that stuff's full of asbestos? Full of it. It killed my son."

I stared into my coffee and said softly, "No, it's not."

"What's that?"

"It's not asbestos, Mrs. Rourke. It's horsehair plaster."

She ignored me. "You know, I'm afraid to breathe down here. A lot of days I tie a wet towel around my mouth." Drywall scraps dropped past the windows behind her. Mrs. Rourke was a victim of progress; it wasn't even my progress and I had to push her. She had maybe six weeks before I moved downstairs. It made me heartsick.

I drove over to Hamilton and I always found my mother in the kitchen, worrying over her paintings. She was always so happy to see me. I sat and watched the anxiety ebb from her body. I always asked, "Where's Dad? Is he up?" And she always shook her head. "He's just lying in there?"

"I'm afraid so. David, I think we should just let him rest."

"Oh, c'mon, Mom. He's been resting for two years."

"Not quite." I made her nervous.

"How's Jonathan? Is he here?"

"No, dear, he's at practice. He should be home soon. Do you want something to eat? A grilled cheese sandwich or something?"

"Sure, Mom, I'll eat. So he's doing better? Jonathan's doing better? He's not depressed, is he?"

"I don't think so. He's playing basketball again." My mother got out the bread and cheese and I went down to inventory the garage. Our old fishing coolers were stacked against the back wall and filled with empty wine bottles. I was furious. My mother was alone and she was suffering and Dad hid away like a coward. I'd been drained of empathy, all pity. I was sick of blaming some mystery, some spirit or ghost. Just like Grandpa, all I had now was rage. I went back upstairs, walked passed my mother, and knocked on Dad's door.

"Dad. It's David. I'm coming in." I charged to his bedside, glared down, and ordered him up. I told him Mom needed him. "Dad, it's beautiful outside—pretty warm, a nice sunny day. It's daytime, Dad. Did you know that, Dad?" My father didn't move; he didn't speak; he just stared at the opposite wall. He played dead and I stood there and watched. I knew how it was; I knew all about this despair. I knew my words worked like knives and I opened his veins. I knew I could kill him. I heard my mother call from the hallway: "Your sandwich is ready, come on, dear, Dad's resting." Peggy and I agreed that our mother's deathwatch had gone on too long. Her sorrow had broken our hearts. We blamed Dad for all Mom's unhappiness, for Jonathan's ghost of a childhood. We blamed Dad for sadness. I blamed him for me.

Dalton introduced me to Daphne at one of his law school parties and we hit it off immediately. I convinced her to visit Gloucester and picked her up the next morning. On the ride I pitched her the story of Dogtown, the site of Gloucester's first settlement. I'd been hunting for the place for weeks—just a string of small cellar

holes somewhere in the woods. The village was largely abandoned after the Revolutionary War and left to its widows, stray
dogs, and the indigent. People in town called them all witches
and named the place Dogtown. It was the stuff of romance—at
least my kind of romance—and Daphne and I spent the day rambling on the trails behind my house, getting lost and discovering
flooded quarries, fields grown over with brambles. After that we
were inseparable.

She was beautiful and serious, with long black hair and dark
eyes. Her father had emigrated from Greece and struggled to
send his only daughter to college. She was grateful and driven,
and had captured a full scholarship to law school. After Daphne
began spending her weekends in Gloucester she asked me my
plans.

"My plans," I said flatly.

"Yes, your plans. You can't stay here. Remember? The lease
ends in June."

"Well, I have to finish Dalton's job. That should take forever."

"That's because you shouldn't be doing it. You should be
applying to graduate school."

"Why? Just because I don't know what I'm doing? I like it
here." I waved my arm over the coffee table. "This is fun." Nathan was in the kitchen sharpening his chisels and avoiding
Daphne. William was upstairs barricaded in the master bedroom
ironing his vast collection of faded secondhand ties. Our third
roommate was upstairs in bed, chain-smoking and reading
Kafka. He'd been there for weeks but when he first arrived he
was cheerfully delivering pizzas and waving *Cannery Row*. He

insisted we call him Doc and aspired to a life of bohemian ease. His outlook had darkened.

"Fun," she repeated, and shook her head. I couldn't afford to lose Daphne; I couldn't afford to scuttle her faith in me. And so a few weeks later I applied for a graduate publishing seminar. It was only twelve weeks; I figured I could hold it together for twelve weeks.

Nathan and I hired Doc to help out in Charlestown and each morning we stuffed ourselves and our tools into my Volkswagen Rabbit. Its starter was dead, so I parked on a slope and we rolled, and I popped the clutch and we smoked until we hit Boston. The lumberyard had put my account on hold; materials were scarce so Nathan and I were making bricks out of straw. Doc was the only one still enjoying the job. He was philosophical and spent weeks stripping paint from the original woodwork with a brass-bristle brush. He wore a series of disintegrating yellow rubber gloves and wrapped himself in Zip Strip fumes and cigarette smoke. By January I no longer cared about doing the work right; I just wanted it done, slapped up. Nathan took issue with this and held on to his pride. Doc and I just left him alone and re-paired to the second floor, to Dalton's apartment. We raided his stash and smoked bong hit after acrylic bong hit until all the anxious drama boiled out of the place.

Mrs. Rourke's complaints became a daily occurrence. We locked ourselves away upstairs. The beautiful apartment we had set out to make filled with end cuts and ill will. Dalton hid his bong and his dope and began tallying the numbers daily. Each week I'd present a punch list of tasks to Dalton. Each week he would check our slow progress against my good intentions. It had become pretty obvious to all what was going down by the time we sat in Rosie's Diner on Main Street and watched the space shuttle *Challenger* launch on the twelve-inch television behind the counter. It showed the doomed teacher and astronauts, and then the shuttle would launch again and explode again all through our lunch.

The budget was dead and gone, but every afternoon I'd report downstairs to Dalton's apartment. He'd offer me a beer and I'd sit covered in dust with one or two knuckles bleeding. I'd make my excuses while my friend listened patiently with his necktie and checkbook and notes. "Look, Dave," he kept saying, "it's not your fault. This is a big job, bigger than either of us imagined." I smiled at the floor ruefully. "The third floor's almost finished and buyers are interested. I'll pay down the lumberyard and we'll get the third done. After that you can start with Mrs. Rourke's. We'll adjust your old numbers and blow out the walls."

"Okay," I said, unconvinced. I wished he would just fire me.

"Jennifer and I are going down to the city in a few weeks. A friend of mine's throwing a party. You should come down."

"Maybe," I said. Dalton valued my friendship more than the numbers and that made me feel awkward. I questioned his judgment.

Radcliffe called to schedule an interview but I was stoned and scribbled the time and address on the back of an envelope. I lost it and a week later I arrived just past three. "Sorry I'm late," I said. "The parking was tricky."

The director looked up from his desk. "Late? Your appointment was for one p.m. You're two hours and ten minutes late." I stared, thunderstruck. "I have others scheduled, I'm afraid, but thank you for coming." I suggested rescheduling and he thanked me again. I drove over to Daphne's apartment and she sat me down. She said I wasn't ready to grow up and that she had big plans. She wanted a law firm and a forty-foot sailboat. She quit me; it hardly mattered. I agreed with her, told her it was a smart move. I decided to go down to New York with Dalton, drink heavily, and quit.

I got to Gloucester late Sunday night. I wanted to sleep and then I wanted to drive into Charlestown, collect my tools, and then sleep for a week. I got to the door and Nathan pulled it open, grabbed my arm. "Where have you been?"

"I went to New York with Dalton, you know that. I think we worked out a—"

"Never mind about that. Look, your dad's not right."

"What? What are you talking about? What do you mean 'not right'?"

"He means whacked," Doc clarified from the kitchen. "Crazy." Nathan nodded. I narrowed my eyes and looked at him. He was grinding his teeth. "We've been, um, doing a few lines," he said sheepishly. I threw my bag down, walked toward the kitchen, and found Doc sitting in front of a mirror.

"It's all gone," he said. "Just as well."

"What the hell do you guys mean, my father went crazy?"

"Dave," Nathan said calmly, "your grandmother called us."

"Grandmère? She called you?"

"Yeah, Grandmère. The Matriarch. She was trying to reach you, obviously. She needed you to go over to Hamilton and see what was going on. Your father called her in Woodstock and freaked her out. We told her you were in New York and then Doc decided we should go over and see."

Doc nodded proudly. "You need to call the Matriarch."

"And tell her what?"

"That your father is 'crazy.'"

"It's after midnight."

"Doesn't matter."

"What the fuck do you mean 'crazy'?"

"Okay, okay, calm down," Nathan said. "I'll tell you."

"I need a drink." Doc found some whiskey while Nathan continued.

"Everything's all right, now. Don't worry. Your mother's fine."

"Christ, could you just tell me what happened?"

"No one answered at your parents'. I don't know where your brother was. Anyway, after your grandmother called, Doc and I jumped in the car. It was, I don't know, about three this afternoon."

"We were kind of high," Doc allowed.

I had told them all the great family stories, the same Professor Lovelace lore that circulated through Peniel and the seminary. They knew my parents and now they had spoken with Grandmère. They were high, excited for some wacky Lovelace adventure. My family was a bit odd, that's all, not a problem. Cars were blown up, snakes lost in libraries, boats sunk, iguanas left on curtains and children at gas stations. So what? We were eccentric and fun. We were madcap. My friends thought it sounded fun and mostly it was, until our disease made it serious.

Whole seasons had been lost to despair, and spring most of all, curled to a desiccate brown outside our bedrooms. When one of us was well we set food out for the others. We left them in silence and waited our turn for the sadness. It was all so horribly polite. We didn't want a fuss. We weren't crazy. It was spiritual, we said, and we almost believed it. It wasn't that hard to believe. Until this point my family had suffered only from night sickness. None of us had stared at bright blindness, not one of us had struck toward the sun. My dad was the first.

"Wait, wait. What exactly did Grandmère say?"

"She said, 'Richard sounds terribly excited.'"

"'Terribly excited.' All she said was 'terribly excited'?"

"Pretty much." Nathan shrugged. "But she sounded pretty scared."

My grandmother rarely called us, but Dad called her dutifully. The most unsettling thing the two had ever discussed was Grandmère's Christian Science church. None of us discussed our feelings with Grandmère, our sorrows and fears, our joys. Quite frankly, my grandmother was more interested in the proper placement of flatware. And now after thirty-odd years came this phone call. God knows what my father told his mother, what terrible floodgate had opened.

"Really," I said, considering. "So you went there?"

"Sure. We figured we could help."

Apparently Dad had been watching for cars because he met my friends at the garage. He cracked open the door and demanded, "Who is it?" He seemed all right. My friends were disappointed; they'd been hoping for drama.

Nathan smiled and said, "Hi, Doctor Lovelace. It's me, Nathan Sargent, David's friend. And this is Doc."

"Peter," Doc whispered.

"I mean Peter. Doc's his nickname."

"It's about *Cannery Row*," Doc interjected.

"He's not a real doctor," Nathan clarified. "Anyway, we're David's housemates over in Gloucester."

My father relaxed and swung the door open. "Oh, yes, yes. Of course. Come in, come in. Friends of David Lovelace. Welcome." My father smiled broadly. "Welcome. Please call me Richard." Something was off. My reclusive father had thrown his arms open wide. My friends smiled furtively at each other. The synthetically high had met the real thing. "Please, please, come up the stairs."

My mother stood in the kitchen. She immediately moved toward my friends. "Richard's feeling a bit frisky tonight," she said with a crooked smile. She was afraid they might leave her. "It's nothing, really. Where's David?"

"He's down in New York. It's just us," Nathan said. "What's going on?"

"He's been singing hymns," she whispered. "Since this morning." Dad glared down at my small, helpless mother.

"Okay," Nathan said. "That's okay. I'm sure we can—"

"We need to sing!" my father thundered, and he grabbed Nathan's hand. He grabbed Doc's. "Do you boys know 'Michael, Row Your Boat Ashore'?" They stared at him. "Come on, you must know it." They stood in an awkward circle beside the refrigerator, embarrassed. Nathan and Doc avoided looking at each other; they tried not to smile.

"I don't know it," said Doc. "I don't think we should sing it."

"You're going to sing it." My father raised his voice. "Now, please take Betty Lee's hands and we'll begin." Doc stopped smirking and Nathan sobered up. My mother held up her hands to my friends and Dad started in his strong baritone. "Michael, row your boat ashore, alleluia, Michael row..."

Nathan leaned toward my mother. "Where's Jonathan?"

"He left this morning. He's over at the—"

"Keep singing. You're not singing."

My mother wouldn't sing. She stared at the floor. "High school. He's at the high school."

"Sister helps to trim the sails, alleluia, sister...Come on, now. Sing." Nathan and Doc mumbled the chorus. It was all chorus. My father ran out of verses and Michael kept rowing back and back. It wasn't funny anymore. It was never funny and the song made my friends queasy. Finally my father stopped and everyone dropped their hands, relieved. Suddenly it was quiet and scary and no one knew what to do. My father went to the window and checked the driveway.

"How did you boys know to come?" my mother asked quietly.

"Grandmère called us. She was worried. I guess he called her."

"I heard that." My father swung around. "I heard that! Grand-mère called you. Get out. Both of you. Get out now! You are agents of my mother. You came to spy for her." Doc and Nathan watched dumbstruck as my father's face darkened. He squared his shoulders and moved toward them. "Get out! You are agents of Grandmère."

"Honest, Dr. Lovelace," Nathan said. "She just asked us to check on things. David's away and—"

My father pushed past Mom, opened a drawer, and pulled out a large flathead screwdriver. He waved it in the air and then pointed it at Nathan and Doc, his face splotched and red. "You boys are agents of Grandmère. I knew it." He stepped toward them. They bolted and Dad chased them outside. He stopped by the garage and shook his weapon as they scrambled into their car. My father stepped into the driveway and scowled as they sped past. My mother was alone.

I woke her at one a.m. She said it was quiet. My brother was home and my father had been taken by ambulance somewhere. A psychiatric hospital. "Okay, Mom, okay," I said. "It's all right. I'll be over in the morning. Go back to sleep."

The days followed in whispers. We knew very little. "Dad woke me up," my brother said. "He was in the hall around five a.m., just pacing up and down and singing creepy hymns. I mean the scary ones, Dave. You know—minor key, blood of the Lamb stuff. Medieval. He wouldn't stop."

"What did you do?"

"I got out of there. I had stuff to do. I was freaked."

"You just left Mom? You left her alone?"

"She said it was fine. That Dad was okay. So I left." I might have left, too. None of us had seen a full-blown manic break; we didn't know what it was. There had been no discernible warning, no hypomania leading up to Dad's hymns. He spent more than a year twisted in sheets and silent, and then, *bang,* he launched into space. Our family's disease had a second act, a real show stopper. It had us coming and going now, up and then down. The great fear, the madness that had stalked my mother every day of her adult life, that had whispered up crazy from under my child-hood bed, the fear that had driven my sister to Loyola and a de-gree in psychology, had come for us now. It starts with depression, I surmised. So that's how it starts.

The ambulance had taken my father to a nearby psychiatric hospital named Baldpate. I drove over with my brother the next morning. "Baldpate," I said. "They called the fucking place Bald-pate? What is this, the twelfth century?" Jon and I laughed ner-vously. "Sounds like skulls; the Place of Skulls. Nice." We spent the rest of the ride worrying in silence. I was disappointed by Baldpate. I had hoped, perversely, that Baldpate could live up to its name, but it proved a series of low-slung, nondescript buildings filled with addicts and drunks. We passed through security and sat in the visiting area, waiting for Dad. He came through the door slow and stiff. He looked confused and pushed out his words with some effort.

I told him he'd be all right. That he'd be out soon. "Of course, of course," he said, "I'm fine. How's Mom?"

"Good, Dad. She's fine."

We sat there and stared at the floor in silence, and finally we left.

Two or three days later my father called my mother from the ward's pay phone. He asked her to come at six sharp. When she pulled up to his building, my father jumped out of the bushes and into the passenger seat. He looked at my startled mother. "Everything's fine, Betty Lee, wonderful. Now, just drive. Drive." We never went back for his clothes.

Dad didn't go back. He refused. My mother filled the prescriptions called in by Baldpate—an antipsychotic and lithium—and Dad complied. He went back to his bedroom, knocked out and counting his pills in a cotton-mouthed hush. My mother bought him plastic pillboxes with snaps and small trays and he slid his slack-jaw meds like rosary beads. She found a psychiatrist, a Christian involved with the seminary. No one said much.

Dad slept through the days, his eyes half-open in a room filled with undersea noise. My mother's watercolor still hung on the wall—daffodils and calligraphy that read "Rejoice in the Lord always and again I say rejoice." There was no music in the house. My mother answered phones and whispered like a ghost to doctors and friends. It's all right now. We're praying. Yes, thank you. I'd visit and Mom would say, it's all right now. He's all right now, just sleeping.

Back in Gloucester my friends Nathan and Doc worked up their story—a Dr. Lovelace story so strange, so gothic, that it beat all the others. They called each other Agent One and Agent Two. I'd sit by the woodstove and stare and hear the Agents of Grandmère as they laughed in the kitchen. Daphne had left,

Charlestown was in shambles, and Dalton wouldn't let me quit. I owed it to him, he said, to stay and to finish. I took his check for eight hundred dollars. I cashed it and called him and said I'd be back in two weeks. I drove to Hamilton and told my mother I was leaving on a short vacation, that I'd be home soon. I told myself the same thing and knew I was lying.

SEVEN

My father's break confirmed my worst fears. His mania introduced my own demon. There was something more frightening than despair, something uglier and more humiliating, and it stalked me. My medicine, my pot smoke, proved useless against this cold fear. I got high and then I was wing shot and flapping and dread ran me down. I needed to run. I loved my family, they needed me, but I needed to run. I feared my father's sickness was inexorable, pulling me closer toward madness, and so I cut him loose and never looked back. I couldn't hide anymore in Gloucester; I couldn't float on Ipswich Bay. I needed a far ocean. I wanted to sink, disappear from New England, from my family and our devils.

I chose the Blue Hole, a massive dark circle punched through a turquoise reef off the coast of Belize. It drops straight past the bottom of the sea and into a vast subterranean cave system. I packed all my dive gear—my mask, fins, buoyancy vest, and regulator. I packed my tank and a sixty-pound weight belt. Writing would be my excuse, my work. I packed a primitive twenty-pound laptop in one briefcase and a dot matrix printer in another. All this ridiculous weight—these props—announced my intentions and proved my resolve. I bought a cheap flight and paid extra for baggage.

At Belize City the bus driver heaved out my bags. My tank hit the concrete and rang through the station like a great empty bell. I dragged all my stuff into bright sun and the city, a decayed shantytown built by pirates, all its wooden buildings leaning on stilts and splashed with faded turquoise and pink. A clutch of children watched me stagger down the street under my luggage and laughed, jumping over the orange septic gutters and pointing. I crossed an iron swing bridge and found a cheap room overlooking the brown stinking river. Toward dusk I ate fried pork and bought dope at a Chinese restaurant. It was everything I had hoped and I was happy.

The next morning I caught a speedboat out to a small fishing village called San Pedro on Ambergris Cay, an island just behind the barrier reef. Its main street was short and made of sand, a few cheap hotels and shops with two modest gated resorts at either end. Past those there were just tangled mangroves. I unpacked at the cheapest hotel and went to bed with the best of intentions. In the morning I'd hire a dive boat. But I got stoned after breakfast, too stoned for diving, and wandered beyond town on a foot trail that snaked along the island's edge. I didn't find beaches; the surf crashed on reef a mile out from shore, just a line of white laid before the horizon, a dull distant roar. I found a camp near the end of the island—an empty cluster of tarps and plywood, a tree house that flew Rasta colors. The air smelled foul and clung to the tangled undergrowth. I turned and at the island's north end the reef came close. I floated and kicked above its bright colors and fish.

The second night I found the Tackle Box Bar at the end of a wood pier, just a shack with Guinness and rum. Out front a deck encircled the pier's old turtle pen, a wooden cage about twelve feet across where a morose sea turtle swam circles all day and nosed at the bars. The Tackle Box kept the turtle for tourists but the bartender, Clive, ran the place like his private club. We hit it off and before long my routine centered on the place. By my second week I had scheduled and cancelled trips with every dive boat on the island. I made excuses each morning and had coffee and joints with Clive until lunch. I drank up my dive money fast and I gradually gave up on the idea. I was too stoned to count my breaths coming up, to avoid the bends and drowning.

Clive believed that maintaining a dissolute expatriate writer on premises provided ambience. His bar already had a depressed, endlessly circling sea turtle and now it had me. I became the bar's second mascot—typing ostentatiously at a novel through the afternoons and shooting darts for drinks late into the nights. Every day after lunch Clive ran an extension cord out from the bar and I plugged in and typed. He let me keep my briefcases behind the bar so I could play writer. It was perfect, really. I had rum, a laptop, and fishing boats out the window. I was Hemingway in Cuba without the right words.

"Brother David," Clive asked every day, "how is the book?"

"Oh, great, great. I mean good." I could tell Clive anything. He didn't read and didn't much care. "I mean it's coming along." The novel wasn't coming along, of course. It was floating facedown and unconscious. Every afternoon I flipped it over and poked at it for an hour or two. I had spent weeks sitting in a bar two thousand miles from my sick family and the novel was my excuse, my justi-fication. As long as it didn't die I could stay here at the Tackle Box, a shack at the end of a pier on an island off the Mosquito Coast. But the book was a goner, an absolute dirge. On the bus down I had convinced myself that Ed, a troubled adolescent tollbooth operator from Chagrin, Indiana, would rivet the reader, that Ed could give alienation a fresh face. But by the second chapter Ed just sat in his cold metal box and grumbled. And I sat on an island staring into a blinking, sun-bleached screen, empty and high.

San Pedro is a small village and locals started to talk. The dive shop had given up on me weeks earlier. I stuck to snorkeling on the north end of the island and hadn't used my tank and regu-lator once. One morning an American dive instructor stopped me as I walked on the beach. "You know," he said, "it's not like people don't notice."

I smiled. "Notice what?"

"How you are. How you wander around this place, up and down. Who your friends are."

"What about my friends? You mean the Tackle Box?" He smiled slightly, looked out at the white line of reef, and walked away. I cursed at him under my breath but I knew he was right. I watched everyone now and I knew how they saw me. I wasn't a diver or a writer, I wasn't even a tourist, just a kid staying stupid with hardly a dime. By now, the thought of diving the Blue Hole terrified me, the idea of dropping down along its outer wall, down past all the colors with the black cutouts of sharks hanging above.

I was a coward; I knew it. I had left my family in crisis, my mother in shock and my father gone blank. I left my brother with hardly a word and I blunted my guilt with island rum and smoke and bright water. My novel spiraled into incoherence but I told no one and typed pointlessly, tangentially, for appearance's sake. Clive knew I was broke but he didn't mind; he knew I was wasted but then so was he. I stuck to the bar and when money got tight Clive let me string a hammock after closing and sleep there. My dart game got sharp and I won all my drinks from the tourists.

One evening I noticed a pretty girl from the States. We danced to Clive's endless reggae outside on the pier, spinning and flirting beside the Tackle Box and its poor, hopeless turtle. That was all it took. I fell into some sort of desperate amphetamine love right there in the dark. I blew up against the girl and held on for dear life. June was flattered at first and we kissed. The next day we hiked to the north of the island. I gave her my mask and showed her all of the beautiful fish. We were drunk on rum by dinner when June's friend entered the bar. She gave me a cold stare, moved close, and they whispered together. They stepped outside. Clive leered after them and turned to me laughing.

"I guess I'm screwing up her vacation." I shrugged.

"I'd like to screw up her vacation," Clive said. "Just fine."

June came back, sat down, and looked serious. "This isn't real."

"What do you mean, this isn't real? It's real." I knocked on the mahogany bar. "We're sitting right here. In Belize. In Clive's bar."

"Home is real. I go home in a week. I have a boyfriend at home and he's real."

"Okay, okay." I backtracked. "This isn't entirely real, but so what? You're not home. You're on vacation." She looked skeptical—drunkenly skeptical, but a tough sell nonetheless. "It's not supposed to be real."

"Exactly."

"What's home, anyway? Is that all you want? Wisconsin?"

"Illinois."

"Whatever, the Midwest." I waved an inebriated hand. "Look around. Look at this place. Look at me." She smiled but I knew my logic was failing. I knew it wasn't even logic. I was bluffing and ordered more rum.

"When are you going home, David?"

I shrugged. "Who knows?" I laughed and picked up my drink. I tried to act insouciant but June shook her head sadly. Her pity scared me serious and I looked down at the bar. "After I finish the book, I suppose."

We danced again and drank. I told her I loved her and thought that I did. I was hypomanic by then, clever and charming. I could seduce anyone and wanted to try. I was madly in love with a girl I'd known for a day and I wanted to prove it. I asked June down to the beach and tried to undress her. I couldn't convince her; I couldn't seduce her; "It's not real," she kept saying.

"All right then," I said. "I know what to do. Let's make it real and get some tattoos, matching tattoos." She smiled and thought I was joking, and I was when I said it. No one had tattoos back then, just bikers and sailors. "Yeah," I said. "Let's go. I dare you. So when you get home you can prove this was real. You pick the design." She started to laugh. "It can be small."

She pushed back at my chest and considered my smile. She

stumbled and kissed me. "All right, okay. I'll do it. Let's do it." I was charming, all right.

I knew there was a barbershop and tattoo parlor straight up from the pier, and I knew it stayed open late, a place where fishermen played cards and drank quietly. No one smiled when we walked in. No one spoke; a radio somewhere played static and salsa. The men stared at June. They looked her up and down without expression, grave. The owner moved behind his desk and asked, "What you want?"

"We want tattoos, both of us." Someone whistled low. The card players frowned and shifted in their seats.

"No, you don't want any tattoos." He looked at me skeptically. "Where you been? The Tackle Box?"

"Been on the beach," I said. "What's it matter? We want tattoos. Can you do it?"

"Yeah, man. I can do it. But you don't want it. Your lady there, she doesn't want it. What you want to mark her up for?" I looked back at June where she stood in the doorway. "Sure she wants a tattoo," I said, and showed him my money. "The lady chooses the design. Go get your book."

"Okay, okay. Yes, sir," the barber said. He was done reasoning with drunks. I intended to brand a young woman and the men against the wall stared contemptuously.

In retrospect, the love of my life chose poorly: a complicated little seascape featuring two seagulls, a palm tree, and a trite sunset that took a half hour to carve into my ankle. When it was finished, I stepped out from behind the curtain and June was gone. The men chuckled and shook their heads. I saw her once more on a sandy backstreet. She looked up, panicked, and ducked into a tourist trap. I knew not to follow her. She was frightened and her fear knocked me out. I'd been dizzy for weeks like a punch-drunk fighter and finally fell down.

I was scared, too. The locals just stared at me. I was sure they were talking about me, joking. I hauled my dive gear down to the Tackle Box. I laid out my new, shiny-chromed regulator, my mask, my fins, and my buoyancy vest on the bar, stood my tank in the corner. I was broke and I needed to leave. My ankle hurt and I felt humiliated. Nothing was real. The diving was a lie, the novel was a lie, and true love was just an angry red blotch above my left foot. Clive put the word out; some local divers ran over and the bidding lasted fifteen minutes. I gave away unnecessary clothes, sold my backpack, and cut my luggage down to a rucksack. Clive let me leave the laptop behind the bar. I said I'd be back in a few weeks, when my money ran out.

Years later, when I returned to the Tackle Box, Clive yelled, "Brother David! We have your machines! We have your machines." The cases were stashed in the rafters and dusty. I traded Clive my sunglasses for them. The turtle was gone. "The tourists complained it was dying," Clive told me. "It was bad for business."

"I suppose you're right." I smiled. "Greenback turtles are an endangered species, you know."

"Yeah, yeah, I know. So what?"

I boarded a boat for the city at dawn and caught a bus for the Guatemalan border. I crossed in the morning, moved through by young soldiers with rifles. My scuba gear netted good money and Guatemala's poverty doubled it. The checkpoints and soldiers continued all day through the jungle and right into Tikal, nothing but local color to me. I felt just fine away from the ocean, free of my book and blue holes. I met some American kids on the bus and none of us were tourists. We claimed to be travelers deep in the northern jungles of Guatemala and headed for Mayan ruins.

Tikal's ancient temples rise from a vast tract of jungle filled with partially excavated and buried palaces, temples, and tombs. There are parrots and toucans and the roar of howler monkeys at dawn. The place was transcendent and crawling with soldiers. Guatemala had been at war with itself for thirty years. Four rebel armies hid in the mountains. The soldiers fanned out from a barracks just past the ruins, patrolled the whole region, and blocked every road.

My friends and I decided to sleep in a temple. We hid in the jungle while guards and soldiers cleared the park. At dusk we climbed a half-buried temple, using roots and undergrowth for hand- and footholds. We saw the last of the sunset from a small room at the top and watched the jungle fade into gloom. All of us made wild conjectures concerning Mayan spirituality. One of my friends expounded upon Quetzalcoatl and the ancient Mayan calendar. It promised, she said, the apocalypse in 2012.

Apocalypse. I wasn't quite right, and like many before me I found the word itself intoxicating. I loved the very sound of it. "Look around," I said. "Look at this place. Apocalypse happened a long time ago. Look at the soldiers. Apocalypse is happening right now." The howler monkeys had started up, a low wall of sound from the jungle. We watched flashlights move up and down the main temples. My friends unrolled their sleeping bags and slept. But I couldn't; my mind was too fast. I thought about the Mayans, about human sacrifice, the Last Supper, and cannibals. I sat until morning, wide awake with the jittery ghosts of disease and religion. I figured I didn't need some fool sacrifice; I had road dust to cover my sins.

I got to Antigua and found Doña Luisa's restaurant. It wasn't hard—gringo hippies buzzed around its entrance like bees. Doña's interior courtyard functions as the central switching station on the gringo trail and its corkboard is plastered with notes: "Darien Gap—Safe?"; "Elvis from Puerto Barrios is a COP!"; "Need starter for VW bus"; "Sally from Denver: I was sick. I'm sorry. Headed to Copan. Meet in two weeks?" I scanned Doña's board for something, some reason to stand there short on cash, miles from home and pushing for farther. There were relief work and Spanish lessons and yoga.

I stood in the white stucco entrance with my pack slung down sideways and I fell for it all, for the never going back, just the endless south, its jungles and deserts and ruins. I saw the women around me all lovely and tattered, the ones who rode high on the roofs of ancient Bluebird school buses lumbering down through the hills. I fell for the happenstance jigsaw of traveling broke, the beautiful puzzle before lostness got found by e-mail and cell phone, before the global got positioned by satellite. I loved it more than the ocean.

My crumpled tollbooth novel still lined the bottom of my pack and I settled on its old, time-tested excuse. I ordered coffee and eggs and wrote my own note: "Typewriter needed to rent or borrow." I would find an old black Royal and type it all over again in this ancient colonial city. I'd learn Spanish. I would live with the people. But first, I needed a typewriter. I was quite clear on that. A writer needs his typewriter and my quest for the perfect black Royal bought me a month of leisurely, unwriterly days. Every morning I would check in with my note and spend the remainder of the morning drinking coffee, meeting Americans, and plotting far-flung itineraries.

I moved into a hostel and secured a fine room surrounded by English-speaking stoners for three bucks a night. I fell in with a tight group of travelers—a Norwegian photographer named Per, my American friends from Tikal, and a traveling love triangle involving three Germans. We spent our afternoons in the ruined cloisters of a colonial monastery, playing guitars, scribbling poetry, and studying Spanish. I climbed through the ruins ecstatic; my thoughts frayed and snapped in the wind like blown sails. I smoked my pot to let go of the wind, to spill the sails and just drift. I was in love with the sky now, a small band of friends, and every woman who smiled.

I sought out my highs. I slept with the German women, took full advantage of their stalled love triangle, but I soon fell for Elizabeth, a quiet student from California. She studied Spanish through the afternoons, her picnic blanket laid out on the cloister's grass courtyard, her long, elegant legs delicately tucked beneath lovely cotton skirts. I spent my days gazing down from the arched ruins above her, utterly smitten. It was quiet most days and peaceful, but once a large group of tourists descended. Their leader moved toward Elizabeth and I jumped down from the stones like Errol Flynn. I could move from dewy-eyed love to swashbuckler rage that fast.

"Yes. Yes," the woman kept saying to Elizabeth. The word gave her speech a rhythm, a sort of clockwork, reflexive peace. "Yes. We're gathering to invoke the spiritual essence of this place. Yes." Elizabeth smiled politely. I looked around at the convent, screwed up my face, and asked, "The essence of what? Catholicism?"

The woman stepped back and stiffened. "No, no, oh God, no." Her face, twitched. "Yes. No, it's not that at all. It's more, you know, the life force, its energy." I looked around at the broken stones and pocked walls that had seemed so beautiful, so ruined, before this woman appeared.

"What," I continued, "sort of a nun energy?"

"Well, yes. Yes and no. This place was a sacred Mayan site long before the Spanish arrived, long before Catholics."

"Really?" Elizabeth asked wryly.

"A Mayan site?" I offered. "You mean a temple? Human sacrifice? That sort of thing?"

"Hey, listen, pal." A swarthy man garbed in batik, heavy wooden necklaces, and chest hair stepped into my face. "The Mayans never fucking sacrificed humans."

"Well, actually I—"

"Now, the Catholics. Don't get me started on the Catholics."

"Bill, please." The woman stepped in front of the strongman. "Look. Why don't you just join us? There is room for all faiths, all spirits here. Yes." Evidently, Elizabeth and I were now considered crackpots, some sort of retro-religious Catholic throwbacks, and this by a group cozying up to Quetzalcoatl. They murmured and pitied us. "Yes, come. We are going down into the holy catacomb of this place to chant." Elizabeth smiled.

"All right, all right," I said, laughing. "Lead on."

Their holy catacomb was an old cistern, damp and smelling of toads. I grabbed Elizabeth's hand as we descended the broken stairs into pitch darkness. Someone sparked a lighter, then a few more like a rock show, and we saw the room—circular, with its roof curving in from stone walls. It resembled a hollowed-out subterranean gourd, one infested with hippielike moles. Our leader spoke. "Please, quiet please. Is everyone down? Could we please douse the light?" We stood now, silent, expectant, and deeply claustrophobic. "Could we please everyone hold hands? Good." I was already holding hands with Elizabeth and had no desire to hold hands with anyone else, ever. I pulled her back, out of the dark circle. The group started humming; everyone in the hole started humming ferociously and then they just stopped. Everyone waited and I could hear the walls drip. I couldn't see a damn thing. People kept waiting. Silence. A few stragglers across the cistern started up humming again, unsure and nervous, and then suddenly all hell broke loose with the hums. I kissed Elizabeth quietly, her shoulders pushed against the wet holy stones.

My money was running out fast. I ate bread, avocados, and onions every day, bought harsh Guatemalan cigarettes in pairs, and nursed beer at the bar. I'd been in Antigua three months, I'd overstayed my visa by two, and my friends were drifting away. Elizabeth flew home to California, Per back to Norway, and the

Germans went south. I still had a ticket, a flight out of Mexico that I'd pushed back indefinitely. I figured to get to Mexico I needed two hundred bucks if the ticket still worked. I didn't want it to work but I still needed money. I hadn't called home in four months. If my father had recovered I knew he'd order me home, and if he hadn't I didn't want to know. I still had some time, I thought; I planned to enjoy it and figured I was.

I sat in the plaza across from Doña Luisa's and watched the new kids arrive. I'd have to start all over again, learn their names, where they were from and where they were going. They'd find the cloisters soon enough. The great cathedral towered behind me; pilgrims and wafts of incense pushed through the park. I loved the smell of that pinion smoke. I loved Antigua but I couldn't stay. I walked across the plaza toward the bank, past all the soldiers, and pushed into Guatel, the national phone bank.

Wooden booths lined the walls. Benches were packed with strung-out travelers, Mayan mothers, old men, and children. Every few minutes a name and booth number were called from the desk but I had heard it took hours. I waited in line, took a ticket, wrote down my name and my family's number, and sat down to wait. Then I was too nervous to sit and stood by the door smoking. I could still leave. I lit another cigarette and tried not to think of Mom alone in her kitchen with the house gone quiet, or worse, my father still broken and singing. I thought of my brother, orphaned and left all alone. I couldn't go back; I'd get sick. I'd get stuck.

I stubbed my cigarette on the wall and put it behind my ear. I cut in at the desk and spoke fast, ragged Spanish: "*Disculpe, disculpe.* I'm sorry. *Mi numero es mal. Otro numero.*" I felt panicked, grabbed a pen and waved it. The woman found my card. I scratched out my parents' number and jotted down Nathan's. Forty minutes later they called my name and I jumped.

"Hello. Hello."

"Bueno, señor. Adelante."

"Hello?"

"Yeah, hi. Is Nathan there?"

"Dave? Is that you?"

"Who's this?"

"Shit, it is you. This is Chris."

"Chris. You're living there now?" Chris was a friend of Doc's.

"I took your room. Listen, have you called home? Your parents have been calling everybody—me, Nathan, that guy in Charlestown. You need to call home."

"Yeah, I know. They want me to come home. I know I haven't—"

"Man, listen to me. They *need* you to come home." Chris paused. "You don't know, do you?"

"Know what?"

"It's your brother, man. He's in the hospital." Chris waited for me to respond. I didn't. I didn't breathe. "Dave, you still there?"

"Yeah."

"He's okay, he's okay. I don't know much but he went off like your father did. He punched your father out, broke into someone's house."

"Punched him out?"

"Your dad."

"He went crazy?"

"I guess. I mean I don't know." Chris was embarrassed.

"When?"

"Maybe three or four weeks ago. Someone called the cops. He's at some hospital in Boston, I think. Lookit, you've got to call your parents. You need to get home. They need you." There was no air in the booth. It was hot and collapsing. "Dave, you there?"

"But he's okay, everyone's okay?"

"I guess. You need to call."

"I will, I will. Listen, I was looking for Nathan. I'm broke. I need like two hundred dollars."

"Your folks will give you that. It's not a prob—"

"I can't ask them for it. It's complicated and I can't explain it right now. How about one hundred? Can you wire me a hundred? I'll pay you back when I get home. I need it to get to the airport."

"Look, man, I—"

"Shut up, Chris! I can't talk anymore. Goddammit. These calls aren't cheap. I'll give you the bank information. All right?" I read off the routing numbers. My notebook was shaking. "Get it from Nathan if you have to. Scrape up two hundred or two hundred and fifty if you can."

"Okay, okay," Chris said. "Just come back, all right?"

"All right, man. I will. Thanks. I gotta go."

I hung up and pushed back against the dark booth. I slid my foot against the door and felt myself buried. I heard dirt hit the coffin. It was my kid brother gone now. They had locked up my kid brother, the sweetest guy in the world. He didn't even do drugs. I was smothered already and knew I was next. We were God's twisted joke, some kind of wrecked trinity: the Father, the Son, and me in this holy ghost town.

I wanted more distance.

Our father's manic break drew my brother and I together. It rattled the knob and opened the door we both feared. Like my own sickness, Jon's hypomania built through the weeks after Dad's hospitalization. His mild temperament gave way to anger. His basketball game grew increasingly rough. He cursed referees and friends and fouled out in minutes. The long-standing tension between Jon and the neighbors' boy escalated into a feud with lockers trashed and lies spread. My brother stomped around the house for weeks. He stopped sleeping and then he blew up.

He started yelling about the neighbors. He yelled at Mom—she wasn't listening. He was going to settle things once and for all with that kid up the hill. "I'll kick the shit out of him," he said, "and then I'll forgive him." He went to his room and made some sort of cape and tied it over his shoulders. He stomped back to the kitchen. Dad appeared. "I'm just going up to forgive him," Jon said. "That's all. I'm going up to forgive my neighbors." Jon headed for the door and made it to the driveway before Dad caught him by the shoulder.

Dad tightened his grip and Jon spun and coldcocked him, pushed Dad's glasses into his eyes, cut him up, and he fell to the ground moaning. The neighbors' kitchen door was locked so Jon punched his fist through the glass and fumbled for the lock. The neighbors leapt up from their dinner screaming.

"I'm forgiving you," Jonathan announced. "I'm forgiving you with my blood." They ran for the back of the house. "I'm not going to hurt you," Jon called. "Don't run away. Look, I'm forgiving you." Blood dripped down onto their carpet and Jon smeared gory lyrics on their walls. He was singing them when the cops arrived: "The public gets what the public wants but I don't get what society wants / I'm going underground, I'm going underground." He bolted out and down through the woods and the cops were out of breath when they cuffed him. Jon was sent to the Human Research Institute in Boston, where they strapped him down and dosed him with antipsychotics.

But I didn't want to hear my brother's story, not in Guatemala. And I didn't want to hear it later. I didn't ask him about it for years. Someone banged on the phone booth. I dug my way out and went to my room. I knew what was happening back home was bad and believed it could kill me. If I tried to rescue my brother he'd pull me under for sure; if I returned now I'd never come back. I packed my filthy clothes, counted my money, and walked to the plaza. The cathedral was behind me, Doña Luisa's beside me, and Guatel straight ahead. After twenty minutes I walked toward the phones and straight past to the bus station. I caught a bus toward Panahachel. I'd wait for my money there.

Panahachel is made for prodigal sons, a sad little Riviera beside a deep mountain lake. The mountains look quiet and peaceful and the lake is braided with blue and green currents. Nightclubs play the latest American hits and the video bars show all the latest American films. The only violence in Pana is entertainment on small screens in English. Every morning Mayan widows come from across the lake and sell woven bracelets and embroidered clothes. There are hummingbirds in the gardens and retired US career soldiers, too; the air tastes like spring and blood carries oxygen and alcohol and we share copies of *USA Today* where they worry about crime in Miami. And we worry, too: about the long ride to Tikal or the phone lines and exchange rates, and always the water. What about ice cubes? Can we use ice cubes? In Pana the currents tangle across to the murderous mountains and if we get sick the *farmacía* sells antibiotics that poison the small things inside.

I belonged there and I hated the place. I ate organic yogurt and granola each morning just like the rest. I drank at the Circus Bar and waited for money, for my next round of friends. I carried my bible, *The South American Handbook*, everywhere and plotted my itinerary south. One night an American commandeered the bar. He was over six feet, covered in wiry red hair, and barraging the bartender with terrible Spanish.

"*Zapato*," he said loudly. "*Mi nombre es Zapato*." He pulled off his sandal and held it next to his face. The bartender found this hilarious; we all did. He told me his last name was Schuster—or Shoe—hence the nickname.

"It's Zapata," I said, "with an A."

"It's Shoe, my nickname is Shoe. It's masculine."

"Not the revolutionary?"

"Not the revolutionary."

I smiled. "Too bad." He moved back to his table and rejoined a tough-looking blond kid. Zapato was loud and kept gesturing. He was selling something the kid didn't want.

"What do you mean, dangerous?" Zapato blustered. "The whole damn country's dangerous. If you don't want dangerous, you shouldn't have come here. Right?" The kid didn't answer. "Look, what I'm saying is we could have an adventure, see the place." Zapato swung his arm up toward the lake. "Look at those mountains. Look at all that. Do you want to just sit here and listen to fucking Michael Jackson in some gringo bar, or do you want to explore?" I liked this Zapato.

"Listen, my truck is full of shit and the roads are bad," the blond kid said. "I've had three flats since Mexico." I decided I liked the kid too; he had a truck.

I turned and said, "The roads aren't that bad, not if you go slow."

"That's all right," Zapato concurred. "You got to go slow, Jim. Hell, I'll buy you a spare if that's all you're worried about."

"And the gas," I interjected from the bar.

Zapato glanced up. "Yeah, and the gas. We'll pitch in for gas."

Jim stared at me. "Who the hell is this guy?" Zapato shrugged and Jim continued. "Look, it's not the gas, y'all. There's a fucking war up there."

Zapato dropped his hands to the table, exasperated. "Nah, not really a *war*, Jim. Just some guerrillas. Way out. There's roadblocks up there but there's fucking roadblocks all over."

I pulled out the guidebook, joined their table, and flipped to the index. "Now," I asked, "where are we talking?"

"Nebaj, Cotzul, you know." Zapato gestured dismissively. "Beautiful weavings, real Indians, quetzales."

"Quetzales? You mean the bird?" Now I was skeptical. The

animal boasts a close relationship with most Mayan gods, and is extremely rare. It's almost mythical. Male quetzales sport a crest and a long, iridescent tail that streams out behind them. They resemble a sort of holy Dr. Seuss bird. "We're not going to see any quetzales."

"We might, you know."

"Jesus Christ, y'all," Jim blurted. "I don't give a damn about birds. What about the soldiers?"

"It says here the security situation is improving," I said helpfully.

Jim turned to me. "Oh, really. Are they still mowing down Indians, or what?"

"They don't seem to be ...," I said inconclusively. I scanned the book. "'For lodging Nebaj has Las Tres Hermanas—delightful. Alternatively you can get a room in a private house for slightly less. There is also an army camp.'"

"Exactly," said Jim.

I ignored him. "'There are magnificent walks from Nebaj along the river or in the surrounding hills, but north of the town is still not safe.' Well, there you go," I said, "we just won't go north. 'All houses have been burnt between Nebaj, Chajul, and Cotzal; no one lives in this area and most traffic is accompanied by military personnel. Views of the Cuchumatanes Mountains are spectacular.'" The book wasn't helping. I pushed it across the table, away from Jim.

Zapato kept buying rounds until Jim agreed. We'd go for a ride up into the mountains, spend a few days away from it all. The next morning all three of us crammed into Jim's truck and drove slowly and rather stupidly toward the Ixil Triangle and its three Mayan towns: Cotzul, Nebaj, and Chajul. There wasn't much to see: the land and its people were in shock, featureless, almost blank. At points along the road the dust were nearly black from ash. We encountered few people and all we had were each other and Jim's tiny pickup—a white Ford Ranger with Texas plates, a silver camper cap with a blue surfboard proudly lashed to its top. By noon we were dehydrated, stoned, and relatively optimistic. By the noon the next day we were dehydrated, stoned, and sick of each other. The truck's fan belt started squealing and Jim's mood worsened.

He slapped at his dash. "Why the fuck am I driving around in these mountains?" he asked. "I could be surfing, goddammit." Jim had a couple of grand and told us he was headed to El Salvador for the surfing.

Zapato had maybe five hundred bucks, a fortune, and just wanted to "get laid," which meant any number of things in his cosmology: go on a bender, climb a volcano, screw a German tourist. I had twelve bucks US, enough, I hoped, for the bus back to Antigua after throwing in for the trip. It was tight and I tried to pawn Jim my Nikon. He had a camera—"a perfectly good fucking camera, thank you very much"—and wasn't interested. I wasn't too worried—Zapato lent me cash against my money wire. I wasn't worried about anything as long as we didn't drive home.

We were off to see Indians but there weren't many around. After the military coup in 1982, the civil war had escalated into full-scale genocide and thousands were butchered. Four hundred forty Mayan villages were razed in the four years preceding our tour. Cotzul was a ghost town: less than one hundred Mayans

were left from a city of twenty thousand; the rest were dead or in
hiding. Death squads used late-model trucks much like Jim's. We
were scary and most survivors just ran from us. We pulled into a
small village and a young boy began screaming while his mother
stood slowly and gathered him up. Jim tried to illustrate our ir-
relevance by gesturing to his surfboard but it merely furthered
the confusion. Soldiers stared at our chests but never our
eyes. Inevitably, Zapato would try to lighten the mood, but all
he had left was sarcasm. "Well, this is a friendly town. Nice place
for dinner."

Jim kicked at the stones. "Fuck this, y'all. This fucking trip of
yours sucks. Look, it's my truck, and if I say, we just turn right
around." Zapato and I groaned and turned away. We'd heard this
before. "Listen, I'm the fucking captain of this ship."

We bickered by the town well and smoked cigarettes till the
children came out from hiding. Zapato juggled something and I
gave away Chiclet gum. Their mothers, and some men now, called
from dark windows and the children ran off again laughing. It
was clear no one would die. We strolled down a few blocks and
turned back toward the store. The Mayans quietly gathered our
items and spoke softly to one another worriedly in Ixil. We
bought stale bread and tinned sardines, cigarettes and warm
beer—a few dollars—and then we left quietly with our heads
down, ashamed and strangely triumphant. We had seen Indians
and they had seen us.

Those mountains are more haunted than my family ever was,
more haunted than a thousand asylums, and I hid there. The Ixil
Triangle dwarfed all the guilt that I bore for my family, all my
impotent, cowardly love. I couldn't return to my parents and kiss

them and pick up my brother. I couldn't think of them for the fear but I could drive through a genocide. I could rage against strangers; I could mourn for their untold victims, but I couldn't face home.

On the third day we drove past Acul—just a grid of concrete huts, high on a hill and surrounded by soldiers. This was the first of Guatemala's new "model villages" and was made for the widows and orphans of Nebaj. The televangelist Pat Robertson built it with Guatemala's first evangelical president, General Rios Montt. Robertson paid for Acul's construction with a fund-raiser he called the International Love Lift. None of us commented as we passed the dreadful place. We were exhausted by then; even the truck felt worn out and sad. Three kilometers later we hit a checkpoint.

"Where's the pot?" Jim asked, and threw his beer under the seat.

"Under the seat," Zapato answered. "Fuck. Under the fucking seat, fucking brilliant." Zapato whistled softly.

I lit a cigarette and a soldier leaned into Jim's window. *"Buenas tardes."* He smiled, sizing us up. He put his right hand on his holster; his left he placed on the surfboard. He gestured at it with his chin, still smiling. His teeth were rotten, brown and wet.

Jim sat stone-faced. "El surfboard," he said slowly, staring at the uniformed boy, daring him to laugh. Zapato and I groaned, started whispering something about money, bribes, *mordida.* There were four or five soldiers total, ranging in age between about sixteen and nineteen, bored and dressed in fatigues. They had been sitting at a plank table under a makeshift thatched sunscreen by a blank dirt road in the dry hills. They were bored and encircled our truck. A transistor radio played tinny salsa. The others were up and circling the truck. It was over eighty degrees outside and way hotter in the cab. The one in charge stepped away and Jim began slapping his palms against the wheel.

Zapato pulled at his red beard. "Put out that cigarette, Dave, will ya? Christ." The soldiers were now standing in a tight circle in front of the truck, alternately smiling then stopping as the oldest spoke and gestured—bad gestures, short chopping motions, fists into palms. We couldn't hear a goddamn thing. Fifteen minutes passed. One leaned against the quarter panel; one had a boot up on the bumper. It became apparent they were laughing at the surfboard, pointing at it. One held out his arms, moved his hips in a slow circle. Soon two others jumped in, adding surf moves—hilarious. They watched us, laughing and jerking in the road. Jim watched and shook his head slowly. "Fuck this, y'all," he said. "This sucks, this really sucks."

A brown dog moved up to the leader nervously, sniffed at his boot, and jumped back. It was the kind of dog you see anywhere poor—useless and starving. It was covered with mange and dust. The dog began moving in a strange ocean current himself, slipping sideways between the surfing boys, moving forward and back, whimpering. Then the soldier kicked it sideways, his boot catching the dog's exposed rib cage and landing the sad thing beside the others. And immediately, like they'd done this before, like this was their job—and perhaps it was—all the soldiers lifted their rifle butts and brought them down on the dog and kicked it and crushed it.

Zapato was out of the truck before it had finished. "*Muy mal, señors!*" he screamed, *"muy mal!"* I followed Zapato out and dragged him back into the broiling truck. The dog was dead now and twitching. It hadn't made a sound.

"Shut the fuck up, Zapato." I said. "Please just shut the fuck up." The boys with their guns were laughing louder now, pointing at Zapato, pointing at us. After a time, the soldiers moved back under their thatch and sat down. Two Mayan women appeared from nowhere and dragged the broken dog down off the road and away. Ten minutes passed and the serious soldier stood. He waved our truck through, smiling. They were all laughing now beside a bloody smear in the dust. I waved and said, *"Gracias,"* and meant it, as Zapato beat the dash with his fingers and Jim cursed into the wheel. He said he was sick of this stupid shit, that he was going surfing.

We drove straight through to Antigua and the retreat made us fast friends, *compañeros.* We talked about summer work in Alaska and made future plans to meet in Seattle. I got my two hundred bucks and Jim left a day later for La Libertad, El Salvador. I saw him a week or two later in Livingston, Guatemala. La Libertad was a ghost town, he said, just soldiers and dogs. Jim said there were two Aussie surfers left. He said they ate nothing but Frosted Flakes and seemed damaged. He stayed with them for two days then headed back north. Zapato headed south for Costa Rica, a country without a standing army, without soldiers.

I cashed out my wire, booked another room, and returned to Doña Luisa's. Funds were short but I figured I had three or four weeks left to find the next windfall. I met some more travelers and played the life of the party even while I cut my budget down to the bone. An American couple, a woman named Katherine and her friend Jeff, moved into the room next door and we struck up a fast friendship. We cooked dinners in the hostel's kitchen and drank coffee together each morning. They were unhappy. I showed them the cloisters and hikes and places to swim while they argued quietly. They suffered their friendship in the hostel, on the buses, over coffee and beer. Katherine knocked on my door early one morning and climbed into bed. This trip was all her old boy-friend's idea, she said, a way to woo her back. She wanted to leave, she wanted to go home to Washington State, and she asked me to come. I said sure, why not, that makes sense. I knew I had to get back to the States. I needed money. I'd go to Alaska if I could swing it. I'd stay out west if I couldn't and find a quick carpentry gig. I'd find the farthest point from my family where I could work and save money, and then I'd head south, really south.

Katherine and I took buses as far as we could till we ran short on money. Buying bus tickets farther, to Tijuana, would break us and we'd have to cross the Sonora hungry. We sat mute and ex-hausted in a dusty town square across from a bus station. To-gether we had done it: two middle-class American kids had managed to find themselves out of money, sick, and staring at the desert, almost and finally lost.

We were fine, I assured Katherine, just fine. I was high as a kite, hypomanic, and I joked about stopping in Mexico City. "We could paint murals," I said. "Or I could. I know. I'll be Diego and you could paint those painful self-portraits, like Frida."

Katherine ignored me. "If we could just buy some plane tick-ets, get up to San Francisco. I have friends there."

"We could try," I said, and pulled out my last card, a blown Visa.

It was good for an imprint; beyond that my Visa was worse than useless—it was larcenous, thousands over its limit. For months, I had strategically deployed my bad credit throughout Central America at places too isolated for card authorizations. I spotted a promising travel agency just across the *zócalo*. It looked defunct with its blind drawn, with its sun-faded posters of Machu Picchu, the St. Louis arch, white women on white beaches.

Katherine and I took our best shot. We sat across from a travel agent and exuded all the American confidence we had left. I booked two flights to San Francisco and handed my Visa to the polite man with excellent English. My stomach was shot already but it gurgled in earnest when he reached for the phone. I kicked Katherine's foot and shot a glance at the door but it was too late. The agent set down his phone and he smiled. For the first time he really smiled, looked straight into my gringo eyes, and said, "I'm sorry, señor, but they have instructed me to destroy your card." He drew the scissors from his desk with a flourish, like a matador, and he cut my card in two, slid the pieces across his desk, and sniffed. There wasn't much to say. Katherine stood and left. I asked for the bathroom.

We bought avocados, bread, and bottled water and then took the next bus bound for Tijuana. The bus was packed with peasants, all of them grim-faced but friendly, all of us headed to the north. Things changed. The desert began to undulate beside the bus and I loved it. I loved the bus driver's salsa music coming over cheap speakers. I decided I loved Katherine. I loved the upholstery.

The bus idled at a truck stop and Katherine slept as I watched a man perform at the curbside. His hands moved fast in the hard desert light as he worked his shell game. I knew I was the mark; he had come for me. I rose and stepped into the sun. I knew I could win because of the sway and the change—the hallucinatory wave of heat off concrete, my wasted body, my mind all quick like a blink—and I followed the rhythm and put money down and lost and knew I could stay and beat this and win. A Mayan woman grabbed my sleeve and said, *"Cuidado, señor."* I shook her off irritably and put more money down. The men were laughing. Women on the bus woke Katherine and pointed at me, shouting. The shell man stood from his squat and gestured angrily. We got back to the game. Then Katherine appeared over me with her brown hair like a snarled halo and she grabbed my wrist and our money and pulled me back on the bus.

Tijuana was a mess, and I don't remember how we made it north to Olympia because my mind moved faster than we ever could. And I don't remember Katherine as well as I should; she saved my life.

EIGHT

Olympia, Washington, was dense and green with summer, a rain forest after the desert. My brain flooded with dopamine and I was walking on water. I was walking through Eden on soft carpets of moss. We stayed with her friends in a huge converted barn. Katherine busied herself with chores while I wandered. Everything—the houses and barns, the roads, the telephone poles—was painted in myth. I stood in a story I began telling myself and I shook symbols out from my pockets. I kept them all hidden from Katherine at first and she thought I was happy. My mind swooped in sudden, exhilarating gusts. I knew I had changed and I liked it, almost. I could have gotten better; I could have found help.

Summer solstice hit on a full moon that year. I soon gathered that as astrological omens go, this was a biggie. Preparations began for a traditional Olympian blowout, complete with innumerable bonfires spread out through the woods, Kesey-like supplies of hallucinogens, a fourteen-foot stack of tripped-up TVs, and just a remarkable number of women in sundresses. It was like Altamont had never happened.

When we arrived Katherine found friends and I wandered

into somebody's kitchen and a four-gallon pot of simmering mushroom tea. It looked bad and smelled worse—a vat of boiled liver bits, bats' wings, what have you. I tried just a sip and it wasn't half-bad. Those resourceful Olympians, with their vast stores of fennel and years of alchemical experience, made the stuff almost tasty. Right then I knew I was standing at my brink, resolving to pull some subconscious pin and blow things to hell. I stood alone by the untended pot and drank the stuff like beer. Dosing myself with hallucinogens was not heroic, despite what I thought. I was not embracing my destiny. I wasn't even embracing my stupidity. I lacked the judgment necessary for stupidity, let alone courage, but in my mind I was brave Orpheus plunging into the underworld to rescue my family. I was delusional and valiant and drank two more cups.

I weathered the night in a broken-down hippie bus in a bad-smelling sleeping bag without Katherine. I stayed awake all that night and through all the nights after. Every day I ran through primeval forests and epic adventures. After a week I knew it wasn't the mushrooms anymore. I had stood on druggy cliffs before but this time was different, very different. I was way, way higher and I'd jumped past the ledge. I was falling and I just couldn't hit. I couldn't wake up and I wasn't asleep. I gave up sleep. I gave up food. I didn't have the time.

Thought rose out of its banks and it spilled through sex, God, and dreams, mysterious places the mind should not trespass. Mania flooded my tidy little village of memory and constructs, the sunny little place where I play, where I keep my desires amused. All lines fell and connections sparked and went black and hissed through the water.

What I knew of the world mutated continually, all a huge metaphor now—broken and heavy and rolling straight toward me. When I pulled on a thought it unraveled to trees, asphalt, spilled horizons, and suns. I needed to look away and I knew it was already too late; I was blind and just babbling. This is it, I thought, this is madness and my family was chosen. I wanted my father, my brother, and I knew I could talk with them now, that I could meet them out on electric fields. I knew why my father held hands and tried to share these visions. And I knew why my brother punched him out trying to save them.

My thoughts moved so fast they began to hum, and that humming was music, absolutely sublime movements strafed with dissonance and twelve-tone. My father sang all his hymns because everything did. Twenty years later, I know that music well. It's symphonic and fast and above all it is inclusive and sung by everything—every tree, rock, and smokestack. These song cycles draw a skein up under experience, increasing its tempos, tightening the harmonies, connecting it all. There's a transcendental romance to mania, to this drawing together. And I believed, still believe, that this music is true, that the scattershot visions of madness are holy. They are also fucking crazy and hopeless and sad. At its core the transcendental manic experience remains one of great loneliness. It transcends, but it rarely translates. True visions find their grounding and validity in the universal, the spiritual, but these visions are poured into each cooking skull, one at a time. You'll burn down before you can share them. The face of God blinds and it burns, make no mistake. Approach these breaks in a sentimental fashion and you'll find yourself seduced by nervous, chattering ghosts, maybe lost there for good. Worse, put your vision in a pulpit, wrap it up in some patchwork doctrinal robe, and you're absolutely finished, done.

In Olympia that summer I fell into a bottomless, unpeopled hell—the absolute cold knowledge that I'd gone quite mad, that no one could ever hold me again. Still, I thought maybe I could work out the sense. I needed to remember it, write it, and speak it. I needed to organize and so fell to my knees, gathering rocks and muttering. So what if I was mad? Of course I was mad. Everyone should be mad.

To hell with all the people who stared. I had done it, broken through Ahab's pasteboard mask and harpooned my whale. I would justify my mania, all this quicksilver. I would speak it and write it before it all burnt, before it was smote down to ash and forgotten. The others would see, the ones who stared at the floor to avoid my fucked eyes, who whispered while leaving and never came back. I wrote broken poetry; I spun and I shouted past all the sweet music.

I was a god and I was scared shitless.

But Olympia was beautiful and Katherine loved me. She held my hands and led me down through the woods to the water. She told me to eat; she told me to sleep. She surrounded my bath with incense and candles. She gave me tinctures and teas while I shuddered and twitched. Every evening Katherine laid out the tarot, insisting it would prove therapeutic. She was wrong, of course. Dealing tarot cards to a psychotic is like pouring shots for a drunk. Katherine continually turned over the death card. "That's good," she would say. "It means change. Really."

When she was asleep I'd steal out of the barn and walk through the woods, collecting portents—bits of twigs, stones. Often I'd walk through to the college, look for someone awake, anyone, an audience. The lush smell of the forest, the rhythmic buzz of the insects, and the yellow streetlamps reminded me of Vietnam. A student walked by and I said, "Excuse me, excuse me. Doesn't this seem like Vietnam?"

He stopped and looked me over. I was shirtless and bathed in sweat from running through the woods. "Huh?"

"Vietnam. I think there should be helicopters. Don't you think?" His face screwed up with suspicion and he backed away. "Hey," I called after him. "I asked you a fucking question." I was gravely disappointed in him. People are so unimaginative. Fucking MBA pre-law frat dick. Hate those guys. He'd probably call security.

I walked into a dorm and wandered its halls looking for like-minded enthusiasts. I found them drinking beer in a cinder block dorm room and invited myself in. I was great and they loved me. We were all messed up and figuring it out. I taped some typing paper together, took a marker, and diagrammed our collective purpose.

I placed Man and the Word in the center with scribbles radiating out. I underlined the word "sphere" repeatedly. One of the kids downed his can and stood up. "Yeah, yeah. That's it. Sure, that's fucking it." He took my work and held it up. He taped it on their wall. Everyone approved absolutely. I was their fool and my cosmic schema a souvenir. They loved me. Of course, who could blame them? We drank a lot more beer and when security arrived I did not panic. Evergreen College security would understand me; I could teach them. They weren't interested. I was disappointed again. Nevertheless, I convinced them not to call the actual police and they dropped me off campus.

I found a pay phone and called my cousin back east, a psychiatric nurse. It was the first time I had spoken to anyone in my family in months. I told her I was fine but thought I'd check in. I hung up. I called my friend Paul in San Francisco and told him to get the fuck up to Olympia. I told him it was like Vietnam and William Blake and thought he understood. I might have told him I was William Blake. I told him Katherine was a witch and had spells. I asked him to help me and he came the next day.

If Katherine seemed conflicted upon my departure, her friends seemed delirious. I was too busy talking to kiss Katherine good-bye but as Paul grabbed my arm and pushed me into his rental car, I swore I'd return. I rolled down the window and spoke of Alaska, how we had to keep moving. All the way down the dirt driveway I stuck my head out the window like a kid and kept talking. Paul never told me to shut up, not once.

Katherine and I had seen Paul weeks earlier in San Francisco, after the desert. I had been at sea. I sat on his couch waist-deep in the saltwater flats of Sonora. I talked at Paul late into the evening, incessantly, symptomatically, all the while watching the horizon just across the room, how it curved with the earth's surface. I was preparing to drown.

None of this troubled Paul too terribly. Paul had one passion, Russian literature, and short of Blakean visions, nothing prepares one for madness quite like a passion for Russian literature. Paul himself had never gone mad but he openly admired, even envied, those who had. He aspired to a sort of controlled, manic transcendence and described it with longing and reverence. He spoke admiringly of a brilliant friend, a doctoral student who became "unhinged and enlightened." In that particular case Paul blamed Hegel, straight up. "Have you read Hegel?" he'd ask.

I would lie and say, "Some." I knew the word "dialectic."

"If you read Hegel, I mean really read Hegel, you will go insane." He loved this.

"Really. Insane."

"Absolutely. He encompasses so much, everything. And it's all paradoxical."

"Dialectical."

"That's right, exactly," Paul would say excitedly, and then, before you knew it, you would be in Montreal or Prague or somewhere.

So when Paul flew to Olympia and rented the rescue car, I believe he anticipated real metaphysical drama—a cogent struggle with existential dread, a chance to referee my wrestling match with God. He was sorely disappointed. All he got for his ticket were sleepless nights and a perfectly excruciating flight back to San Francisco on his dime.

At the gate, waiting to board, waiting for the VIPs to settle first class, one inevitably spots the problematic—individuals of large girth; harried mothers with colicky babies; loud men strutting with cell phones; certified lunatics. I was the latter, the person with and to whom Paul had to sit and listen. Listen while I studied the cloud columns beyond my small plastic window, comparing them to Michelangelo's "phony clouds," noting any number of likenesses, wondering aloud if clouds could be read for portents, like tea leaves or entrails; listen while I asked the concerned stewardess for two cups of tea; watch while I ripped open the tea bags and sprinkled the tea into my peanuts.

I asked Paul if he'd ever met an oracle. I asked him to drop the oxygen mask and then I bid him farewell. I space-walked to the bathroom, shut myself in that plastic closet, all lit up and flying. I stood there a long time, wanting to get off, frightened by the whoosh of blue flushes, worried for the pilots. When Paul finally retrieved me and escorted me past the small, irritated crowd assembled by the bathroom, I forgot all about crashing, all about the wreckage of living. I asked the stewardess for a cigarette.

Paul's wife, Jehanne, picked us up at the airport. Jehanne spoke Russian and was busily earning a Stanford doctorate in Slavic literature. Anytime Paul suspected a botched translation she quietly clarified matters. She clarified me right out of the gate. As soon as she heard my broken syntax and jagged statements, she knew what to do. The drive home from the airport to East Palo Alto mirrored the flight. I continued my commentary from thirty thousand feet up while Paul and Jehanne exchanged worried glances.

Most sane people possess an irrational fear of mental illness, see it as a contagion. Frankly, you're more likely to catch a broken arm in a ski lodge than brain disease in a psych ward; nevertheless few civilians dare contact with the crazies. Perhaps it's superstition, a primal fear of possession. Perhaps the demons that Jesus cast out are still in the neighborhood.

Paul had no such fear; he was positively nineteenth century in his romantic vision of madness. Sentence by run-on sentence, I took apart that wistful romanticism. Free association is not always a poetic tool; sometimes it's just a shovel in a dead field full of holes. Paul, my dear and brilliant friend, was exhausted—even disillusioned—by the time we got home.

As for me, I found my return to San Francisco tremendously

invigorating. I was so excited by the time we arrived at the apartment that Paul and Jehanne immediately announced they were off to the movies. They made me promise several times to stay put, pointed out the fridge and television clicker, and then fled my company.

Okay, I thought, okay. I'll just settle in. I'll get out some stuff so I can show them where I've been, figure out where I'm headed. I dumped out my pack by the door and kicked away all my thin, sour-smelling clothes. From a gray plastic bag I drew out a *huipil*, an embroidered Mayan blouse, an heirloom that granddaughters sell for nothing to tourists. This particular one was a real bargain. I worked the woman down just at nightfall, just as her bus was preparing to leave. It was yellow, my mother's favorite color. I laid out small weavings, bracelets, gifts and mementos from travelers and lovers scattered over the continent.

I found books on Paul's shelves, marked the right passages with pencils, pens, and paper clips. I laid them down in a circle. I got some food, some fruit and cheese. I opened a trunk, found blankets, and searched for old letters. A photo would strike me and of course it had to go next to that bit by Melville, or under that window. Everything, every beautiful fucking thing in that apartment, in my pack, in my head was connected, and I circled it round through the rooms, retracing and refining and scribbling footnotes.

Before I broke through, all of this stuff was just junk, just cardboard props standing in for the real. But now it was all heavy as hell, shining and sucking everything toward it. Here I was, little old me, tidying up the event horizon, aligning the chunks of a collapsed star.

Four hours later and it was nearly done. It was just about making sense when Paul and Jehanne swung open their door. Shoved it open, actually, pushing some framed prints out of the way. "Careful of those," I cautioned. Their faces dropped and I smiled reassuringly. "Don't worry. I can explain this. I can explain myself. It's all here."

Jehanne went directly to their bedroom but Paul listened politely, picked up some items, and carefully placed them back on the floor. He moved slowly and with great feigned interest down through the installation and toward their bedroom. "I haven't got to the bedroom yet," I said apologetically as he closed the door.

The cops arrived twenty minutes later. Paul and Jehanne were sitting on their couch, quite close together and not saying much. I was sitting on the floor talking, surrounded by a trainload of meaning all hitched onto items—some of them mine, most theirs. When I saw the flashing lights out their front window, I stood and acted decisively. "Right," I said. "Time for a shower."

I went into the bathroom, shut the door, locked it twice, and stripped. I'd just adjusted the water temperature when the knocking commenced. "Yes, just a minute," I said hospitably.

"Sir, could you please step out?"

"I'm in here. Who is it?"

"The police, sir. What are you doing in there?"

"What do you think I'm doing? I'm taking a shower." I shook my head. "Obviously."

"Open the door, sir."

"Just a moment. It will be just a moment. I've got shampoo all over the place."

"Where?"

"Specifically? On my head, in my hair. Christ." I could hear the cops—there were at least two—talking to each other and then to Paul. I couldn't hear much but I knew what they wanted. Was I dangerous? Suicidal? "I'm not dangerous," I called helpfully from the shower. "I'm not suicidal."

That's when they started banging at the cheap hollow door and shaking its knob. "Open the door or we'll be forced to open it for you. You don't want me to kick your friend's door in, do you?" I pictured Paul and Jehanne, seated on their couch and shaking their heads.

"All right, all right," I said, feigning exasperation, smacking the chrome mixing valve down. "Hold your horses."

"Open it."

"Just a sec. Drying off." And then I looked in the mirror and grinned. I couldn't resist. "Do I have time for a shave?"

"That's it. We're coming in." I opened the door on cue, dripping, a towel wrapped around my waist, the perfect, imperturbable host.

Both cops were huge, one of them black, one white. They stayed serious as I genially fended off questions. I consciously slowed myself way, way down, editing my words for the first time since Olympia. "But of course, of course, I can see how it might seem that way, officers. If you would just allow me a moment to dress, I'm sure we can sort all this out. Actually"—I gestured to the cluttered floor and laughed nonchalantly—"I've been sorting things out all night." I shrugged. "You know how it is—traveling." I got up to get dressed; they sat me right down. Still so serious.

At the time, East Palo Alto had one of the highest murder rates in California. They didn't have time to waste on fucked-up white kids. I rated a clear waste of time. They led me to the bathroom, watched as I pulled on my jeans. An ambulance arrived. I got pissed and I spit out a question. "So, you gonna cuff me or what?"

The white cop shook his head. "No, we're not going to cuff you. You're just going to walk out to the ambulance with us."

Shit. I wanted them to cuff me, I wanted the drama. "Fuck you," I said. "Fuck all of you. Fuck this," I said, and I kicked all the shit out of my way as they led me outside. Paul stood by me, close to weeping. Before I climbed into the ambulance, he embraced me and said he was sorry. I quoted our beloved Dylan and said, "Jesus was betrayed by a kiss." He smiled grimly—"I knew you would say that," he replied—and I climbed into the ambulance, messianic, radiant, and sadly mistaken.

I remember commenting on the ambulance driver's boots, combat boots—heavy-soled with tight-laced canvas uppers. The kind of boot you'd wear to kick picket fences or teeth back into their roots. "Nice boots," I said, making conversation, sarcastic and strapped to a seat in the back while the two-way radio popped with squelch. She glanced around toward where I sat grinning and cuffed, and she sneered as she spoke to her radio. Coordinates. The streetlights like helicopters.

"Where's your shirt?" they asked at the hospital and I had to explain that the cops dragged me out without a shirt. "Where are your shoes?" I explained how they dragged me out without shoes.

"I know how this looks," I said. "I was taking a shower." They wheeled a guy past in a straitjacket and tied to a gurney who kept shouting, "I'm gonna fuck you up! I'm gonna fuck you up!" He said that all down the hall.

"Don't worry about him," they said. "Are you on drugs?"

"Not particularly."

"Where's your family?"

"On the East Coast."

"What's their phone number?"

"I don't recall."

I Love Lucy was on the television mounted to the ceiling of the waiting room beyond the desk. The guy on the gurney kept frothing "fuck" over and over and that corny Desilu Productions heart was on the television screen above the triage doctor, who said, "Give him a piss test." I focused on the TV. Lucy was in trouble and Desi seemed exasperated—a Batista lost in Fred and Ethel's apartment building. I mentioned it but the nurses tended to ignore conversation. Just: "Are you allergic to any drugs? Is your family on the East Coast?"

I pissed in a cup in a washroom with stainless steel mirrors and stuck the soap in for laughs.

"Test this," I told them with all the cracked bravery of a lost kid who'd walked past the strapped-down convulsions rolled into the corner, the concrete underworld-lit Lincoln Tunnel, past the doors that stop screams, toward the desk where I placed the hot piss and the soap on the admittance forms, refusing to sign, watching a commercial for *PM* magazine in the room beyond. "Test this."

They were disappointed. One nurse told me she had had a long night and really wished I could give them another sample, so I complied and they led me into the waiting room, where I sat with a black guy dressed as an orderly on break who said he wasn't allowed to give me a smoke. We watched Mary Tyler Moore and I decided he was watching me, not Mary, and this was no break.

I took some notes with a borrowed pen on the back of a magazine. I made connections between situation comedy and the poor bastard raving in the hall. I quoted Melville to the guard and included Hendrix, and he chain-smoked and wanted none of it. After a while a nurse came in and said, "The doctor wants you to drink this." She held out a plastic cup with the words LILLY CORP stamped on its side. It held thick orange syrup. I asked what it was. "It'll help you relax," she said.

"Well, hold on, I'm just finishing this project," I said, and pointed at the magazine, where models smiled up under my scribbles. It was a standoff, I guess, but the orderly just watched the tip of his smoke. So I listened and I gave in and I downed the syrup okay. I walked past the front desk out of the magazine room to a room with just me and they slid the bolt shut but the TV kept going. I listened all night and it took forever to end.

There were no windows and I slept through that day and well into the next. I woke underwater and slow, and the nurses swam by, gurgled, and left. I lay unrestrained on a gurney in the center of a white, featureless room. I knew where I was and why, and my tongue felt swollen and dead, stuck to my teeth and palate. I tasted of sickness and I spat a thick white paste into the sheets. I sat up and waited out the dizziness for—what? Five minutes, an hour? Finally, I swung my feet from the gurney. I stood up and stumbled forward. I caught the bed and pushed at my legs till the knees locked. I saw I was scared and knew I had nothing. I'd lost my body and they'd repossessed my mind. I understood, then, that my brave spiritual quest was just a cartoon, and I just stood by the bed, rubbery. I felt like Gumby, after the humans got him, after they had put down Pokey.

A cute nurse entered as I slowly took stock. I steadied myself beside the gurney and made a sort of smile. I wore a blue hospital shift and I wondered if it covered my ass. The nurse stood across from my thin, tangled blanket. "How are we today?" We? I thought. We? She was one of them. She wasn't so cute. I worked my mouth and asked for coffee. "I'll bring you some juice," she promised, and left. I twisted around to check my ass but couldn't. I could not turn my head. I reached up and the muscles in my neck were taut and hard, like vulcanized rubber. I got back into bed.

It didn't matter. I wasn't bored. I wasn't going anywhere. There was nowhere to go and I had no one to go with, not even myself. The nurse returned, cranked up my bed, and gave me the juice. Some spilled over my chin and she caught it in her cupped hand. She gave me another plastic cup, more bittersweet syrup. I shot it back into my throat without questions. I would go back to sleep.

Near-death survivors speak of white light and often describe floating serenely above their dying body, the nurses and surgeons and loved ones. After the drugs I lay on my back covered in sheets and departed. I saw fluorescent light tubes. I saw my body lying there perfectly well, rosy-cheeked and ready to walk but for me, the dead mind in the corner, the ghost watching his body and longing for life. I called for the nurse. I gave her the number in Hamilton and then I slid under.

The nurse reached my house and Mom woke my father. "Richard, it's David. It's a hospital calling." My father pulled at his sheets, swung his legs over the side, and climbed out from his haunt. He was dizzy and frightened and picked up the phone. The nurse told my father what he already knew: another child had his sickness, another son had been damaged. She said I was resting and that I'd be fine. She described my symptoms and assured my father that mania was not permanent, that they had medicines now, and my father asked her to stop. He didn't need a tutorial, he knew it all cold. He knew what it was, now, and it wasn't St. John's dark night, or Satan's temptation, or even the whim-whams. He knew what it was: just genetics, our birthright, our brain disease. The nurse explained California's laws on involuntary commitment. If he did not sign and accompany me out of the hospital soon, I was in for weeks of observation, no exceptions.

Dad told my mother just what the nurse said: that I was all right, that we had medicines now, and that nothing was permanent. But it was and he knew it and we all know it now: that our sickness is chronic and there isn't a cure. My sister is well. She isn't bipolar. But the rest of our family—my parents, myself, and my brother—must take medicines for the rest of our lives. We've learned that our happiness will always be suspect and simple sadness must taste of despair.

My father went back to his room and flipped the light switch and packed a small bag. He called his travel agent and booked a red-eye round-trip. He shaved in front of a painful mirror and then knotted his tie. Dad arrived in the morning. Paul met him at the airport. They drove straight to the hospital, where Dad met with a doctor while the nurses pumped me with antipsy-chotics. I was virtually paralyzed when I met my father and Paul by the front desk. They double-dosed me for the plane, I'm sure. "I'm sorry, Dad," I said. "Sorry that you had to come here." I was wearing my jeans, the blue hospital gown, and some slippers.

Paul said, "I've got your pack in the car, Dave. Let me go get a shirt and your shoes."

"Sorry," I said, and stared after him.

My father squinted in the bright hospital light. He had been pulled from his shell and forced to seem confident, well. I knew then that he loved me and that he was brave, and I wanted to tell him how much I had missed him. "Dad," I said, and made a rub-bery smile.

"David, we've all missed you. I'm glad you're coming home."

"Sorry, Dad," I said, and went back to numb.

"Don't worry, David. Don't worry. I'll get you home and then we can talk."

Paul drove us to the airport. My father realized he hadn't bought me a ticket. When his credit card bounced just like mine, Paul paid for my flight. I couldn't even thank him. I avoided Paul's eyes; he left us long before our departure. I hadn't seen my father in months. I'd traveled thousands of miles to join his secret bipolar circle and now we were mute, with our roles reversed. I wanted to ask my father, ask him what would come next, but my tongue felt lifeless and sticky. Dad steered me onto the airplane and got me to my seat. He bought earphones, tore open the plas-tic bag, and listened to Mozart. The hours moved as I stared straight ahead, drooling—just the back of a beige headrest, the engines, and black windows.

NINE

It was late when we arrived home. My father went straight to bed. I found a small watercolor on the kitchen table—a note from my mother. "Welcome Home, David!" it said. "We love you." And it showed a boy with a thatch of black hair standing outside a happy storybook house. I pushed into my old room, climbed over some boxes, and slept in my clothes.

My mother had been up for hours when I finally got up. "Good morning, dear," she chirped. "I'm so glad you're home, David. It's an answer to prayer." She kissed my cheek. "We've been worried sick."

"I know, I know, Mom. I'm sorry," I said. I lifted my arms like dead weights and hugged her. "I'm sorry."

"No need to be sorry." She stepped back and looked for her son. The kitchen was bright and loud but I didn't talk. It felt wrong, not talking; I retreated into the bathroom. It was a slow and reasonable decision, I thought, quite sane. I am sane, I told myself. I closed my eyes in the dim light and sat on the toilet. I spat at the floor and wiped gray slime from my thick, clumsy lips. I needed water and stood and reached for the faucet and steadied myself. There wasn't a cup. I leaned slowly down into the sink. I turned my head to drink and my shoulder came with it; water spilled over my cheek and into my ear. I looked at the mirror and my face hung from its cheekbones. I came out, worked my jaw, and smiled.

"Do you want breakfast, dear?" I stared and my mother decided. "I'll make you some eggs." I sat down and the table was set: a glass of orange juice, silverware, a plate, and three pills.

I drank the orange juice and pushed my tongue forward and back. "Mom," I asked, "what are these pills?"

"Those pills? I'm not really sure, dear." She paused and worried. "I think one of them is lithium." Pills have always confounded my mother—such powerful mysteries in such small secular pieces. She's afraid of making mistakes, afraid of her confusion. Since January her family had collapsed all around her, suffocated with medicines and silence. I was dazed with antipsychotics and my dear mother was heartsick and shell-shocked. "Richard told me their names," she said. "Was it Thoritane, Thorzone?"

"Thorazine. What's this pink one?"

"I just don't know, dear."

"Can I have some coffee, is that all right?"

"Yes, yes, of course." My mother moved hurriedly with the coffeepot. I watched her hand shake as she poured it. "Your father gave them to me this morning, I—"

"Never mind, Mom," I said. "It's all right." We stopped talking. Mom stood watching my eggs fry. The coffee had cooled and I slugged the pills down in one gulp. "Where's Dad? Where's Jonathan?"

"They're both in bed. I imagine Jon will be up soon. He's excited to see you."

"Yeah. When's Dad getting up? I want to know where he got those pills."

My mother sat down beside me and crumpled a napkin. "He's not. He's not getting up." She was grieving alone and she watched my blank face. "He's not getting up. He's on leave from the seminary." Her voice got quiet. "He's drinking, David. I found wine bottles in the garage."

Wine was the least of her worries. Wine was nothing. The room looked small, the pine cabinets tired and shot full of dark knots. My forearms rested on the sticky table as I waited for the drugs to hit. How could I help her? I stood slowly. I wanted to leave but there was nowhere to go, so I just stood.

My brother came into the kitchen. He looked gaunt. "Hey, Dave. Welcome home. How you doing?"

"I'm home at least. And you? You graduated?"

His face fell and he glanced toward Mom. "Yeah, yeah, I did, Dave. Barely. It was hard, really hard going back." He looked up and smiled. "I'm going to Gordon in the fall."

"Good. You're on campus, right?" He nodded. "Good. You need to get out of here."

"Dad's not doing so well, Dave."

"I know. Mom said. What do they have you on?"

"Who?"

"You know. For pills. What are you on?"

"Lithium, mostly."

"Did you ever have pink pills? Do you know what's pink?"

He shook his head. "Never had pink."

"Maybe it's lithium."

"I don't think so, Dave. My lithium's white."

"Well, I've got pink, whatever it is," I said. "And I'm on Thorazine. I know that."

"That sucks. You got to get them to take you off that stuff. It's hard-core."

"I know, believe me," I said as I sat in our old kitchen, waiting for it with the back of my neck, for the paralysis. I shouldn't have taken those fucking pills.

"Mom," I asked, "where did the pills come from?"

"California," my mother said softly. "They gave them to Dad in California."

"My shrink's in Hamilton," my brother informed me. "He's not bad. He's Dad's shrink."

"You mean that Christian place?"

"Yeah, Haven Associates. It's not that Christian, Dave." I stared at him. "I mean they're real shrinks. They don't just pray over you."

"Screw that," I said, and finished my coffee. My mouth leaked and coffee dripped from my chin. "I'm not going there."

"Betty Lee," my father called from his bedroom. "Betty Lee, please come here." He'd been listening.

When Mom left, Jonathan rolled his eyes and whispered. "It's bad, Dave. He doesn't even get up to pee anymore. He's got a jar under the bed."

I couldn't turn my head toward him. I heaved my legs and spun my whole body to face him. Was it good to be home? Was it good to see my brother? Like this? "It's fucked. Jon, this whole place is fucked. Get out. Help me get out." He just stared at me and then Mom was back.

"Richard says you have an appointment today, David. This

afternoon. Jojo set it up. You know she works over in Gloucester at the hospital. In the psychology ward or something." Everyone knew I trusted my cousin Jo, that she was the only one I called from Olympia. Mom handed me a note. "Here. Richard wrote down the address and the doctor's name. Jon can drive you." She took my plate. "Do you want any more coffee?"

"No, Mom. No. I'm just going to lay down for a bit." My brother moved from the doorway. "See you, Jon." He nodded gravely and my mother turned to the sink.

"Yes, dear. You must be tired."

We were all so very tired.

My mother woke me up for my appointment. I was already dressed so I went outside and waited for Jonathan. I picked up Jon's basketball and tried to dribble but it bounced all wrong— too crooked and fast. It scared me how bad I'd become, and I let the ball roll away. I had no idea what Jon was on, but I was on all of it. Shut down. Our ride to the hospital was quiet. Jonathan wouldn't go in with me. He hated the place.

The psychiatrist was quick; my cousin had briefed him. Manic or possibly mixed state. Bipolar type I—both manic and depressive history. Strong family history of the disease. Father, brother. Mother? He wrote two prescriptions: lithium and Thorazine. On a separate sheet he wrote out careful dosage instructions and the names of two local therapists, and shuffled me out.

I was old-school now, a classically doped mental patient on time-tested pills. In 1986, psychiatry was on the cusp of major breakthroughs, but in Gloucester, at least, the docs stuck to the old guns. I was taking drugs from the 1950s, the old standbys. I have no quarrel with lithium. Lithium was proven effective against mania in 1949 and remains among the best mood-stabilizing drugs known. Lithium made me sane and it continues to make my life livable. Drugs such as lithium and Depakote regulate levels of dopamine, a neurotransmitter associated with pleasure. My basic—and primitive—understanding is that too much dopamine and thoughts can speed out of control; too little and depression often results. Some enthusiastic neuroscientists even claim that profound religious experiences, visions both ecstatic and hellish, are essentially dopaminergic—just dopamine and nerve endings—the result of too many or too few neurotransmitters. It appears reductionism is a professional hazard among brain chemists.

Thorazine is another thing entirely. It is not a mood stabilizer; it's a mood strangler, a blunt instrument. Thorazine arrived in 1954 and is the founding member of a group known as the "major antipsychotics." They are neuroleptics, literally "nerve-seizing" medicines. They don't regulate dopamine as lithium does; they shut it down. They are faster, stronger, and more dangerous than the mood stabilizers and they feel scary as hell. If lithium is a glass of merlot with your dinner, Thorazine is a quart of scotch with your breakfast. Long-term use of neuroleptics is primarily limited to chronic schizophrenics, but in the short-term these drugs remain the front-line weapons against mania. They stop patients cold and keep them quiet for a week or so until the long-term mood stabilizers like lithium kick in.

Thorazine was the first of these blunt instruments to be

approved and was used extensively through the 1950s and '60s. It is a quick-acting sedative and proved especially useful through the psychedelic years, when it became known as the "LSD antidote." It remains one of the fastest, if not one of the safest, drugs to treat delusions, hallucinations, and manias. Administered as a syrup it can drop a maniac in minutes, although I'm proud to say it took a double dose to knock me out in San Francisco. Possible side effects include withdrawal, autism, and tremors. A severe movement disorder called tardive dyskinesia can be triggered by long-term use of the drug. Tardive dyskinesia doesn't stop once it starts, and there's no known cure for its muscle spasms and tics, tongue protrusion and finger twitching. It is constant and lifelong.

I don't claim to comprehend neuroscience. I understand the role of transubstantiation in Holy Communion more than the dopaminergic causation of visions. I've been accustomed to mysteries, holy and otherwise, since I was a child. Some of us care for orphans, amass fortunes, raise protests or Nielsen ratings; some of us take communion or whiskey or poison. Some of us take lithium and antidepressants, and most everyone believes these pills are fundamentally wrong, a crutch, a sign of moral weakness, the surrender of art and individuality. Bullshit. Such thinking guarantees tragedy for the bipolar. Without medicine, 20 percent of us, one in five, will commit suicide. Six-gun Russian roulette gives better odds. Denouncing these medicines makes as much sense as denouncing the immorality of motor oil. Without them, sooner or later the bipolar brain will go bang. I know plenty of potheads who sermonize against the pharmaceutical companies; I know plenty of born-again yoga instructors, plenty of missionaries who tell me I'm wrong about lithium. They don't have a clue.

Back then, though, just knocked down from my high, I despised the pills and considered them all the same—the balance of lithium and the death haze of Thorazine. I hated the fact that I needed them. I had been pulled from the road back to Hamilton and my friends had all scattered. I felt stranded. The Morrison place was just a winter rental; Doc was in Baltimore and Nathan out west. My mother had saved a card that arrived for me from New Mexico: "Dave, Get down here. We've got a house surrounded by mesas and cacti. Tam and Tony are here. Bob's here. Need spiritual guidance. There might be work. Nathan."

I would have gone in a shot. I wanted to go. I wanted to stop eating their fucking pills and head back west. I couldn't help my family, not like this. My brother was on his own. He just needed to leave. It was too late for my father. He had chosen his life—curled up in a dark bedroom at noon. My father's drugs made living death possible, a blank still life with pills. I hated the smarmy psychiatrist's cure that hollowed me out and stuffed me with cotton and headaches and fear. But I hated my damaged mind even more. I knew I'd been crazy; on that I was clear. I knew I was still crazy and thought if I missed a dose I'd be gone. So I kept taking the stuff. I was scared of myself.

I convinced my mom to give me the keys. I told her I had a doctor's appointment and insisted upon driving. There was no stopping me. I had my old car and drove back to the winter rental, back to the Morrisons'. I knew they were back for the summer and that the main house was full. I knew the Morrisons had enough grown children to pack the place, but I also knew that Pat, their mother, loved me, and that she gathered strays up, made them breakfast, and put them to work.

Pat's son Tiger had his eyes on the stone water tower out back. He planned to break into the cistern itself, which comprised the tower's first sixteen feet, and create an apartment. But he was fishing on a trawler off Maine, so Pat let me move in for the summer. Butch and the goats lived downstairs, stabled next to the cistern, and I had the top floor, a round room of stone circled by small arched windows and topped with a cone-shaped roof.

Byron and Shelley are completely correct. There is no better place to go crazy than a stone tower in the forest. Romanticism fed and enabled my madness. My aesthetic was made for madness and madness made it. I would not give up and rot away in Hamilton. I would find as romantic a tomb as possible. I would light a pyre in my head, stand by the sea, and throw sparks. I now had my tower. I had the haunted wood. I had my goats with satanic eyes. I even had a llama whose significance I had yet to plumb. I had it all. I had everything a young, romantic poet could need, excepting opium and the ability to walk, speak, or think well.

I tried to get better. I kept taking the drugs. In fact, I took a lot of the drugs. I avoided doubling up on the lithium but I began loving the Thorazine . . . I seemed to remember the shrink telling me it was fine. "Take two if you are still feeling racy." I'm sure he said that. Apparently, Thorazine was having a paradoxical effect on me. I believe it sped me up, way up, back up to where I wanted to be. And as soon as it did I downed another and took to the woods or the ocean. It's a difficult feat—almost impossible—but I developed a pronounced taste for recreational antipsychotics. I wandered Cape Ann happily stoned.

I found my old boat, *Strider*, half-swamped in its berth at Gloucester Marine. It was a wreck but I cleaned it, pulled its battery, and swapped in my car's. I flooded the engine and waited impatiently, chain-smoking beside the tank. I pretended I was headed to England. It wasn't hard. I could play make-believe at will. The more outlandish a notion, the quicker I claimed it. I wasn't completely insane: part of me recognized the impossibility of a transatlantic voyage but I suppressed the killjoy in me. I loved playacting, took the absurd seriously, and loved to tell others about it. It was, after all, remarkable.

I fueled the boat downriver at Lobster Cove, bought some beer and ice. I pounded out the mouth of the Annisquam and into Ipswich Bay. The bay opened to the northeast, toward Maine. I planned to pass Lane's Cove and Folly, round Halibut Point, cut across Sandy Bay past Pigeon Cove and the Dogbar, then shoot behind Straightsmouth and out to Thatcher's Woe. I knew that Thatcher's Woe is the island where Salem's minister had wrecked en route from Ipswich, all hands and his family lost, all but him. I knew this and I had the chart in my head; I had its poetry. I knew where the names came from and I thought this made me heroic, unsinkable. After Thatcher's were Milk Island,

Pebble Beach, Good Harbor, and Gloucester. I'd dart through the cut and gas up again, just to be sure. Then it was "straight on until morning," for "they that go down in ships": George's Bank, the open Atlantic, England—at least through the first tank.

I got lucky and found glory much sooner, in the monstrous, injection-molded shape of a cabin cruiser, drifting out near Salvages. An overweight man in a tangerine sweater and shorts waved from its flying bridge, his arms making the international symbol for distress and a clear call to destiny. I cut back the engine, threw out some fenders, and pulled alongside. A bikini-clad woman moved in the galley.

I tried to sound competent. "Trouble?"

"Yes," he called down. "Do you have a radio?"

"What? You don't?"

"I dunno. It's not working or something."

"Flares?"

"What?"

"Flares. Do you have flares?" I love flares.

"What the hell are you talking about, flares?"

"Flares. Morse code. All that stuff." He stared at me blankly. "Listen, do you want help or what?" The man looked disgusted and started down the ladder.

We would have a gam. According to Melville, a gam occurs when two boats, preferably whale boats, meet at sea and exchange news. I was insane—nautically proficient and insane, a time-honored tradition. The guy made it down and commenced to sweat. "Listen," I said. "How 'bout I give you a tow into Rockport? Where you out of?"

"Newburyport."

"Yeah, well." His boat was two and a half stories of solid plastic, a thirty-eight-foot slab loaded with every inoperable navigational and nautical convenience known. It weighed more than most marinas. I wasn't towing him to Newburyport.

"Okay, Skip. Tell you what. Throw me the bowline and I'll tow you into Rockport." This was better than imaginary transatlantic crossings. This was real. I could really rescue this guy. I could pretend he was sinking, even.

He stared down at my presunk craft and her ancient Evinrude. "I don't know," he said, and scanned the empty horizon.

"Just throw me the line. C'mon, Skip. I don't have all day." I caught his line. Fed through a chock on his bow, the line dropped at a sixty-degree angle down to my stern. The *Strider* was nearly under his boat. I could have added line but hadn't the time—he was sinking. I cranked the engine and we were off, marking maybe two knots. My engine coughed and the bow pitched strangely. I lost steerage intermittently.

Twenty minutes into the operation I glanced over my shoulder and I saw Skip yelling at me. He started waving his arms again. The international sign of distress. Of course, he was sinking. I waved him off. We waved at each other for another five minutes until my boat jumped forward and the towline shot over my head. He cut it, cut his own line. Nice one too, one-inch braided. I looked back. The guy was screaming and I just gunned it.

You try to help people out and they just cut you off. You try to teach people a thing or two and they run. After my thwarted ocean rescue, I retreated to my tower, to solitude. No one understood a goddamn thing. I wrote run-on poems. I tried to reread *Moby-Dick* and turned its margins black with my scrawls. My situation was seriously dangerous, and this welcome realization filled my days with adventure. But the nights, the nights were horrible. The tower had no electricity; all I had were candles and a gas camp stove. I spent the hours pacing and muttering, full of fear and paranoia, waiting for the bats to flit down from the ceiling. I thought of my father and how if I did what everyone wanted—if I got sane—I'd end up like him, half-dead and laid out. I slept less and less.

When the Thorazine ran out I grabbed the empty bottle, walked through Dogtown and down into Gloucester. The drugstore refused to refill it and said I should call the doctor. No chance. I walked down to the Main Street Café, sat down, and pulled out my notebook. It was a mess, fat with notes and scraps, filled with exclamations and cosmic errand reminders. I pulled out a Guatemalan road map, consulted, and set to work on my epic poem, *Extranjeros*. I still have that notebook. The poem features dead, bloody tongues, clubbed bluefish, and churches. It was art. The best thing I had ever written, I was sure, but it wasn't quite done. It needed more. Everything needed more.

So I got back to it, scraping away at that notebook in the empty midafternoon café. I thought I cut a dashing and unusual figure for Gloucester, carrying notebooks like it was Cambridge, ostentatiously flipping the ruined pages of my talismanic *Moby-Dick*. When the young waitress walked over I redoubled my effort. I held my finger up and asked her patience as I scribbled.

I looked up. She was beautiful. "Do you know, by chance," I asked, "how to conjugate the verb 'murder' in Spanish?"

She didn't skip a beat. "Past, present, or imperfect? What do you want?"

"Um, coffee, I mean past." I was impressed. "You know Spanish?"

"Sure." She smiled at the papers I had spread over the table, turned, and walked off for the coffee.

"What's your name?"

"Roberta."

"I'm David."

"I didn't ask."

"You from Gloucester?" I asked. "You don't seem like you're from Gloucester."

"Sure I am. Lanesville." She looked me over. "You're not."

"Well, no. Not exactly. I've been in Guatemala. Mostly. Colorado."

"I went to school in Colorado."

"Huh," I said. What I wanted to say was, *Jesus, you went to school in Colorado? So did I! When? Exactly! This is no coincidence. It's fate, pure and simple. Quit this place and let's go back. I have friends outside Taos!* But fortunately all I could manage was, "Huh." It's incredibly difficult, nearly impossible, for a maniac to effectively chat up a girl, but I soldiered on.

Roberta smiled. "You've been traveling. Me too. I just got back from Greece and Africa. Now I'm figuring out what to do."

"Wow," I said, completely agog. "Greece. How long?"

"Six months or so."

"Where'd you stay?"

"Under a sort of bush."

"A bush. You lived under a bush?"

"It was a large bush. It was down by a beach. A number of us lived there. We picked olives." Roberta had lived under a Greek bush by the ocean. I was in love.

"What about Africa?"

"I might tell you later. I don't know." She glanced over at her boss. "Listen, I've got to get to work."

Roberta, Africa, Greece—I was clobbered with romance. I was in love again and planned to sweep her off her feet. I began writing love letters immediately: tearing sheets from my notebook, jumping from prose to verse, sketching far-flung dreams for our future. I drew a treasure map of Gloucester with an X marking my tower. I had pages and pages and I left them on the table with a five-dollar tip. She shrugged it all off and figured she'd never see me again.

I left the café, walked down Main, and entered a hair salon. I don't have the faintest idea why. The last thing I wanted was a haircut. Romantic poets do not get haircuts. Before long I was explaining the subconscious to an amused hairstylist named Diane. I had *Moby-Dick* out and open to the masthead chapter. I must have seemed harmless, because before long we were comparing pharmaceuticals. I'd found a fellow enthusiast. I littered the front counter with various pills and my scribbled descriptions and dosage instructions. I shamelessly traded three Thorazines for two Percocets. I made Diane promise to read *Moby-Dick* and I tried to give her my copy. And then Roberta walked in.

I looked up and we startled each other. Diane jumped up and smiled mischievously. "Hey, Bert. Let me introduce you to Dave."

"We've met." Roberta rolled her eyes. "He was just in the café."

Diane laughed. "Really. Did he make you read *Moby-Dick*?"

"I did nothing of the sort," I interjected while collecting my pills from the counter. "I just suggested she should read a few chapters. Do you know the masthead chapter?"

Diane smiled. "No, I can't say I've read the masthead chapter."

Roberta and Diane smiled at each other.

"Well," I explained, "the masthead chapter just hammers transcendentalism—all that fuzzyheadedness."

They laughed out loud and then Roberta said, "Listen, David, we have to pick up Di's brother at the airport. It was nice to see you again."

"Oh, sure, sure," I said, and hurried outside, feeling suddenly foolish. I spent the rest of the afternoon wandering the town: Pavilion Beach, Halfmoon, Rosie's Wharf, the galleries over on Rocky Neck. I made people nervous and knew it, and so I kept moving. By nine o'clock I was in Blackburn's Tavern, drinking beer and sharing random thoughts with the bar's disc jockey as he set up. I was tangential. I was global.

"Have you ever considered classical?" I asked.

"Classical," he scoffed. "No. Why would I play that?"

"Just for a break, a sort of breather between, I dunno, Bob Seger and Aerosmith."

He smiled. I was amusing in short doses, good for cameo appearances. He kept fiddling with knobs, pulling cables from milk crates.

"How about African drumming?" I asked. He looked past me and I heard Roberta's voice.

"What are you, everywhere?" I turned and there were Roberta and Diane, Bert and Di, back from the airport and laughing.

"Ubiquitous," I said. "Like the whale."

"Hey, this is my cousin," the DJ said. "The one I was talking about. She's the one whose boyfriend does all the work in, what, Nicaragua?" We both looked at Roberta. Her eyes fell and she nodded, then she and Diane wandered off.

I looked for them later but they were gone. No matter. I learned from my new friend, DJ Mark, that Roberta was staying with him up in Lanesville, a small village to the north. I thought I knew Lanesville. At least I knew how to walk there through Dogtown. I knew its granite cove and the quarries scattered through its woods. I didn't know Roberta's family owned two of those quarries, or that her family spread through the woods and down to the bay. I didn't yet know that dating Roberta meant courting all of Lanesville.

Mark said his house was on Emerald Street. I was in luck. There was only one house on Emerald. I sat on its front steps and waited for Roberta to come home. Mark pulled into the drive around 1 a.m. I ran out from the dark and said, "Hey, Mark. How'd everything go?"

"Jesus!" He jumped. "What are you doing here?"

"Waiting for Roberta, I guess. Do you need any help unloading stuff?"

"Roberta? She's not here?" I shook my head. "Shit. Wait here for a minute. I'll see…" He stopped at the door. "Oh, just come in already. Just for a second."

I was in the living room flipping through his records when Mark tracked Roberta down at Diane's. "Bert," he said in a stage whisper. "Listen, that guy's here...The guy from the Black-burn...I know, I know...Yeah, I figured. He was sitting here waiting for you. Huh? Well, what am I supposed to do with him? Shit. All right, all right. I'll take care of it. Christ." Mark stepped into the living room. I smiled and he threw me out fast, like a bouncer.

Most women would have gotten a restraining order, but not Roberta, not after living under a bush and hitchhiking through Zimbabwe.

The next day I was still out of Thorazine. The situation was desperate. I couldn't go to the doctor, out of the question. But my cousin Joanna, down at the hospital, she could get me some. I showed up at Addison Gilbert just flying. Joanna looked concerned. "This doesn't seem to be working out, David."

"What do you mean?" I blustered. What had tipped her off?

"Your situation. Where are you staying?"

"In a water tower. Out in the woods."

"Right."

"By Dogtown. Do you know the history of Dogtown? It's fascinating—"

"Right. Forget Dogtown. Have you been taking your meds?"

"Yeah. Sure. I took all of them. I need more. Especially the Thorazine. I've run dangerously low on Thorazine."

"I see. Why don't you give me the name of your doctor?"

"Short guy," I said. "Mustache and glasses. Works next door in the other wing."

"Right."

By dinnertime I was locked in the psych ward over at Beverly Hospital. My father had driven me over. "Just for an idea you might want to consider, an option," he said. I found the nurses quite charming. We chatted forever and then they invited me on a tour, which sounded lovely. They had me sign some papers—just a formality, they said—in order for me to view the entire facility. And so I committed myself. It wasn't voluntary, more of a bait and switch. They explained I was stuck there for at least four days, and then they gave me the complimentary syrup.

The next morning I sat down to a fine breakfast of oatmeal and drugs. Afterward the nurses sent me down to the psychiatrist's office. He was reviewing some papers when I entered.

"Hmm." He set down his glasses and looked me over. "Have you ever been on Trilafon?"

"What the hell is that?"

"An antipsychotic. It seemed to be effective on your brother."

"Another one. How much of that crap is out there?" I asked.

"Quite a bit."

I was in a fog and sat for a moment. Trilafon. It looked like I'd never see Thorazine again. I blew that. The doctors had me where they wanted me. They were going to run down the list of chemical options until they hit pay dirt. "Okay," I said. "Bring it on; bring on the Trilafon."

Trilafon was a disappointment but the hospital itself was a pleasant surprise. The psychiatric ward at Beverly dispelled the standard images of bedlam I carried. When I was a kid in neighboring Hamilton, we didn't call each other nuts or mental, we just said, "You're Danvers." Danvers's State Lunatic Hospital had warehoused the region's chronic, violent, and hopeless since 1878. It was an astoundingly gothic structure set high on a hill. It was so astoundingly gothic, in fact, that it inspired H. P. Lovecraft's Arkham Sanitarium, the one featured in *Batman.* Its spires and turrets are visible for miles and dark legends about it are numerous. The hospital had seventy-seven acres that once belonged to John Hathorne, a judge in Salem's infamous witch trials. People spent their whole lives behind those walls. Its graveyard doesn't have stones, just small metal markers with numbers, no names. Before lithium, before its approval in 1970, I would have gone there and I might have stayed there, institutionalized.

Instead I played *One Flew Over the Cuckoo's Nest* in a sunny common area with compassionate nurses. Granted, I was manic, but I loved the place. My fellow patients took me seriously and I befriended two in particular, a kid my age who was in for attempted suicide and a young schizophrenic woman. I fancied myself Randall Patrick Murphy, gambling for cigarettes and telling tall tales.

And then suddenly, I was sane—not completely well, but fundamentally sane. The Trilafon stuff worked, just as it had for my brother. The hospital wasn't an adventure anymore; it wasn't a novel or movie, it was just dull. I was actually bored. The depressed guy was depressing, the nurses humorless. Only the schizophrenic could get me to laugh. She was brilliant. By the second week I reached an understanding with the nurses. I would take my medicine if they would let me out after the morning's group therapy. I promised to return for dinner and meds. I had more leverage than I realized. Technically, I had voluntarily committed myself; I was free to go whenever I wished.

As soon as they sprung me I headed back over to Lane's Cove. I spied Roberta sunbathing on the bow of a lobster boat and the sight filled me with courage. I hoped I could explain—or at least distance myself from—most of my madness. I approached Roberta because I believed she could understand me, that she wanted to understand me. But first, I had to get past the phalanx of lobstermen on the boat's deck. New England's lobstermen are an insular bunch, suspicious of all outsiders. Any out-of-town mental patient who expresses interest in their young female relatives can expect formidable opposition. I knew that. But hell, I was a New Englander. I was a New Englander on medication and I was up to the challenge. I walked down the ramp to the float and the lobstermen stared. "Hey, guys," I said. "Nice day."

"What? Are you that guy from Danvers?" They chuckled. Evidently, I needed no introduction. My questioner drained his beer, threw his can toward a white five-gallon bucket, and missed. All of them looked a bit sunstruck and beery.

"Not exactly," I said. "I'm living up in Dogtown."

This was greeted with general hilarity. "Dogtown? You live up in Dogtown? No one lives up in Dogtown."

"Well, I mean I—"

"You're that crazy guy that knows Bert and Di."

"No, ha ha. I wouldn't say that, ha ha. I'm not really crazy. Ha. Just a misunderstanding." They leaned on the rails and waited for my story. This was becoming difficult. My newfound sanity had eroded my ability to chat up anyone—cops, waitresses, stonewalls, or lobstermen. Where was Roberta? Hadn't she seen me?

"Yeah, well, listen, guys. All right if I go forward and say hi to Roberta?"

Mercifully, one of them stepped forward. "Yeah, fine, fine. Knock yourself out. You want a beer?" I took it gratefully and pushed around the wheelhouse.

Roberta immediately jumped overboard. She was treading water under the bow and I could hear the lobstermen laughing. "Roberta. Roberta, come on. Look, I'm better now. Honest. I'm straight. I want to apologize." No answer. I knew her options were limited. She could swim for it—melodramatic and awkward—or she could climb back aboard—just awkward. A few tense minutes passed on deck, just me and the guys. No one said much. Then Roberta swam down the length of the boat, climbed over the transom, and smiled.

My chances with Roberta had improved substantially along with my mental state. I told her about Olympia, about my break and the hospital. I even attempted to listen, a difficult feat for any man but especially taxing for the manic gentleman caller. The afternoon moved slowly, so slowly it was tonic. I came back to the cove the next day, and Main Street Café the next, and I still made it back for lockdown and meds. I asked Roberta to lunch and took her to the Willow Rest, a gas station lunch counter. I bought her a Superburger for two bucks and told her I couldn't stay long; I had to get back to the ward. Last Christmas she gave me a Willow Rest mug.

TEN

I wanted out. I promised the nurses anything they wanted. They arranged for a therapist and I promised to see her. They found a psychiatrist and I promised to take all his pills. I promised to avoid "excitement" and "overstimulation." I vowed to eat vegetables, drink plenty of fluids, and swear off hallucinogens. I meant it, too, every last word. I didn't need Yeats to tell me the center could not hold. My gift for metaphor, my free associations, had reached past poetry and into illness. A phrase or image spilled into my mind and flew back in splatters, a kind of dreadful spin art. I wanted sleep and I wanted more sleep; I wanted to wake under a medicine spell and drift into whiteness.

I went back to the tower and considered all the tiny altars I'd built throughout the room, little piles of meaningful bits: a broken blue bottle, scrawled notes, a key, a ball of wax. I swept them up with my boot and pushed them from windows. I had nothing left beside the pills and my family and still I wouldn't go home. I feared the sadness; I feared I'd stay sick with it, never leave my father's dark room.

Instead, I pushed back at sadness with long hikes and carpentry's hard, physical work. I was lucky and strong enough to dodge mania's blowback depression. I renounced mania and faced down its subsequent humiliations. And yet, I still loved my poles. I always will. After Beverly Hospital I walked a fine, dangerous line between romanticizing the aesthetic of madness and courting disease. I wanted quiet but not some hospital hush. I needed a beautiful calm, a capital-R Romantic calm. My recovery required the proper setting and architecture. I didn't want a room; I wanted a landscape, a painting, and I found it in Rockport. A friend introduced me to the owner of the oldest house in Pigeon Cove. Nadia lived elsewhere in Rockport and the house needed a caretaker. I was to sleep in the house, call the plumbers or the fire department if necessary, and pay fifty dollars a month.

Nadia's place was off the Byronic charts; it out-Shelleyed even the stone tower. And it had heat; it had glass in the windows. It was hidden from the road by massive oak trees but everyone knew the place and called it the Old Witch House. According to local lore, two Salem brothers had fled to Pigeon Cove with their mother, an accused witch. They built the house in 1692 and hid themselves away in the woods. It certainly looked like a witch house: a dark brown garrison with swirled glass in diamond-pane windows, low ceilings, and high fireplaces. Hallways went back and back through centuries of cobbled additions. I remember opening a closet to find another nest of rooms, and another and another until I was lost.

The rooms were all very beautiful, but it was the barn that I loved. It had sheltered the boyhood of Nadia's son, who had committed suicide. Model train tracks ran through the rafters and the bookcases bulged with Jules Verne. There were notebooks and drawings and old wooden toys. And then he grew up, moved to the city, and returned; he stepped off the Stone Pier and swam out to sea. He met death just as I once hoped to meet it, by drowning. I never touched his things, never moved them, but watched the room, all quiet and ghostly. It was the antipsychotics that kept me so still. I could sit for hours, watching daylight crumble, watching the shadowy brooms sweep it away. The barn frightened me with all its heartbreaking little pieces that Nadia never boxed or hid away. And yet I was drawn there by its melancholy undertow. I found it fascinating and lovely and all this was dangerous.

My psychiatrist said I "wasn't out of the woods" and I would need to be on a low dose of antipsychotics for some time to come. He said I could expect, eventually, to maintain proper equilibrium with lithium alone. I could look forward to that, he said. I stayed alone at the Witch House and took the doctor's drugs two, three times a day. I took care with the doses and times. I bought a watch.

I avoided friends. I saw their sadness as I tottered around and answered their questions with rubbery, stupid words. Dalton came up from Charlestown once. My housemate Doc was gone and William was just too crazy to visit. Nathan came back from New Mexico and tracked me down at the Witch House. "Hey, man. It's good to see you," he said. I marked his dismay. "We got your cassettes down in Taos. We loved them." I didn't remember making tapes. I didn't remember sending anything to New Mexico. "We listened to them every night like they were some kind of surreal *Prairie Home Companion*." I winced. "They were a frickin' riot."

I spent my mornings dividing up doses, my afternoons tromping through Dogtown, and my evenings convincing Roberta to see me. She was calm, quieting, and she never gave up on my mind. She stayed over on occasion and we slept together and I had hopes for the future. But I was fresh out of a psych ward, unemployed, and blunted by drugs, by the Trilafon. I remained physically awkward and my tongue was bloated and dry. Roberta was understandably noncommittal but I pressed on with a sort of primitive, Frankenstein-by-the-well charm. It was all I had left, and it worked.

One morning I sat down with my coffee and shook out my daily dose on the scarred kitchen table. Roberta walked in and said, "That stuff's going to kill you."

"What, the coffee?"

She smiled. "No, those pills. What is that stuff anyway?"

We'd been through this before. "This capsule's lithium and this here's Trilafon."

She sat close and touched my arm. "You seem a lot better, David. You're not crazy at all. That stuff scares me. It's industrial."

"Would you say it's a chemical straitjacket?" I smiled. I just loved that phrase. "A way for the doctors to keep me down?"

"Seriously, do you really think this shit makes you better? Cures you or something? It just shuts you down."

"Okay, I'll grant you the Trilafon. It's not exactly fun, but it did get me down in a hurry. They've got me on a low dose now." I held the gray pill up between my thumb and forefinger, considered, and popped it back like a chocolate.

"It's a sedative."

"Actually, I think it might be a horse tranquilizer. Really. I'm serious." She didn't laugh. "Look, I don't want to go nuts again, just go off. Ever. I'm taking this stuff until they tell me to stop. I don't think the lithium is all that bad, at least that's what they tell me. It's not as bad as the Trilafon. It's not an antipsychotic."

"What is it then?" She turned to the stove. "Do you want some eggs?"

I nodded. This was exhausting, the longest conversation I'd had in weeks. "Lithium? Lithium's a salt, that's all."

"A salt?"

"Yeah, it occurs naturally. In groundwater. It's good for you. I think they drink it at spas."

"They make batteries out of it."

"True," I said. She had me there.

I enjoyed my assigned therapist. She was pleasant and caring. She was brilliant and addressed the practical and philosophical ramifications of psychopharmacology while I stared and drooled on her couch. I voiced Roberta's concerns. I complained about my slow, rubbery body and the sludge in my head. I asked about lithium batteries. She did her best to downplay the side effects and stress the therapeutic necessity of the medicines. She knew I couldn't afford a frank discussion of tremors and tics, kidney and thyroid functions. I didn't need excuses. She said I'd be off the Trilafon very soon, that my dose had been lowered. She said lithium's side effects were far less pronounced than the antipsychotic's. But it was very likely, she said, that I'd need lithium the rest of my life.

I didn't believe her. I couldn't separate the antipsychotic's gruesome effects from the lithium's workings. I took them together and I lumped them together: the zombie pill Trilafon and the mood-stabilizing lithium. It was all or nothing in my mind. If I dumped the Trilafon the lithium went as well. I wanted my body back. I wanted my soul. I craved just a touch of dopamine grace. Compared to bipolar's magic, reality seems a raw deal. It's not just the boredom that makes recovery so difficult, it's the slow dawning pain that comes with sanity—the realization of illness, the humiliating scenes, the blown money and friendships and confidence. Depression seems almost inevitable. The pendulum swings back from transcendence in shards, a bloody, dangerous mess. Crazy high is better than crazy low. So we gamble, dump the pills, and stick it to the control freaks and doctors. They don't understand, we say. They just don't get it. They'll never be artists.

I needed Roberta but I knew she wouldn't coddle a head case forever. She wouldn't shack up with Frankenstein. She had been threatening to leave for New York City. A few of her lefty college friends were squatting in a building on the Lower East Side. They promised her plenty of room. New York was clearly the next adventure and I wanted her to go, even without me. She couldn't stay in Gloucester any more than I could live in Hamilton. I told her I'd join her as soon as I could, as soon as I was all better.

I still thought that way, that I could get better—all better. That I could recover, dump the drugs, and move on. I wasn't about to surrender and sit quietly in a pale-colored room with a pill tray and Muzak. It took me years to understand that the only way to recover from the disease is to greet it each morning and raise a lithium toast every night. I didn't want that. I wouldn't listen. I wanted to pitch the pills and go off with Roberta. But deep down, I knew I needed the quiet of Dogtown and the Witch House and time. I still needed my medicines.

By the early 1980s Manhattan's Lower East Side was a mess of empty, burned-out buildings, rubble, and crack houses. Tompkins Square Park resembled a refugee camp, a tent city full of the homeless. Real estate speculators had abandoned their properties and so the city condemned the empty tenements and took possession. It wasn't worth investing in these buildings at the height of the AIDS and crack epidemics. They weren't saleable. They weren't worth fixing. The city was stuck and it blocked up the tenement doorways and windows; it deterred squatters and drug dealers by demolishing stairs and trashing the roofs.

It didn't work. There was a critical lack of housing in New York and, what's more, a critical lack of frontier left in America. Squatters had a reason, a grand cause, to further their adventure. Advance troops crawled through back windows until the squats established themselves, had a critical mass of occupants. Then the sledgehammers came out, the agitprop posters and spray cans. The squat symbol—a circle bisected by a zigzag arrow—announced the new neighbors; a poster told the city YOUR HOUSE IS MINE. The neighborhood had dozens of squats by the time we arrived.

It was late September when I drove Roberta and her belongings down. Her college friends, John and Pete, lived in a fledgling squat on Thirteenth Street, between Avenues A and B. It was hard to miss. The old tenement's brick front was covered with wheat-pasted agitprop posters, defiant slogans, and great swoops of punk graffiti. Its first-floor windows were barricaded with cinder blocks and its metal front door was battered and streaked with rust. To the building's left was Life Squat, to its right Camouflage building, then Squat Theater, and then Sucker's Hole, all of them fortified bunkers filled with politicos, artists, and punks.

A handful of grubby people were smoking next door on the stoop when we arrived. The only clean person on the stoop, the only one without a dust mask dangling from his neck, stood as we approached. He wore camo and combat boots and his hair was hacked into a blunt pageboy.

"Who are you?" he said. "Are you here to see someone?"

"We're here to see Pete and John in 537. We're friends," Roberta said. "Who are you?"

"He's John the Commie," someone said, and then laughed. "Don't mind him. He gives speeches while we do the work."

"Fuck off," John the Commie said. "I work same as you." He turned to us. "Yeah, okay. I think they're inside." He went out to the street and hollered up at the broken windows. "John, Pete, are you up there?" There was a shout and we waited for revolutionaries to pull back the barricades. But there weren't any liberated masses, just another guy covered in plaster, with a big grin and heavy black glasses all white with the dust.

"Berta, hey, Berta. Come in, come in." He slapped me on the back. "I'm John." We walked toward the back and on up a dark stairwell. It was cold inside and dank like a tomb. It was a five-story cave. We got to the fourth floor and John proudly welcomed us into his space. It was windowless and illuminated with Catholic saint candles. A radio played opera and a large tub of wet plaster covered the table. "I put some red into the mix," he said. "It makes for a nice salmon color, don't you think?" It was beautiful and John was beaming. We all were.

"Alex lives upstairs on the fifth," John said. "Come on, I'll introduce you. He was the first guy in here. He's been here all summer." We climbed up. John put his shoulder to the door and it opened out into the back half of the building. Most of the walls were gone, including, I noticed, the main weight-bearing wall. Rubble was everywhere—piles of lathe, tile, and horsehair plaster. Most exterior walls were stripped to gray mortar and red brick. The roof was bad and much of the room was wet. There was pigeon shit in the far corners and glass crunched underfoot, but the room's center was swept and Alex had pitched his blue dome tent in the clearing.

"Alex. Hey, Alex," John called. "Are you in there?" The tent rustled. "Alex, I want you to meet a friend from Boulder. She's going to stay here for a while."

The tent moved again; a flap unzipped and Alex crawled out with a groan. "Alex is an anthropologist. From Princeton," John whispered. He looked the part. Alex wore a graying beard, round wire glasses, and a pained expression. We sat on folding metal chairs arranged around a milk crate and plywood table, a stack of books, two cook pots, and a gas camp stove.

"So, you opened this building up?" I asked.

"Yes."

"Wow," I said. "That's something." He nodded. "John says you're working on your doctorate."

Alex narrowed his eyes. He seemed surprised I knew the term.

"Yes, a doctorate," replied Alex. Silence. Alex didn't have much to say. If there had been a campfire, he would have pushed at it with a stick.

Finally John sprang up. "Okay. Well, I just wanted you guys to meet."

"Did you give them a key?" Alex asked.

"Not yet."

"Humpf," commented Alex. "How many keys do we have?"

John walked toward the door, waved him off, and said, "Plenty." Out on the landing he confided, "It's not that Alex doesn't trust people. I think he just envisioned a more pure experience. He's writing his anthropology thesis and I think he wanted a kind of proving ground."

"Without people?" Roberta asked.

"No, without us. Rich white kids."

"You mean," I clarified, "kids that go to Princeton." John smiled. "Besides," I said, "we're broke. We're not rich."

"Yes, we are," replied John. "Take a walk down to Tompkins Square." He smiled. "We're loaded."

Roberta asked, "So who else lives here?"

"Nobody right now. The front half of the building is pretty much trashed," John said as we stood on the landing. "The third has no flooring and the second is full of rubble from the third. The roof's bad on the fifth-floor front. The front of the fourth floor is pretty much fine. You could live there, I suppose. Or not. It needs a lot of work." In the meantime John set up a futon for Roberta in a spare room. There were plenty of spare rooms. That's all there was: rubble and spare rooms. I carried in all her things and headed back in the morning, back to my rattled mind, my spooky house, and my medicines.

The squat was thrilling. It was one huge adventure and I knew I would move. I figured in two months I'd be right, strong enough to drop the pills and sweep up Roberta and live in New York. I found an old broken coal stove back in the woods and dragged it out. It was perfect for the squat. Its body was rotted but all the castings were good—the door, base, and top. I bent some sheet metal, doubled it up with rivets, and fitted it with stove cement. I wrote well-organized, lamentably sane love letters to Roberta and eventually convinced us both: I was well.

My therapist was another matter. "David, I'm not sure New York City is the best place for you now. A squat in New York City is, well…" She trailed off, shaking her head. "You need quiet and security, David." I thanked her and never went back.

What do these doctors know, I thought, all careful and ordered and rich? They argued against excitement, curiosity, and joy. Rest comfortably, sit still, and listen to Mozart. Drink tea and nap and accept your recovery one day at a time. I'd lost my father to depression. I had lost my faith, squandered my education, lost my job, and lost Daphne. I'd lost my mind. And now, now the doctors wanted to shut out the world. I wasn't about to lose that. I gave their fucking convalescence sixty more days. If I wasn't fixed by then I'd never be fixed. I needed a project beyond my own skull. I wanted a place where I could prove useful and competent and sane. I needed New York and the squats. And mostly I needed Roberta. I missed her terribly.

I gave Nadia notice. I ate the last of my meds and let the prescriptions run out. It took a few weeks to adjust; I had trouble sleeping but pushed through. I didn't go crazy. I'd proven that madness was not in the wings. I was cured, I figured. I was fine, a little jumpy and nervous but that was all right. It was just the old jitters, and so I bought a bag of dope. I bought some flowers for my mother and drove home to Hamilton. I woke my dad. He sat at the kitchen table in his bathrobe. I told them both I was leaving, that I was moving to New York City.

"But, David, you just got home. You haven't recovered. You can't leave now and you certainly shouldn't go to New York City. What's in New York City?"

"Roberta's down there."

"You mean that nice girl we met over in Rockport?"

"Lanesville. That's right, Mom. She's working with an advocacy group down there. For the homeless."

"I liked her," Mom said. "She's very nice."

"Is it with a church?" my father asked hopefully. "What organization is she with?"

"Well . . . she's not with an organization. It's more grassroots."

There was an awkward pause. My father narrowed his eyes. "Grassroots. How do you mean, grassroots?"

"Really grassroots," I admitted, stalling. They kept watching me. "Okay, okay. I'll level with you guys. She's squatting."

"Squatting," my father said.

"Yes. There's a bunch of empty buildings down in the city and the homeless are everywhere. We'll be fixing up apartments for them."

"Like Habitat for Humanity."

"Right, Dad. It's like that. I'm a carpenter and they need me down there. I've got a place to stay and friends. Don't worry," I said, "they need me down there."

"Well, Betty Lee, I think this sounds interesting. I think we should pray about this."

"Yeah, Dad, by all means, pray. This project needs all the help it can get. That's why I'm leaving tomorrow." I had dinner and then I kissed them and said I'd be back. "I'll just be in New York," I said. "It's not like I'm going to Guatemala." No one smiled.

I was pretty pleased with myself. I'd played it just right. I was working for the common good, just like Jimmy Carter and Habitat. As far as my father was concerned, I was back on the job building the Kingdom of Heaven, that shining city on a hill. I had my Dad's blessing, and what's more, I'd told him the truth.

At its best the squatting movement was visionary, a shining intentional community covered in dust. America has a long history of utopian social experiments and the squats were rooted in that tradition. We didn't have rolling lawns and gardens like the Transcendentalists; we didn't host salons in the sitting room; we had punks instead of Shakers; but it was utopian, experimental, and brave. The Lower East Side's squats were vital and sudden and all at once past.

I was needed down there, I knew that. 537 remained a near-empty shell. It needed more people and especially more carpenters. I visited most weekends. I always had tools and sometimes some scavenged lumber or doors. When I pulled up, before I even parked, Roberta and I hauled the saws and power cords up to her room and locked them away. I met Bill on one of my first visits. Roberta and I were resting on the stoop when he walked up. He was tall, loud, and exasperated. He was dusty. We were all perpetually dusty. I was already dusty.

"Who's this?" he asked Roberta.

"That would be my boyfriend, David. David, Bill."

Bill looked me over, whistled, and shook his head. "He'll never make it." He smiled.

"We'll see," Roberta said. "Jury's out." The three of us talked for a bit about the building, the work it demanded, and all of its characters. Before long Bill commenced pacing.

"Look," he said. "I need help. I've got to move Paula over here. She'll be good for the building, don't worry. She's all right. I mean she's all right but she can't stay where she is. The fucking roof's half-caved. She doesn't get it. She just doesn't get it. It's getting cold."

"Okay," I said. "Let's just go get her." We walked over to Eighth for Paula and I felt useful and fine. I was already needed.

We stopped at C Squat, another squat plastered with broadsides. Bill hollered up at the building, calling out various names. A head full of dust in full mask and goggles appeared from an upper window. "I've come to get Paula," Bill yelled. "From next door. I'm Bill from 537." The dust mask waved, ducked inside, and returned with some keys. Bill caught them and we let ourselves in.

The building's layout was similar to 537's but they had electricity. White romex wire hung from bent nails along the stairwell, ceramic sockets were pigtailed, and bulbs illuminated the stairs. Power cords ran everywhere. The place smelled of bleach and urine. "Paula's not exactly in this building," Bill explained. "These guys started freaking her out so she moved herself next door." He looked down halls at every landing. "They say this building's full, but Christ, there's tons of space in here. They could shovel that space out, no problem." Bill was fed up with most of his fellow squatters. "They have no work ethic," he muttered. "Look at that. Wasted space. Throw up some Sheetrock and boom. Two days. Plenty of room."

I followed him back through the vacant fifth floor. He stopped at an empty window frame and pointed across the airshaft. "She's over there."

"You're kidding me." Two two-by-ten boards stretched from the windowsill over a five-story drop and into a window next door. A two-by-four ran from the top of the windows as a rail.

"It's a bit tricky, but it's safe," Bill said. He stopped in the window and appraised me. "You're a carpenter, right? Just some staging here."

"She lives over there?"

"I said it wasn't good. It's kind of a siege situation. She can pull back the planks if she feels threatened."

I scoffed. "No, she can't. She'd drop them for sure. Then what?"

"She'd have to use the fire escape. The stairs are bad and the front's blocked up. Like I say, it's not good." Bill called across, "Paula! You in there?"

A voice warbled across, a sort of muffled patrician voice. "Yes. Who is it? Who's calling?" It sounded as if Katharine Hepburn were trapped under rubble.

"It's Bill. All right, Paula? I'm coming over. Okay?"

"Oh, yes, Bill. Please do." Bill ducked through the window and out onto the boards. He turned. "I think you should wait until I get across." I hesitated and he shook his head. "You're a carpenter, right?" I nodded. Sure, I was a carpenter and I'd built plenty of staging, but this wasn't staging, just two sketchy planks shot full of knots and pushed over a death trap. Bill made it across and glanced back with encouragement. "Don't worry," he said. "She doesn't have much furniture."

The roof had indeed collapsed. Blue sky fell through broken timbers and glanced off bright plaster and red broken bricks. Paula sat in a bed made up of blankets, back in the corner where the roof remained sound. A box of pastels lay beside her and she had a large sketchbook on her lap. She had pinned bright scarves and sheets to the beams; great swoops of color covered what plaster remained. Pigeons fluttered in the corners and dust swirled through great shafts of cold sun. Bill smiled at me. It was a magnificent ruin, epic. The enormity of our project loomed all around us in the broken November light. It was London after the Blitz.

Paula sat in her bed and waved to us cheerfully. "Oh, Bill, really. There's no need for this. I'm perfectly fine." She looked fine, too, smiling amid all the wreckage. Her hair was orange and full of tangling spikes and dark roots. "Really," she said, looking toward me, "he's making a fuss over nothing." But Bill was emphatic and by the end of the day 537 had another starry-eyed tenant. We scavenged plywood, covered most of the third-floor front joists, and piled Paula's belongings there. It was a cave compared to Paula's windswept nest over on Eighth but we framed up some makeshift walls and made her place safe. It wasn't dramatic. It didn't express Paula's creativity. But Paula couldn't stay in her own art installation—not for long. None of us can.

I moved down in midwinter. I couldn't handle my own art, my poetry. I couldn't witness my astonished mind linking strange words, jumping from image to faraway meanings. I couldn't allow that. I couldn't sit in a quiet room and scratch at a notebook. I'd go crazy alone. I wasn't scared of the squats; I was scared of my mind. I could live with anarcho-punks, the dispossessed, the wild and odd. I didn't need electricity or plumbing, a lease or security. I knew the squat would save me from thinking, from my pretty games of artsy roulette, and I was right. The work was constant and demanding both physically and socially. Every day in the squats brought a crisis or a party, usually both.

Bill and I were carpenters, John was a mason, and English Steve was a plasterer and jack-of-all-trades. All of us, everyone in the building, hauled rubble. We were all makeshift plumbers and electricians and Oliver Twists. I felt needed and necessary at 537. The squats were an insane kind of wonderful circus. By contrast I was calm, logical, and competent. If I had been surrounded by accountants and manicured lawns I would have gone mad. In the squats that troubled soul Dave was just Dave, a pretty good carpenter. I avoided the self-styled leaders, the louder anarchists, and all of the Marxists. I avoided the paint-splattered Artists, our requisite radical priest, and anyone else wearing a beret. I'd preached all my manifestos out west and in hospitals. I just wanted to work.

I built a small one-room apartment for Roberta and me. I pulled the lumber from various uninhabited spaces in the building and bought the insulation and Sheetrock. We had a bed, a few chairs, and a table. I replaced half an air shaft window with plywood and cut a hole for a galvanized stovepipe. I pushed it up to the roof and wired it to the parapet. The little coal stove I salvaged heated our tiny home beautifully. Roberta and I fell in love in a small, quiet room during wartime; it was simple and safe and all that we needed.

Outside our apartment door was chaos, a hollowed-out building with half-crazy comrades and piles of rubble and hope. Bill, Paula, English Steve, Cathy—these are the friends I've kept all my life. Past the squats, past Umbrella and Foetus and Glass House and Bullet and Life, the city got cold and crack-headed and desperately sad. Beyond that was New England, the ocean and woods and my family. I called my mother weekly and she was too scared to say it out loud—that something was wrong, that my father was gone and that she was alone. I knew it, of course, I knew how deathly it was, but I was weak. I couldn't stand watch at the wake and sometimes I felt glad she was quiet, glad she couldn't ask me to stand.

I kept busy hauling buckets of water and scavenging firewood from the city. Every morning I ventured out into the icebox building with a framing hammer and stripped lathe from the walls. I'd watch my breath frost in the cold, dim rooms and feel vaguely heroic, a backwoodsman in downtown Manhattan. It was strangely gratifying—burning my house down for heat. At first it was easy; I just opened our door and tore lathe from the hall. Later on I scavenged up and down through the building with everyone else. Half-inch strips of century-old pine burn hot and fast. Our room was toasty with the teakettle steaming in just minutes. The nights, however, were long and cold and we hoarded whatever hardwood scraps we could find. I always checked the Dumpster outside a nearby furniture shop but word spread and everyone hit it and that source got dicey.

The air shaft between 537 and our sister squat, 535, was nothing more than a chimney. Stovepipes pushed through windows on both sides, some cocked and angling up the building, some belching straight out. From the roof the shaft looked positively Dickensian, dangerous and makeshift and blanketed in smoke. All of it was a flagrant and crazy code violation. The entire condemned building was a flagrant and crazy code violation and no one seemed overly concerned. The city had bigger problems than us in 1986. The squat movement was militantly anti-crack and its drug stance created unlikely and critical alliances. Squatters proved to be the lesser of two evils. The cops and the neighbors preferred squats to empty tenements left open to dealers and addicts. Punks hauling buckets of rubble were amusing and harmless compared to the alternatives.

Firemen caused greater alarm than cops. We knew the fire department could shut us down fast. I was alone on the stoop when the fire chief stepped up and flipped out his badge. "Fire chief. Listen, I'm gonna need to inspect this . . . this place. Do you live here?"

"Maybe," I said.

"Can you let me in?"

"No. You're a cop."

He rolled his eyes. "I'm not a cop. I'm a fireman. You guys need firemen, believe me." I sat silently and looked past him. "Listen, I don't give a rat's ass if you guys are in there. It's none of my business. I don't own the building. I'm just trying to keep you from burning down the block." I sat weighing my options. No one else was around. The chief's face darkened. "Okay? You can just let me in, we'll do a little walk-through, and that will be that. Or I can condemn this fricking firetrap—*again*—and let the city come in."

"Damn," I said, "I guess I don't have a choice."

"That's right, kid. You don't."

I felt like a Judas. I broke the squat's most fundamental law, opened the door and let the man enter. We walked into the cold dark and for once I was glad we had no electricity. He couldn't see much and if we had had electricity it would have been bootleg.

"No juice?" he asked.

"No."

"What do you use?"

"Flashlights, just flashlights," I lied pathetically. There were candles and pools of old wax all up the stairwell. I took him to my room. At least I knew our stove was properly installed—properly enough for an illegal stove in a squatted building. I opened the door and there it was, my patched-up, darling little coal stove.

The chief's jaw dropped. He looked at me and then walked over to a window. When he saw all the pipes he shook his head and began laughing softly. "You've got to be shitting me."

"I mean we do have buckets of water," I said helpfully.

He shook out a cigarette and lit it. "No you fucking don't. You don't even have plumbing. Christ." He thought for a moment. "Look, I'll tell you what. Get some fire extinguishers, for Christ's sake. Get some buckets of sand and have them on every landing." I nodded and he walked to the stairs. I hesitated. "Are you gonna let me out or what?" What? That was it? I couldn't believe it. I figured he'd return with all the right paperwork, two trucks, and some axes, but he never did. He was just curious, a sightseer.

We snaked power cords over the roof from Life Squat for our tools and occasional light. That got ridiculous fast, so we pooled our money and paid a guy named Irish Mike three hundred dollars to fix things. He came drunk but highly recommended. He jumped down the manhole out front and in ten minutes he jacked Con Ed juice right into the building. We ran wire all over the building, lit the place up like Times Square, and Con Ed never even blinked.

We never did get plumbing. There were vile, fermenting piss buckets on every floor. We took turns carrying them out and dumped them down storm drains. It was a nasty job and slackers avoided it. For the rest we strategically visited local restaurants. Eventually, a particularly brave group of volunteers cleared our building's main drain so we could manually flush toilets with buckets. We had the hydrant out front for clean water. My friend English Steve, a longtime squatter, had scored an apartment on Fourteenth. He handed out keys to everyone from 537 and we took showers there regularly, day and night.

By midsummer the building was well-established; there were actual, bona fide homeless wanting in, not just punks and politicos but dispossessed families. The building was filling up and we needed more room. So began a major drive to repair the roof and make the front of the building safe and habitable. Bill found the timbers needed for roof joists next to a Pentecostal Spanish church six blocks away.

"It's simple," he said. "There's a pile of them—ten-by-four beams. They got to be twenty-four, twenty-six feet long. They're just laying there." Five or six of us sat on the stoop and watched Bill catch his breath. He was excited.

"Are you saying we should just steal them?"

Bill grabbed at his hair. "Well, we're not going to buy them."

"All right," I said, "but where we gonna hide them?"

Bill grabbed at his hair again. "On the fucking roof, of course. Look, we build a lookout, you know, with a block and tackle and winch them right up. Seventh Street's got a block and tackle. I know it."

"What the hell is a lookout?"

"Whatever. You know. A thing we can lag the block to and stick out, over the street."

"You can't lay it on that parapet," John said. "It'll let go. I wired it in but it sways. Dangerous as hell."

Any ethical issues, any church robbery qualms, were soon trumped by our righteous cause, the Homeless—the college-educated, middle-class Homeless. We were down to the nuts and bolts of the operation now. Bill and I walked down to the church with a thirty-foot tape and the beams measured fine. We stopped at Seventh, yelled up, and got our hands on the block and tackle.

We stole the first beam just before dawn. We walked up empty Avenue A with it on our shoulders, the four of us bent and quiet like strange reverse penitents. I thought of my parents: how they prayed for me, my father's misplaced pride in his son doing the Lord's work. I started awkward, superstitious prayers in my head. First I apologized for stealing the church's wood and asked for forgiveness. Failing that, I began justifying the mission. My father taught me that nothing else mattered but the Kingdom of God. Forget money, forget career; just work toward the Kingdom. Well, this is it, God, I said, 537's all the purpose I've got. That angle failed, too, and then I just prayed we wouldn't get caught. I prayed the whole fucking rig wouldn't come down on our heads.

Three more trips and we had all the beams we needed stacked on our sidewalk. We rousted the squat. We cordoned the sidewalk and cut off the traffic like the Army Corps of Engineers. A group of onlookers formed across the street and a dozen or more people inspected our knots. We moved fast before cops showed. Four of us pulled the thick rope across the street and hauled off. Steve and John balanced the beam and kept it from swinging out into parked cars. The beam tipped and swung vertical but the rope bit into the wood and held fast. We stood in a crowd of dealers, squatters, and neighbors and pulled hand over hand fast. John and Steve appeared above the wobbly parapet, and people screamed directions in English and Spanish as they grabbed hold and swung the beam over and onto the roof. The street broke into cheers. We had them all up by ten a.m. and rebuilt the roof in three days.

By winter, small areas of the squat were almost comfortable. We found a massive potbellied stove and installed it downstairs near the front door, creating a kind of parlor. The stove was four feet across and the iron cast in an ornate Victorian design. We cut a sink into plywood counters for a common kitchen. We held our meetings around a large table and scavenged several cushioned chairs. The meetings were endlessly democratic: any ridiculous suggestion and every paranoid objection could hijack the table for hours. I felt reasonable at these meetings, even staid.

The question of James came up at one winter meeting. James was in his sixties, a dignified black man who always wore the same dark suit. His manners were impeccable. James was the calmest, most philosophical member of the squat, a grandfather figure to Roberta and me. Most mornings Roberta and I found him downstairs. We bought him coffee, he offered us cigarettes, and we sat together, quietly smoking by the stove. But James had been allowing strangers into the building and I was elected to suss out the situation, to reason with James before he was bounced.

"So, James," I started one morning. "There's been a lot of coming and going from your room. People we don't know."

He smiled. "Oh, them? Those folks are my friends, my ladies."

"Your ladies? What are they, living there?" I glanced over at Roberta, who smirked at me. "I mean, why are there so many different people coming and going?"

James's eyes narrowed. "You've seen them?"

"Not really," I admitted. "But lots of us have. It's come up at the meetings."

"Look," James said. "Those ladies are my friends. They have a little business, it's true, but it's not what you think." I looked at

him expectantly. "They sell feminine items. Tampons and con-
doms and such. Hygiene items."

"Ah, come on, James." I sighed. "It's got to stop. You've got
crackheads and who knows what coming in here. They're prosti-
tutes."

"They're my friends," he said plaintively. "The women take
care of me." James didn't do drugs, he didn't even drink, and he
wasn't a pimp. He was just getting by, I figured, getting a little
money for the use of his room. But it was stupid and dangerous,
a complete breach of security.

"It's done now, James. It has to be. It stops now or you'll be
thrown out. No drugs, no crackheads, no whores. That's the
deal." For once it was me. In the lunatic squats mine was a voice
of reason. I was still sick with denial and stoned on my street
medicine. I hadn't transformed so much as adapted, changed my
surroundings to suit my own illness, but I was listened to, respected. James stopped all the nonsense and he stayed and we
were happy to have him. James was a reasonable man, and somehow I was becoming one.

The squats had three rules: no violence, no theft, and no hard
drugs. The first two were easy—any transgressor met with eviction. The last rule was tricky; it smacked of moral judgment; it
made us like cops. Exceptions were made. The movement had its
junkies but compared to the crackheads they seemed harmless.
Junkies entertain themselves quietly for hours. Our resident ad-
dict was Flowers, a black guy who kept to himself. He was useless for work and often bad-tempered but no one threw him out.

Evicting Flowers just promised a struggle and didn't seem worth it. Besides, he kept saying he was going home any day—back to South Carolina—and one day he just left.

Crack and cocaine were different. The rule was immediate expulsion, no second chances. Crack promised instant psychosis and almost immediate trouble. The radical priest sent Charles to us. "He's got a job working maintenance," the priest said. "He just needs a place. He's clean." We had our doubts but moved him onto the fourth floor. Charles wasn't clean. The man aged visibly in a matter of weeks. His cracked eyes glittered fiercely and then went sticky and dead. He moved past our rooms muttering scripture and hellfire. He knew dark scraps of my childhood: the jealous, angry God who leveled Sodom and struck Lot's wife into salt, Satan's foul pit, and six six six. Beyond his religious psychosis and crack there were questions of hygiene. Charles barbecued chicken backs on a grill in his room almost nightly. He left the bones outside his door on the slate stairway landing. "For the cats," he said. Every other night I threw burnt chicken backs into the air shaft. I slipped on the grease. It stank.

"Fucking Charles," I complained at a meeting. "He's still cooking his chicken, smokes up the whole floor. It's monoxide. I've got headaches from it. He won't answer his door anymore but I know he's in there. He could suffocate."

"So what if he chokes?" Bill said grimly. "That's his business. It's the chicken bones. They're drawing rats."

"You don't live next to him. It's nasty." I threw up my hands. "And now he's decided I'm the Devil, the fricking Antichrist." People laughed. "I'm serious. He starts screaming about the Antichrist every time he sees me."

"It's just the crack," Bill said.

"So what if it's the crack? He's psychotic. He probably got wooden stakes and is just waiting to use them. I mean the guy's dangerous."

"All right," Steve said. "Let's throw him out. We need to throw him out, that's all." He stood up.

"What?" I said, backing off. "Right now? It's past midnight. Where's he going to go?"

Steve shrugged his shoulders. "Who cares?" That was just it; no one cared. Everyone knew we were his last chance, the last safety net before the street, madhouse, and prison. None of that mattered anymore; it hadn't for weeks. Charles was crazy as hell and we were scared of him. That's the only reason he'd lasted this long.

"Look," I said. "Let's talk to him in the morning. See how it is." This plan relieved everyone. It seemed sensible but when morning came we avoided each other and, above all, avoided Charles.

A few weeks passed. Roberta was away, it was late, and I had been drinking by the big stove with Bill and English Steve. I climbed up the stairs drunk, kicked the chicken bones at Charles's door, and stopped at the floor's common toilet. Charles's door banged open and he came out screaming, "Satan, you're Satan!" I looked out from the bathroom and saw him slash at the air with a large metal crucifix. "Damien, you're Damien!" he screamed. "The Devil. The Last Days have come." He charged at me, pushing the cross in my face like some psychotic priest. "You're the fucking Antichrist!" He swung the crucifix and I caught him by the wrist and spun him into a wall. He weighed about as much as a doll. He sat for a moment, winded, the horsehair plaster falling down into his hair. I heard the others coming and zipped up my jeans. My hand was bleeding, some skin torn away by the cross. Charles jumped and bolted back into his room.

My friends and I huddled on the landing and agreed on eviction, immediate and final. I was the sane one now and I wanted the crazies gone. They had the virus; I was susceptible and I didn't want it. Whatever empathy I once had, whatever insights I claimed, disappeared. I had no compassion now. My fear and anger had boiled it off. Charles wasn't my problem. I wanted Charles out in the street, knocked out and quiet on the cold fucking pavement.

Billy banged on his door. "Okay, Charles. It's all right. The Devil's gone. We got rid of the Devil." He smiled at me and I held up my fingers like horns. "Come on, Charles. We need to talk about this. I mean, what the fuck? Dave's not Satan. He's not even Damien. How'd you get that idea? I mean think about it." Bill pulled on a Guinness. "His name is Dave, not Damien. Okay, Charles? Dave." We stood there waiting in the dark. The adrenaline was wearing off. We stood making nervous jokes and banged on Charles's door every few minutes. Someone got beer.

Then Charles stepped out fast. He'd swapped the cross for a baseball bat and ran past us and into the front swinging. "Fucking fire!" he yelled. "Fire! The Lord's flames and let's burn the fuck down. God's judgment is fire!" We stood for a moment, dumbstruck. "We need oxygen. Air for the fire and flames!" Then Charles ran at the front windows and bashed them out in a line. When he pushed his head out through the last window and started screaming out to the street, three of us pulled him down into the glass. Bill twisted an arm and kneeled on his back.

"He's out," I said. "Now." Charles started screaming again.

"Shouldn't we call someone?"

"Fuck no! He's out now."

Charles quieted when we pulled him to his feet. His arms and hands were cut and bleeding. We dragged him down to the street and a police radio squawked. We told the foot cop what happened, what the noise was, and he smiled down at Charles. "Sometimes," he said, "sometimes you just gotta kick people off the bus." He barked an address into the radio. Somewhere Charles had family—maybe a mother who took him to church, a brother or sister or someone. But I wasn't his brother. I wasn't family and I wished him good riddance. Paula ran up and gathered his things but by the time she returned the squad car was gone. She stood there with us, holding a plastic bag stuffed with cloth.

The cold was brutal that second winter and Roberta and I agreed to break up the siege. Our apartment cost nothing; I'd earned some cash and our space was secure. Roberta wanted to go down to Nicaragua and pick coffee with Sandinistas for a few months. I supported the Sandinistas but had little interest in picking their coffee. In truth, I was sick of New York's endless outrage, and Roberta's solidarity group promised more of the same. Instead, I kicked around Mexico and traveled down to Belize. I went back to the Tackle Box and claimed my computer. My novel had grown even worse in my absence. Roberta sent postcards from Nicaragua with cute, impoverished children on them. She sent me Neruda poems. I couldn't wait to get home. I got back before her, sometime in March. It was beautiful, walking from the subway stop on Fourteenth. The city even smelled good, cold and clean.

Steve and a young punk were on the stoop when I arrived. Steve hugged me, ridiculed my tan, and introduced me to Misty. "She's staying in Charles's old space."

"How is it, Steve?" I asked. "Is it okay?"

"Good, man, good. It's been smooth. Just the usual paranoia. Nothing's really happened since you've been gone. Are you back now for a while?"

I nodded. "Roberta will be back in a week or so."

"Okay, well, your room's still there. No one's in it. I think Paula may have stored some stuff in there, that's all."

Someone started yelling from deep within the building. It got closer and louder until Bill flew out, clear past the stoop, waving a three-pound sledge. "Flowers! In the air shaft. It's Flowers. We found him."

"Nah," I said. "He's in Carolina or something."

"No. He's not. He's in the air shaft. I mean I think it's him." We stared at him. "Really. Deb's been bashing out cinder blocks in the back. Her windows. There's a body out there. First we saw its hand. But now it's Flowers. He's totally fucking dead."

"Shit."

"He never went anywhere. He's been—hey, Dave, you're back—anyway, he's been frozen out there all fucking winter. Christ." Bill started pacing and working his hands, clenching and unclenching his fists. Deb came out and stood very still. She was beautiful as she stood in the door with long purply black hair and a crowbar.

"It's him," she confirmed quietly.

Bill jumped. "We've got to get him inside," he said, and started up the steps.

"What?" I said. "Are you fucking crazy? We can't move the body."

"Well, we can't just leave him there laying in the trash. I'm moving him." Steve and I reasoned with him. "What are you going to do?" asked Bill. "Call the cops?"

"Damn straight we call the cops," I said. "Nine-one-one. What do you want to do? Bury him?"

Deb said, "I think we need to call the coroner or something." Misty ran inside.

"Whatever," Bill said. "He's coming inside." Steve grabbed him by the sleeve and talked him down.

I went back in. I guess it was Flowers; his face was bloated and obscured by bricks. It was still cold and he didn't smell too bad, just a sickly sweet hint in the wet brick air. Squatters were peering down from the windows above the air shaft. Bill came in with the sledge and knocked out the remaining blocks, and then we knew it was Flowers. His arms were clutched across his chest like he had tried to keep warm.

"Well, I'm calling the cops," Deb said. "Does anyone know his real name?"

We shrugged. "Just Flowers," Steve said.

I walked out to the stoop and noticed a plainclothes cop across the street. He had to be a cop—he was wearing a trench coat and staring straight at our building. He stood, lit a cigarette, and crossed the street. Already? I thought. They knew about Flowers already? Impossible.

"Hey, pal," he said—he'd seen all the movies; he used all the language. "I'm a private eye. Here's my card." I took it and he pulled a snapshot out of his coat. "Have you ever seen this girl before?" The Misty I met had ragged black hair and torn clothes. This one had blond hair, a corsage, and a prom date with acne. The detective blew a fleck of tobacco from his tongue. "Her parents back in Ohio are looking for her. They miss her. She's their little girl. Just seventeen. Well?" I looked at the ground. He knew damn well I had just been sitting here talking to her.

"No," I said. "I've never seen her before in my life."

"Yeah, sure." He frowned momentarily and then brightened. "Hey, I hear you have a stiff over here?"

"Where'd you hear that?" He looked at me and smiled again. "Yeah, all right. So what's it to you?"

"Mind if I take a look?" He stood. "I haven't seen a stiff in a long while." And then he was in. I ran upstairs to find Misty but she was already gone, up over the roof and down through Life. The detective had his look with the rest of us and then left.

Half an hour passed and then four policemen knocked. They seemed irritable, looked at the body, and shrugged as if to say we should have buried him there, gone back to work, and saved them the trouble. Their radios hissed and cracked and it was strange to hear them.

"Okay," one of the cops said. "The coroner's office has been notified. He needs to sign a death certificate before the wagon can come. It takes a while. He's a busy man and gets backed up. We'll post a policeman here until the body is picked up." That was it. No investigation was necessary. Three of the cops left and the unlucky one stood in the back by the rank air shaft and waited. Deb got him a chair. She lit some candles. The word got around and some neighborhood friends showed up and filed past. Quite a few squatters came through, grave and curious and dry-eyed. Flowers always said he had family back in South Carolina but no one found a license or ID or letter in his room. No one knew his name. The city pulled him from the shaft about one in the morning.

When Roberta got back we drove home to Gloucester. It was high summer and we camped near the cove, along beaches and the edges of Dogtown. Every few weeks I headed back to the city for small jobs with Steve or Bill, but our time there was closing. Roberta and I gave up our room at the squat and took an apartment by Plum Cove. Paying rent was an adjustment; by January we were broke and I went back to the city for a quick little job on Wall Street, snipping tin studs and building cubicles. I slept out back on the first floor, across from Flowers's ghost. The room was used for storage, just an icebox without a stove. I found a thin, ragged electric blanket, stuffed it into my sleeping bag, and plugged it in every night.

Weeks passed and I had a dream. I heard screams and then more, and then I heard the word "fire." John the Commie's voice came across the air shaft and snapped me awake. "Come on, you guys. I'm not kidding. It's a big fire. Fire! Get the fuck up!" People were running up and down stairs, banging on doors, rousting everyone. I could smell smoke. Out on the street we tried to count heads but it was useless. No one knew who slept where anymore. Fire trucks showed and shot water up into Life's fourth floor. John the Commie and his girlfriend started screaming at the firemen, calling them fascists and pigs. He said the fire was planned, a plot against the "movement." He pulled at their hoses and tried to block them from entering.

The fire had started in Dawn's room. She was a newcomer to Life Squat but she had been on the scene for years. Everyone knew her and sympathized with her. She'd been burned out of two squats and seemed so unlucky. Now we all knew she was crazy, clearly batshit, setting fires to her life and ours. She'd gone out and left her wood stove open, surrounded it with newspaper. John the Communist lived below her and his room was drenched. "Fucking Dawn," he said, and we all joined in. I stood in the dark winter air surrounded by friends. This time we couldn't blame the city or the government, gentrification, or yuppies. We were all crazy, every one of us.

I cashed in my winnings and went home to Roberta. I was finished. It wasn't the arson. Dawn's fire woke me up all right, but it was just another crisis in a long list of good stories. It was John the C's ugly reaction, the absurd and hateful tirade he unleashed on the firemen, that finished the squats for me. I saw all the changes we'd suffered since the cops drove the homeless from Tompkins Square, the movement's slow ugly warp. Tompkins Square was a police riot—they charged the tent city on horses swinging their clubs—but their violence infected us all. The park was fenced with barbed wire and shut down for years. Freedom and humor drained from the squats and the wide-open anachro-punk scene of the squats; its makeshift beauty, its art, was supplanted by riot, faction, and rage.

———————

Fifteen years later I met English Steve and Bill at Mona's, our old bar around the corner. Roberta and I see Bill regularly and Steve's family visits often—we've all moved on—but on the barstools the old stories turned maudlin. The neighborhood had changed. A handful of squats went legal and now rate as homesteads, but most were evicted and turned into co-ops. Some burned. Steve wasn't sentimental and went home, but Bill and I missed the squats, our fearful and beautiful buildings, our youth falling wide open.

We walked down to 537. Our slogans were gone for good, power-washed from the brick, the battered metal door and cinder blocks refitted with window glass and wrought iron, locks and buzzers. There was plumbing inside and light bills and such. The place almost gleamed but the stoop was the same. We sat there like war buddies returned to Europe with the rubble all gone. Bill went across to the bodega for two bottles of Guinness. We put them in brown paper bags and twisted them tight at the neck. I was in New York on business. In a few hours I would be in a warehouse buying books, but for now we were squatters. We were back on the old stoop. I pushed on the first door and it opened, and so did the next—neither lock had clicked home.

It seemed way, way too bright in the stairwell. The old hallways were serious with their identical doors, and the place didn't smell right. It smelled of floor wax and order—like a high school, like we needed a hall pass. We crept up to the penthouse and pushed through to the roof. Now the roof, the roof was impressive. The owners had improved our improvements: nothing felt spongy; the parapet no longer swayed over the street; the knee-wall surrounding the air shaft had all its bricks.

"I wonder if they left our framing," Bill said. "Our framing was good. I mean it was up to code and everything. Those beams were way beefy enough." He finished his beer. "Definitely beefy."

"Oh yeah, most definitely beefy," I slurred, and stomped the roof.

"Quit fucking making noise!" Bill screamed. "We're gonna get caught."

"Oh, yeah," I said. "Right."

The buildings burned all around like constellations. At about three a.m. Bill turned and asked, "Did you prop the door? The penthouse door?"

"You were the last one out," I said, and walked back to the door. It was locked tight. We considered our options. The fire escape was no help; it stopped at the fifth-floor windows.

"That's doable," Bill said.

"What? It's a half-story drop."

"That's not a half story, not really." I looked at him. "It's not." Bill kneeled at the parapet and hung his head and arms down toward the street. "Look," he said, waving his hands for emphasis, "if you hang from the parapet down it's maybe a four-foot drop."

"You're out of your fricking mind," I said. "I'm not hanging off that parapet. Not that one. The building's not on fire."

"Tell you what. I'll drop down, then I'll come back and unlock the door."

"No, you're not. There's no way you're doing that. You're

drunk. I'm not letting friends jump off buildings drunk. Besides," I argued, "you won't get back in from the street."

"You think the door's locked?"

"All the fucking doors are locked."

Bill considered this. "Tell you what. I'll call Steve and see if he can get in. I'll wake him up." Steve wasn't answering his phone. No one answered their phone.

I tried the door again. "I give up," I said. "We'll just have to wait until dawn and then bang on the door."

Bill never quits. "You know," he said, "the fire escape out back goes right up to the roof. All we have to do is climb over the penthouse." He stepped up on the air shaft knee-wall, stretched, and just caught the penthouse roof. "I can do it. I can pull myself up."

"Well, I can't," I protested. "You're like two feet taller than me."

"I'll pull you up," Bill promised. "You give me an arm and I'll pull you up." And then he scrambled up. He disappeared for a moment and returned triumphant. "Yup. The back escape is doable."

"Doable? You mean it comes all the way up?"

"Yup." Bill lay down, braced himself, and reached over the edge. "Come on. Don't think about it." I cursed and grabbed on to his wrist with my right hand. He pulled and I hung by the air shaft. Bill kept pulling until I found a handhold and flipped a leg up onto the roof.

We got giddy. We dropped down to the back roof and raced down the escape, whooping and hollering past the windows of young bankers and web designers, past Alex, Charles, James, and Deb Lee. We cut through a lot, scaled a fence, and sat across the street laughing until squad cars arrived. Shit.

One of the cops stepped from his car and motioned at us. "Hey, you two. Someone reported two men on the fire escape. Did you see anything?"

"What?" I asked. "On the fire escape?"

"Yeah."

"No. But two guys did come from around back. They climbed the fence there and took off."

"Which way?"

I pointed east.

"Were they black? Hispanic?"

I shrugged and said I couldn't tell. "They were wearing hoods," Bill added helpfully.

The cops headed east and we ran west. Not much has changed. We were middle-class white guys and got away clean. We weren't as young or naïve but we were still game. I slept a few hours, slugged my lithium back with hot coffee, and drove down to the warehouse. I worked all day and loaded my truck, exhausted but happy. I had hundreds of books for my shop, and much more important, I had one last, ridiculous squat story. Trespassing on an East Village rooftop was pointless, locking myself out was stupid, and swinging over the air shaft was extremely dangerous. I am the father of two small children, Mary and Hunter, who need me. Roberta and my elderly parents need me. Hanging drunk off old squats is irresponsible and even selfish. But that delicate sway, that balance between the ridiculous and the reasonable, between crazy stories and dependable bookkeeping, is something I love, a gift that I've learned from my family and from our disease. We have our adventures, our stories and visions. It beats television. It beats selling insurance.

ELEVEN

After New York and the squats Roberta planned a career. We moved to western Massachusetts in 1990. I was stubborn; I held out for a calling. She entered graduate school while I cleaned gutters and remodeled basements. I wanted to write but couldn't sit still. I wanted to teach but I was too jumpy. That's how it was, I figured. I had to keep moving. I lacked clarity and purpose. All I had was excellent taste and dashed expectations. In short, I was a dope-smoking, nail-banging cynic. But I got lucky for a guy with no vision; a poet ran off and left me with his massive used-book shop out in the woods.

"You don't want this place," Jim told me. "Let the bank have it. Trust me. It's sinking. The Bookmill is a floundering ship on a pitch-black sea. Stormy sea. A black ship pitched on a stormy sea. Something like that. Anyway, it leaks money." He took my shoulder paternally.

"Listen," I said, "I appreciate your concern, but don't worry about the shop. I don't need to make a lot of money. I think I can make this work."

He shook his head. "All right, then. Suit yourself. I'm off to make a reasonable living in Florida."

"That sounds awful," I said, and Jim threw up his hands, climbed in his Peugeot, and drove south.

Once again I was surrounded by unreasonable beauty: thousands of books lining the walls of a nineteenth-century gristmill on a trout stream in the middle of nowhere. I'd been working for Jim less than two months, but a combination of luck, fiscal impropriety, and landlord panic left my penniless coworker and me owning the shop: no money down, no capital, no real estate, just good books and a banknote. It was the perfect job for me, quixotic and pure and untainted by profit. My coworker and now business partner was even a card-carrying anarchist. We hosted readings, poetry slams, and concerts—chamber, folk, punk. We hosted a ukulele festival. We added a café and a fine restaurant moved in below us. There was a waterfall just past the windows, rising trout in the pools downstream, and books everywhere.

It was peaceful. It was lovely and the checkbook usually balanced, but I stayed jittery. I was anxious, scared to answer the phone, scared of my accountant, scared of Foucault and Derrida. The only place I stood still was in trout streams, calmed by water and the rhythm of casting. And then I had dope. I had been getting stoned regularly for twelve years, every day if I could swing it. I smoked alone in the woods, at parties, at work. It helped me stand television, tie trout flies, and stay in my skin. And then it stopped working. It no longer soothed my agitated mind; worse, it jump-started my worries and pushed them toward paranoia. I withdrew. I spent whole parties contemplating bone cancer and bankruptcy. I hadn't taken lithium since the Witch House but I knew how things stood; I knew my pot was lousy medicine. I pulled a psychiatrist's name out of the phone book and made an appointment. I walked in, laid out my family's history, and walked out with a prescription.

My parents decided to sell our old house in Hamilton. It's gotten too much for your mother, our father told us. It was too much for all of us. The worst of Dad's depression had passed by then, but the disease had ruined and haunted the place. I called in a thirty-yard Dumpster and dropped it just under the living room window. I sat my mother down in the kitchen with old photo albums, left my father sorting his library, and gleefully pitched everything meaningless straight out the window. The house was bulldozed three days later, replaced by a prefab estate. Landscapers cut the oak trees and mulched thirty years' worth of leaves.

My parents moved out to Saratoga Springs, New York, to be closer to Peniel. It took two years, but I finally convinced them to move closer to us, closer to Northampton. Jonathan Edwards is buried just down the road, I said. I helped Dad find a nice apartment downtown, close to the shops. My mother got involved with a church in the neighborhood. She painted hundreds of cute watercolor cards and sold them from the bookstore. Dad began teaching at the seminary again, part-time. He shuttled back and forth to the North Shore once a month or so, and his lectures were jammed. My father, brother, and I went to Idaho and fly-fished. We drove to the Catskills and flew into remote Maine camps. Dad was happiest, I think, when he was with us and fishing.

By 1994, I had proven my bookstore could fly through the fiscal trees indefinitely. My partner and I teamed with Roberta's sister Betsy and built a second bookstore nearby. Roberta had been teaching for years. I took my lithium, wrote poems, and fished. We were pretty near broke, happy and settled. And now we wanted a family. I was still in the theoretical, advance-planning stage when Roberta began scheduling the children's arrival. We discussed Roberta's teaching career and financial concerns; we discussed midwives, home birth, and hospitals; we considered names, circumcision, and high chairs. Frankly, my family's illness was just another question, a practical concern rather than a moral quandary. We had lithium, we had knowledge and love. I had Roberta, a solid Yankee with Finnish roots whose calm, self-possessed grace had saved me. I liked my chances with Roberta from the start, and they'd only improved.

We knew the odds. My family is a textbook example of manic depression's genetic link. We could have saved Gregor Mendel a great deal of trouble. Roughly 1 percent of the general population is bipolar. Studies are ongoing, of course—and statistics vary somewhat—but if one parent is bipolar the odds of a child inheriting the disease are much greater; the percentage rises 8 to 10 percent. If both parents are bipolar, the odds are much, much greater. Five percent of the general population has suffered from major depression. If one parent has experienced major depression before age twenty, their children's chance of depression rises to 30 percent. My children, Mary and Hunter, are ten times more likely to suffer bipolar illness than their schoolmates.

I hope they've won the gene pool lottery, that they don't carry my disease, but if they do I'll be ready. I've learned my own story and I'm not afraid.

I assured Roberta that I was ready for children. I was excited, I told her. I was ready except for one little thing: Patagonia. I was obsessed with the place. Blame Bruce Chatwin, I said, blame all the rivers, the millions of trout. It's now or never, I said, and I promised I'd return in a month. Patagonia wasn't a frantic bipolar decision; it was just a prolonged adolescent decision, and Roberta has never quite forgiven me for that trip. She was already pregnant but I pretended all questions of wisdom, fairness, and timing had been settled. Roberta read *What to Expect When You're Expecting* and I studied maps and read about rivers and South American mayfly hatches. I began tying flies.

"It says here the bugs are pretty much the same," I assured Roberta. "I bet I could get away with a parachute Adams, a Wooly Bugger, and some sulphurs." She shrugged and went back to her reading. "For nymphing I'll just use a gold ribbed Hare's Ear." She ignored me. Over the weeks, Roberta evinced less and less interest in angling minutiae. It was deflating. I turned back to my tying. I picked up some notebooks, a spare reel, and a rod, and I carefully packed a month's worth of lithium into my fly vest. I felt prepared. I felt reasonable. I told myself I deserved my grand trip, that I needed it.

I knew all along Patagonia was selfish, but one of the least attractive aspects of manic-depressives—even medicated, well-adjusted manic-depressives—is their deep, nearly bottomless capacity for narcissism. They claim to be theologians and poets. They write books explaining God's own will; they write poems, throw readings, and make people listen; they write memoirs. They leave their pregnant wives alone and embark on journeys of self-discovery. A simple fishing trip is never simple.

I'd forgotten all about trout by the time I got to LaGuardia. I started to panic. We were having a baby, an actual baby. It was already real and I was skipping town for a month, maybe forever. Patagonia was a brilliant metaphor for self-destruction, the last and loneliest place. I convinced myself I'd get lost, really, really lost out in the pampas. I'd never get home. My trip was just self-ish, it was self-destructive. I had planned the whole thing, I sud-denly realized, just like Hart Crane. "Good-bye, everybody," he said, and he waved, stepped off the deck and into the Mexican sea. I'd gone looking for my madness and I knew I would find it. I couldn't get on that plane; I was afraid of the flying.

I called Roberta from the airport. "I'm not going," I told her. "I can't get on that plane. I'll lose it. I'll see if I can cash out the ticket or something. All right?"

"No," she said. "It's not all right. You'll regret not going. You'll feel awful." She paused and waited for me to reply. I was too busy hyperventilating. "Look, Dave, what have you got? Do you have any Xanax? Just eat some Xanax and get on the plane. Eat two; that's what they're for. You're not going to go crazy. You have to do this, now. You'll always wonder."

"Okay," I said quietly.

"Good. Now just go fishing and I'll see you when you get home." She hung up and I got on the plane. I caught a train south from Santiago as far as it went and hitchhiked to turquoise rivers. I crossed the Andes into Argentina and camped by the Malleo. I rented a car and drove it farther south, down to Esquel, and then east toward nowhere, just a small spring creek. I took my lithium with Argentine beef and red wine. I ran low on money and pan-fried my trout. I had gone south again, farther this time and still all alone, and I looked for the brink. I caught beautiful fish and I proved my return was now possible. I came home proud and happy and ready for children. Mary was born the next fall and Hunter four years later. We bought a house.

It was an old farmhouse upriver from the Bookmill. It was a young carpenter's dream and his wife's worst headache—the eternal remodel. By the time Mary was eight I was almost done with the kitchen. She and Hunter were both happy, beautiful kids. They had a barn to explore and a pond full of frogs. The bookstore was breaking even at best, but it still looked pretty handsome after ten years. I still had good books and concerts, and the Mill had a growing, albeit underground, reputation. In 2003 I decided to upgrade the Mill's café with more food, a beer and wine license, and an extensive remodel. I formed a new partnership with one of my longtime employees and his girlfriend. We took out a business loan and I tore into the carpentry. We needed the café reopened fast. I worked an intense schedule, installing counters and sinks while juggling the bookstore. Roberta took the kids out to Gloucester and I hoped to join them in a few weeks when the café reopened.

I was excited. I had a new business venture, a great family, a beautiful house. I was a success—broke, maybe, but a success. At

least I wasn't a wreck. I wasn't nervous or crazy or stoned. I
hadn't had a manic break or depression in years. I was steady,
and so were my parents and my brother. I was just a little bipolar,
I thought, or maybe I'd grown out of it. In truth, I was tired of
taking my medicine, all this drug dependence. I felt addicted to
lithium. It still gave me headaches. It slowed me down. I didn't
need lithium if I just used common sense, if I avoided the obvious: hallucinogens, crack, civil war. I quit in late June—on the
solstice, in fact—and the weather was beautiful.

I drove to the city and bought a beautiful old mahogany bar
from a salvage yard, hauled it up to the mill, and cut it and fit it
just right. It was perfect. I felt fine. I felt better than fine. I was
efficient, productive, and decisive. I cleaned out my barn and
dragged everything flammable out to the field. I built a bonfire
full of broken chairs and wardrobes, pine scraps and oak pallets
and saplings. There were boxes of overstocked titles and just
plain dead stock in the barn. I pulled them all out and staged
every bookseller's dark fantasy, a book burning. I was selective. I
burned self-help and new age; I burned romance and thrillers; I
burned some sociology and all the psychology. I kept the poetry.

The café still needed finishing, I knew that, but first I needed
to explain my vision, describe its unfolding in the fullness of
New England time. I drove to work and called my new business
partners. I told them it was an emergency and demanded they
rush to the mill. Bring a video camera, I said. We need documentation. I had my carpenter take a break, cleared our tools off
a bench, and pushed back the tables. I scavenged the building for
various props—a block and tackle, iron wheels, art books, and

ancient machinery. The bookstore had been given a beautiful scale model of the mill, cut by a local model maker and assembled by an elderly town resident, that had made the cover of *Model Railroader;* in my hurry I dropped it down the stairs. I grabbed pine scraps from the café floor and paint, made signs, and placed them out front.

My new partners arrived. They were clearly annoyed. "So, Dave," Matthew asked, "what's this all about? What's going on?" His girlfriend Sarah glowered at me.

"You'll see," I said. "It's an installation. We need the camera. Did you bring the video camera? That's the main thing. Did you bring it?" He held it up and nodded. Good. I needed documentation; I needed proof I was right. I ran out and gathered an ad hoc audience of mystified customers. And then I jumped into my dramatic presentation of the mill's epic history.

"Welcome," I said, "and thanks for coming at such short notice. The mill is at a critical juncture in its long history. One that we all must recognize and honor. The building you stand in was built by Alvah Stone in 1832-ish. He ground grist here. This is a gristmill. Can anyone tell me what grist is?" No one raised a hand. "Of course not! I'm not surprised." I looked out over my nervous audience. They shifted anxiously; they whispered; they weren't prepared. "Quiet, everyone!" I commanded. "Please bear with me. I promise this will make sense." I desperately needed it to make sense. I lined items up on the workbench just as I had in Paul's apartment in East Palo Alto years earlier. I wanted a well-ordered defense, a windbreak for my flickering mind. I wanted to reassure my new partners, friends, and patrons that my free-form business plans, my vision for the old, venerated building,

made sense. "Quiet, please." I stared down my witnesses and returned to the broken scale model. "You see, the water ran through
this penstock and then into the turbines—"

"David," Sarah interrupted. "You're scaring the customers."

"No, I'm not." I looked at the small group remaining. "What?
Am I scaring you?" I bullied them. "This model's scary?" My
friends shook their heads unconvincingly; most left. My show
wound to an inconclusive close. A friend stepped up and called
the show brilliant and his girlfriend called me an artist. My rattled business partners were less impressed. They waited for me
outside. "So, what did you think?" I asked. "Did you get it all on
tape?"

"Yeah, Dave, we got it all on tape." Matthew looked at me
quizzically. "But, I don't know. It seemed a little, well . . .
incoherent."

"That's putting it mildly," scoffed Sarah.

I drew back. "No, it wasn't," I huffed. "It was not incoherent.
It was multimedia." I stomped off. My partners lacked vision.

Later that evening I crashed their potluck and jumped from
one conversation to another. I told my friend Mick the town's
selectmen wanted to close down the bookstore: "The old Yan-
kees in town hate the place. They'd rather have it empty and
haunted." I harangued a pregnant woman at length about cloth
diapers: "Disposable diapers are better for the environment, for
all of us. I have one word," I said after talking ten minutes.
"Bleach. Bleach is a killer." Afterward I returned to the mill, sat
at a window overlooking the river, and waited for ghosts. They
didn't show so I wrote them a letter: a sprawling historical poem
on the old mill and the Sunoco station nearby. I was grappling

with the Civil War when the store opened the following morning.

I knew I was fucked. I knew what was happening and I needed my family, I needed to get to Gloucester. I slipped out of the shop by a side door and drove home for some clothes, a few odds and ends. I managed the clothes and a toothbrush. I stayed focused and made it past all my books, past my music and photos. I pushed out to the truck but the barn caught me. I went in for some fishing gear and came out with a plan. I dragged out my skiff and slid it onto the bed of my truck. I decided to take my family by surprise, to approach Lane's Cove by sea with my skiff flying black flags and bones. I wanted smoke bombs and bottle rockets and considered a fireworks run to New Hampshire. Cherry bombs, roman candles, and quarter sticks—the kids would just love it.

I was lashing all my gear down when three friends pulled up beside the truck. "Where are you going, Dave?" my friend Kate asked. She's a therapist and she knew the score. She'd brought another close friend, Karen, and she brought Matthew, my business partner. All of them were obviously upset. At once I sensed they weren't thinking clearly and acted quickly. I sat them down in my kitchen and tried talking sense.

I talked over them, refusing to listen until Kate dropped the bomb and said, "Just face it, Dave. You're manic." And then I looked down. I was a cartoon; I was Wile E. Coyote run past the cliff and just hanging. I looked down and I plummeted. Poof.

"David, are you taking your lithium?" I sat frozen and finally quiet. Lost. "David?"

"Huh? What?"

"Lithium."

I looked up at Kate. I held her eye and bluffed. "Hypomanic," I said. "I'll give you hypomanic. Slightly hypomanic." I knew I couldn't bullshit her. I stood up, shirtless and scraped from hoisting my pirate skiff. "That's it," I said. "I'm not full-blown."

"Are you taking your lithium?" I shook my head. Suddenly I wanted to get better. Mania wasn't fun anymore. It wasn't creative or visionary. It was mean parody at best, a cheap chemical trick. I needed to stop and get better. I'd take whatever they gave me, I pledged silently. I'd take Trilafon or Thorazine or whatever. I just wanted to sleep.

Kate called my psychiatrist, Dr. Bryant. She made an emergency appointment for the morning. She left messages for Roberta in Gloucester. Matthew spent a sleepless night standing watch and in the morning delivered me to the doctor. His waiting room had always seemed pleasant, a few depressives, a few embarrassed neurotics, but reasonably pleasant. Apparently I was scheduled on the more hopeful days, the good-prognosis days. It was an entirely different kind of waiting room I had been squeezed into that morning. It was filled with heavily sedated, chronic patients—schizophrenics and the permanently damaged. I just sat in the chair next to Matthew, thinking: This isn't me; this isn't me; this isn't me.

Roberta returned that afternoon and relieved Matthew. At first she seemed skeptical and, quite frankly, peeved at the whole business. I hadn't been manic for years, she reasoned. It was an anxiety attack and my friends were exaggerating. David could have driven to Gloucester but no, they hauled the whole family back from the beach. It was just drama.

That defense fell apart in the driveway, as soon as she saw my eyes. I was terrified and I told her. "It's not good. I'm not well. I'm sick mostly and I think I fucked up." The kids were hungry and cranky right out of the car. I hugged them and hoped they were still happy to see me, that they weren't scared. I carried Hunter inside and bounced off the walls with him as Roberta made lunch. She was nervous and I tried to reassure her. It wasn't a crisis, not really. She was angry, too. She'd had the kids for a week straight and now she had me. The kitchen was trashed and it looked like I hadn't eaten in days. She pulled out some frozen burritos. She sliced open the packages hurriedly. I came close; she slipped and cut her thumb open. She cursed and threw the food down. She turned to the sink, flushed her hand with cold water, and the stacked dishes swirled pink. Hunter and Mary began crying.

"Dammit. It needs stitches. I've got to get stitches." She had started to panic. My fear was contagious. I tried to slow down.

"It's okay, Roberta. Stitches are not a big deal. I'm fine. I'm all right. Okay? I'm all right. Just go get some stitches. We'll be fine."

"Really? You're okay?" she asked fast.

"I'm okay," I said. I was shaking. Nothing will happen. I'm crazy but I'm really all right. "The kids will be fine. They're happy to see me."

"You stay here with the children and I'll run down to Dr. Allen's. That'll be faster than the emergency room. You'll be okay. I'll call. The food's on the counter, all right? All right, David?"

She held my shoulder and caught my eyes. "David, you'll be fine with the kids." I nodded. Of course.

Roberta rushed out of the kitchen and the three of us stood there. "Mom's going to be fine," I said. "It's not a big deal. There's nothing to worry about." Hunter latched onto my leg. I looked over at Mary. She had stopped crying and was watching me, and I wondered if she knew. "Mom's going to be fine," I repeated, stalling until I could focus. Lunch. Hunter wouldn't let go and I lurched over to the counter with him. I pushed the burritos into the microwave and pushed four seconds. It beeped and I jumped. Dammit. Four minutes. Careful, now, conservative. I'd move slowly, that's all. I knew I was sick. I wasn't right but I'd just move slowly. I pushed my mind down and stared at the ticking machine, waiting for the beep. Hunter let go and he and Mary moved into the living room. I poured out some milk. How could she do this? How could she leave me with the children? What if something happened? What if I ran off? What if I scared them? Fuck.

"Dad. Hey, Dad," Mary yelled. "Hunter just took my clay. He's throwing it."

"No, I'm not." Hunter started screaming. I charged in. Mary had her brother's arm as she peeled green bits of clay from his hand.

"Mary," I yelled angrily, "let go of your brother this instant. Goddammit. He's only four. Just share with him." I was shaking again. I stopped and sat down on the couch. Both kids stared at me. I couldn't look them in the eyes. The microwave beeped and I jumped. "Okay?" I said quietly. "Just share. Please. I can't handle this now. I just can't." I took deep breaths and sat with the children silent and watching. Hunter's screams and the bickering, Roberta's cut thumb and the microwave—all of this was sudden and loud and it lit up my head, shot me full of adrenaline and fear. My heart pounded and my mind rushed through the house.

I stood. "All right, come on, let's go out on the porch." I had to keep them happy. If I kept them happy they wouldn't scream. I wouldn't scream; I wouldn't lose it. "Mary, you bring the clay and we'll make stuff." Mary smiled and grabbed her plastic bag full of clay balls. Hunter laughed and followed her out to the porch. The kids were fine, I thought. They were happy to see me again, even now, even like this. I smiled after them. I heard them laughing just past the screen door. I was overcome with love and I started to cry. "Goddammit, Dave," I said softly. "Pull it together." I wiped my eyes and walked outside. "Okay," I said loudly, deci- sively. "Okay. Listen, we're going to make stuff out of clay."

Mary looked at me quizzically. "We know that, Dad. We al- ready are." She and Hunter already had two snakes and a horse between them.

"Okay," I said again, and I sat down and crossed my legs. I concentrated and made a red car with blue wheels. I made a goat. These kids deserve better, I thought. They deserve better than a fucked-up father who yells and cannot be trusted. What was I thinking? I can't have kids. I'm too sick. My family's too sick. What if they find out? What if something happens? Roberta doesn't understand. How could she? She just left me here. I looked at little Hunter and I wanted to cry.

I brought out the phone. "I'm going to see how Mom's doing," I said. I called down to the doctor and got a recording: *"If you want to schedule an appointment, push one . . ."*

"Oh, goddammit," I said.

Mary looked up. "What, Dad? What's wrong?" She knew already. She knew I was wrong.

"Nothing, darling. Nothing. Keep playing. That's a nice... whatever it is."

"Elephant."

"Right.

"... for prescription refills, press two; for referrals, press three. If this is a medical emergency, hang up and dial nine-one-one."

Christ. I hung up and dialed 911. "Hello, this is Officer Blaine of the State Police. This call is being recorded. How can I help—" I hung up fast. Shit. What the hell was I thinking? State troopers. They're the worst—fucking Nazis. I stepped off the front porch, away from my children. I was panicking and I didn't want them to see. Officer Blaine called back.

"Who am I speaking with?" Oh, shit. "Listen, we're sending a car out now. Hello?"

"Please don't send a car," I said. "Everything's fine."

"State your name and the reason for your call."

"David Lovelace. I'm David Lovelace. Look, everything's fine. My wife just cut herself, that's all. She's at the doctor's and I'm—"

"What doctor?"

"Dr. Allen in Amherst. Listen, I'm here with the kids—"

"Are they all right?"

"Will you fricking let me finish? They're fine, they're fine." I turned back toward the porch and found Mary right behind me. "Mary, go help your brother. I need you to help your brother." I scooted her back toward the porch, away from me. "Look, I didn't mean to call nine-one-one. I was just trying to get a hold of my wife at the doctor's. It was a mistake. Please don't send a car here."

"We already have."

"Look, it's like this. I'm bipolar. I'm, well, I'm a bit off, manic. I mean, I'm fine. But if you send a car I might lose it. Okay?" Officer Blaine waited a beat. "Hello, are you there?"

"I'm here."

I started pleading. I was terrified, standing on my summer lawn with my beautiful children and waiting for the worst—screams and guns and all of it. "Look, call the doctor. Call him now and my wife will explain." He agreed and, suddenly, he hung up.

"Is everything all right, Daddy?" Mary asked. "Are the police coming? Did you do something wrong?"

I pulled my children close and sat down on the grass. "No, darling, nothing is wrong. I'm fine. Your daddy's just fine. All of us, we're all doing fine." They both hugged me and held me and kept me from falling. Finally I said, "Mary, go get the clay and bring it out here. Let's make some more stuff."

I made a yellow dragon and then the phone rang. "David, this is Dr. Allen. What's going on up there? I just finished speaking with the State Police."

"Where's Roberta?"

"She's fine. I sent her home. Listen, she told me—"

"That I'm manic? I am. I can't have the cops—"

"They're not coming, Dave. Don't worry. Are you okay? Everything all right?"

Sure, I said, everything will be okay. I'm taking my medicine again. Thank you.

I ate my lithium and within a week or so I was level. I am fortunate to have friends with whom I can trust my history, who know how and when to intervene. That whole scary afternoon—the whole week—all of it was needless and stupid.

I called a meeting with my café partners and quit my own project. I was too humiliated and they were too scared to continue with me. It got emotional and Sarah raised her voice. "This whole thing was awful. Do you know what we did for you? Matthew had to spend the night at your house. We covered for you. Do you have any idea, any idea at all, of what you put us through?"

I did. I had a very good idea. I was out and that friendship ended. My family and I drove back to Gloucester and I went rowing and fishing. I built sand castles with Mary and Hunter, and we built fires and boiled lobsters and mussels down on the rocks. I had scared my family and friends; the episode cost me a business and a friendship, but it clarified things. I now know for certain that my mind and emotions, my fix on the real and my family's well-being, depend on just a few grams of salt. But treatment's the easy part. Without honesty, without a true family reckoning, that salt's next to worthless.

Shame fosters the denial that guarantees a return. Without treatment the episodes get worse, the cycle speeds up. Two years after my café break, my family got slammed again—the double-header with my Dad through the roof and my mom on the floor. It was easy to save my mother's life—just call 911. But once she was saved, it took all my family's compassion, every ounce, for us to recover. It took all my bipolar experience—both real and delusional—to feel my way through this horrible house of genetic mirrors, to understand and not simply react. I'm still angry; we all are. We are all still recovering.

My mother was dying; she was slipping away. It was a straightforward medical emergency, and the hospital moved fast. My father was slipping as well, but differently, strangely. He wasn't bleeding, he wasn't hurt. It wasn't his appendix or his heart that landed him in the ER. It was his brain. Bipolar disorder is a brain disease, but too often the health care system—the insurance companies, the lawyers, and even some doctors—blame the mind. To many in the ER, my father's illness was his fault, some moral weakness, something shameful. It wasn't really medical, it was emotional. It was subjective, his treatment a legal quagmire. Bipolar disorder, many insurance companies argue, cannot be covered because it cannot be proven. It won't show up in an autopsy, they say. My father wasn't dying and so the hospital sent him home, twice.

On the third day he locked his apartment door and hid. I moved back to the patio and spied on my father as he paced through trashed rooms. I began tapping on the glass door. I stood there and banged on it until my father had had enough and stepped out.

"Dad, we've got to go back," I said. "To the hospital. We can see Mom." Mom was my trump card.

He looked me square in the face and said slowly, "I am not going to the hospital. I'll see her later. I am going to church to pray for your mother." And then he took off, cutting through backyards and cul-de-sacs. I kept up with him and reasoned frantically. He waved me off and I fell back and tailed him.

When we got to the church my father climbed the steps, turned, and said, "Don't come in here. You're not welcome."

"Ah, come on, Dad," I pleaded impatiently. "I'm not fooling around." He turned and opened the door. "What?" I asked angrily. "Are you claiming sanctuary or something? That doesn't work, Dad. This isn't a war." He just turned and went inside. I followed but lost him. I wandered the church until I found the pastor's office. I heard laughter, knocked, and found them both drinking coffee.

My father gestured at me proudly. "Dan, this is my son, David Lovelace."

The minister stood and assessed me. "Very pleased to meet you, David. Your father has told me a great deal about you."

"No doubt," I replied.

"Please, sit down and join us."

"I'd rather not. I'd rather take my father over to Cooley Dickinson. My mother is there."

"I'm sorry to hear that. I trust she's all right?" The minister looked toward my father and he started to speak but I cut him off fast.

"She's not. Not really. She's in the ICU," I said. "I have to take my father to the hospital."

"I'm fine, Dan," my father chimed in. "There's no reason on earth for me to go to the hospital. Betty Lee is much better now and there's nothing wrong with me."

"With you, Richard?" the minister asked. "What could be wrong with you?"

"Nothing. Nothing at all. It's my son here—"

Now the minister cut him off. "Hold on, Richard. Let's see.

David, why don't you step out and give me a few minutes with your father?"

Thirty minutes later he found me outside on the steps. "Your father seems—"

"What? Crazy?"

"Well, excited, but…"

"Crazy. He's manic. He locked me out of their apartment so I broke in and found my mother lying on the floor unconscious. She'd been there for days. He was just singing hymns and mixing protein shakes."

The minister went white. "Oh. Well. I see."

"He's off, manic. I need to get him to the hospital, get him back on lithium." I caught my breath and slowed down. "Look, I need to get help. Can you see my father home?"

"Um, yes, I suppose. I'll try."

I thanked him, ran to my truck, and sped back toward the shrink's. I called my cousin Joanna en route, the same cousin I had called from Olympia, the same cousin who had helped commit me. She said I needed a Section Twelve, a doctor's order for involuntary psychiatric commitment. No more interviews, no more bureaucrat suckers drawn in by Dad's act. I arranged an emergency meeting with Dad's psychiatrist. I told Dr. Bryant I needed the order—no more phone calls, no more recommendations. Just Section Twelve—the men in white suits.

"Of course," Bryant said nervously. "I can't believe they refused to admit him. He needs hospitalization. I spoke with the hospital and made that quite clear."

"Yeah, well, it's been ridiculous," I complained, "just stupid. I don't blame my father for not going back. I don't want to go back, that's for sure."

"I don't blame you," Bryant said sympathetically.

"Why didn't we use a Section Twelve to begin with?" It was a rhetorical question. I knew the answer: lawyers. No one wants to sign committal papers.

"A voluntary commitment is preferable, less traumatic, and two days ago he was willing. They should have admitted him immediately upon my recommendation." Bryant produced the dread Section Twelve and signed it. "Look, this will work. If they don't have beds this time we send him to Holyoke. We need him safe. Take this to the Northampton police."

"The cops?" He nodded. "That's good." The men in white coats were cops and they were the good guys. My world was a jumble.

"Yes, they'll need this and they'll call for the ambulance. This will go fast, I promise you." He shook his head in exasperation. "I can't believe they put you through this." I nodded. I was exhausted. "How is your mother?"

"Still unconscious. Still in ICU. I don't know. Her signs are better, I guess. Stable. They thought it was a stroke but the MRI showed nothing."

"Well, I'm conferring with your mother's doctor there, making sure she has the right medications. Now let's take care of your father. Take this to the police station. And don't hesitate to call if you have questions or problems."

Section Twelve worked. It summoned a squad car to my father's apartment in ten minutes. I walked up with the police, explaining my dad as fast as I could. I saw his figure dart past a window and the living room lamp switched off, then the bed-room. One of the cops rapped on the door.

No answer.

"He's in there," I said.

The cop rapped again. "Mr. Lovelace, sir. I'm Sergeant James of the Northampton Police Department. Your son..." He turned.

"David."

"Your son, David, is here, sir. He's concerned. Could you come out, sir? We'd like to speak with you." Silence.

An ambulance swung in with its lights flashing. Great, I thought, that always helps. "You're not going to need handcuffs," I said to the cops. "Really." Right then my father opened the door calmly. He even worked up a smile.

"Gentlemen, David Lovelace," he said, "welcome." He ush-ered us in with a grand sweep of his arm. "As you can see, every-thing is wonderful here." Dishes were piled on the sofa; the place reeked. "Everything is wonderful," he repeated, stalling and shrugging his shoulders. He lifted his open hands to the police. It was showtime. He'd start with the shrugs and light banter and then he'd wow them with his Presbyterian book bag of tricks.

Not this time. Not with a Section Twelve. "Yes, Mr. Love-lace, sir. Mr. Lovelace, we are bringing you to Cooley Dickinson Hospital. They'll get you checked in."

"I've already spoken with them, numerous times. I've been there for days. Everything is fine. They sent me home already." My father rose up and said deliberately, "I am not going back."

The cop touched my father's elbow lightly. "I'm afraid you

need to go back, sir." My father stood scowling. "Now, sir." And then, quite suddenly, my father just smiled, shouldered his book bag, and walked to the ambulance.

We both returned to the ER with newfound confidence. My father knew the system; he'd tied it in knots. But I was ready this time. I had Section Twelve. My father went from the ambulance straight back. No waiting room this time. The triage nurses eyed me warily. They started to whisper. I was back again. Would I threaten a social worker this time or just take a swing at an orderly? I swaggered up to their counter, glowered at the meanest, most bureaucratic nurse of the lot, and spread out my paperwork, my royal straight flush.

"Oh," the nurse said. "I see."

"Could we expedite this process now?" I said with just a trace of malice. "Perhaps my father could see a *doctor* this time? Immediately?"

The nurse didn't flinch. She simply checked the form's signatures. "Yes," she said. "Of course, Mr. Lovelace. We do have a short intake procedure, I'm afraid. I'll get someone down to talk with your father immediately." She buzzed into the back. I sat beside my father's gurney. He had his wallet out and was shuffling through business cards. He said he wanted to call his lawyer. He said the whole church was praying for me—praying bad things, he said. He told me I was manic, that I needed help, and then he turned quiet. We had him dead to rights and he knew it. When the orderly wheeled Dad toward the elevator a nurse stopped me from following.

"It's better if you just see him later. It's easier this way," the nurse told me. "Go home and get some rest." She was right, of course. I couldn't help anymore. I didn't have any questions. There was nothing left to see and I knew the drill.

I didn't go home. I took the elevator up to intensive care instead. My mother was straight ahead and laid out by machines across from the nurses' station. She was awake. Her body lay still but her eyes darted over the room and bounced from my face. "Mom," I called softly. "Hey, Mom, it's David." Her eyes stopped on me and then her face relaxed. I saw her jaw work but her mouth seemed stuck, broken. I reached for some water and watched her eyes rattle away. I called a nurse.

"Betty Lee has been conscious for five or six hours now," she said, and picked up a cup. "She's still dehydrated. She hasn't spoken, not yet." She worked a straw past my mother's pasted lips. Mom's eyes grew wide and watched the nurse as she drank. I told her I loved her, that Dad was okay. I held her small hand—a dry, translucent leaf, a thin tangle of veins.

Over the following week my mother grew stronger and was moved from intensive care. Peggy flew in from Colorado; Jonathan and his family drove from Gloucester. I briefed them in the hospital lobby. I said, "Mom almost died and she looks it. She whispers some but she's confused. She's paranoid." I told them stroke had been ruled out by the doctors but her legs were weak, the left almost paralyzed. They had run all the tests. They weren't sure what had happened and Dad couldn't help. "All he keeps saying is that she seemed more herself, that she was getting better."

"Yeah, right," Peggy said. "Sure." We had our suspicions, and sadly, they all centered on Dad: maybe he messed with her medicine, gave her too many pills or none at all. My father had stopped taking lithium—that much was horribly apparent. I thought Mom had taken too much. I'd watched her suffer lithium poisoning once and it looked like this. It's too much that will kill you, I reasoned, not too little. I was wrong.

I led the Lovelace hospital tour. First stop was Mom. She was sitting up now and had the use of her arms. "Mom," I said, "look. Peggy and Jon are here with me."

"Really?" my mom asked softly, and brightened for a moment. There were flowers, boxed chocolates, and grave kisses. Peggy smoothed her thin hair. My brother and sister smiled at Mom but their shock was apparent. She had lost a great deal of weight. Her skull was visible and her eyes sank behind her cheekbones.

I opened the chocolates and popped them while Peg and Jon leaned over the bed. "Hi, Mom. Mom, it's me, Peggy. And Jonathan's here." I thought she wouldn't speak; I knew it was hard.

"What a surprise," she whispered, and closed her eyes with the effort.

"We came to see you, Mom," Jonathan said, "to see how you're doing." My mother saw or heard something, something other than us, and her brow crumpled with fear. "You had us all worried, Mom." She started blinking, clearly agitated. She forgot us.

"Mom, hey, Mom," said Peggy. "I see you have your Bible." Peggy picked up the worn leather book, filled with notes from before we were born. "Great."

My mother put her hands to her eyes and tried to speak.

"Her glasses," I said. "Shoot. I know, Mom. I forgot. I'll go get them right now."

"Don't let them see," she whispered.

"Let who see?"

"The nurses."

"The nurses? Mom, the nurses love you. They want you to have your glasses."

"No," she said, "no."

We leaned toward her with crooked smiles and said, Mom, the nurses love you, we all love you. We were afraid; she frightened us.

My mother looked away. "Where's Richard?"

"He's around, Mom. He's close," I said, and smiled ruefully at my sister. "He'll come and see you as soon as he can." I kissed her and turned to my brother. "Listen, I'm going to go and get her glasses. Dad's upstairs on the fifth floor. I've got to go. I'll see you later tonight."

I picked up her glasses, dropped them off with a nurse, and went home. I took Django, my daughter's puppy, up into the woods along old logging roads. Afterward the two of us just lay in the sun by the barn until my children ran from the bus stop and jumped us. It was simple, this happiness, and I felt it passing.

My father had gotten high, cut my mother's lithium, and replaced it with protein shakes. Without lithium my mother's fear came to kill her, and as my father marched fearlessly—even happily—into psychosis, my mother withdrew into a stupor. By the time my father had become God's own physician—his wife's only healer—she was catatonic. Her mind had retreated to hell. She

lay on the floor for days, unable to move, but she was never coma-
tose. It's even possible that on some level she remained conscious
through the ordeal. My mother regressed to a primitive state:
mute, unable to move, literally frozen with fear. She erased herself. She fell down into the pit, closed her eyes, and drifted toward
death while my father sang hymns, while he prayed over her.

"The good news," a doctor told us, "is that it wasn't a stroke. A
stroke could have disabled her permanently. We've been hydrat-
ing her and feeding her intravenously. Now she's eating solid
food. We've got her back on her medications—lithium and
Seroquel—and that should help get her out of the woods."

"So," my sister said after the doctor had left, "that's the good
news. Dad took Mom off her meds and let her get sicker and
sicker."

"Dad was high as a kite," I countered. "You can't blame him."
And so Peggy and I played a high-stakes hand in an old, familiar
game. I defended Dad and she stood in for Mom.

"Dad made the decision to ditch all the meds before that—
before he got sick," my sister countered. "He watched her get
worse."

"So did I, Peg. I mean I drove her to Rockport like that. She
was in a stupor. I saw her like that and I didn't do a damn thing.
I went camping in Colorado, for Christ's sake."

"Nah, Dave, it wasn't just you," Jonathan said. "I was there,
too, practically the whole family. I didn't do anything. None of
us did. We let them go crazy."

"All right," Peggy said. "I'm sorry. It's pointless to blame anyone. We should just move on and see what comes next."

———————

A week later my mother's doctors sent her to a nursing home for rehabilitation. She was getting stronger. She still couldn't walk, but she could sit upright and feed herself. She always recognized Roberta and me and she was happy to see us, but we spent each visit keeping her demons at bay. They always returned after we left.

"There's a boy that comes out," my mother said. "Every night."

I leaned forward. "Who do you mean, Mom?"

"A boy, a little man comes out when you leave and he helps them."

"Who?"

"The nurses. They think I'm Jewish. They think I'm a Jew."

"No, they don't," I said. She nodded slowly. "So what? What does that matter?"

"The ovens." My mother held her curled hand close to her mouth. "The boy, he comes out from under my bed and he helps them."

"No, Mom. You know that's crazy. There's no boy. And the nurses all love you. You need to stop thinking like that. It's not true."

She made a grim smile. "Yes, well … you don't know. You're not here when it's dark."

She'd been in the nursing home two weeks when Roberta and the children brought her some clothes. "So how was it?" I asked over dinner. "How's Mom?"

"She was weird," Mary said, and looked down at her plate. "She said weird things."

"Well, she's still sick, sweetheart. Don't pay attention."

"She said the nurses skinned Django, Dad. She said they had Hunter locked up in a closet." Little Hunter looked up from his plate and laughed. I felt sick.

After work I'd drive to the hospital, stand at the fifth-floor lockup, and buzz. "It's too soon," the nurses kept saying over their intercom. "Your father won't see you." My sister had flown home and my brother was back in Gloucester when Dad finally relented. I entered with trepidation but I was pleasantly surprised. The ward wasn't bad; it was fine. Not as nice, perhaps, as my ward in Beverly but better than East Palo Alto. It was bright and lacked the sick, antiseptic smell of the hospital's other floors. I saw my father before I reached the nurses' station. He was beaming.

"David! Come in." He put his hand on my shoulder and introduced me to the nurses. "This is my son, David Lovelace. He's the reason I'm here." All was forgiven, apparently, but not forgotten.

"Well, not exactly, Dad." I laughed nervously and the nurses all smiled. My father was popular. It was good to see him.

Dad pulled me toward his room. "Come on, come on. Let me introduce you to my roommate, Franklin." Franklin wasn't there. "Oh, where'd he go now?" my father muttered. "Wait here. I'll go find him." The room was small, just enough room for two single beds, two dressers and end tables. My father returned hauling a young white guy with dreadlocks. "Here he is," he said proudly. "Here's Franklin." Franklin smiled sheepishly. "We've been having great theological discussions. Isn't that right, Franklin?"

"Sure. We've been talking a lot about, um, music. And things."

"Franklin's a musician. He plays reggae."

"Really?" I said. "What instruments do you play?"

"Well, um, all of them pretty much. Like church." Franklin was sweet and vague. He was confused—I could see that already—but open and friendly, just like a kid. I wondered about his label. Was he schizophrenic or just a doped manic? In Beverly I befriended a schizophrenic girl. The nurses warned me that I shouldn't get too close. They said I would get better but that she never would. I hoped Franklin wasn't schizophrenic. I liked him already.

"Music is a spiritual practice," my father explained, "even reggae music." He leaned toward me and dropped his voice. "It's a bit one-celled, musically, but it's quite spiritual. Franklin has reminded me of that." Franklin looked positively radiant. "And, just between you and me, Franklin's also taught me that just a little marijuana can be helpful. Ritually, of course."

I smiled. "Well maybe, Dad, but I don't think now's the time to go—"

"Of course not, of course not, David." He swept his hand toward the hall. "I mean, pot's not even allowed in here."

"So. You've been talking about Rastafarianism?"

"Sure, why not?" My father smiled and shrugged.

"Hey," Franklin asked me. "You want to see Jesus Christ?"

"Sure," I said, and glanced at my father. "Who doesn't?"

He rummaged through his dresser and found what he was looking for, a shirt tie-dyed red, green, and yellow. "Here," he said, pointing at a poor silk-screened likeness. "Here he is."

"Who's that?"

"Haile Selassie. Jah. He's Jesus Christ."

"Oh. Well I suppose you—"

"And why not?" My father chimed in supportively. "You say tomato, I say tomato. *À chacun son goût.*" I laughed and I wanted to hug them both, right then. My father was sick—he wasn't thinking clearly—but he was well enough to love his odd bed-fellow, to find room in his world for Franklin, reggae, and Haile Selassie. I knew my father's reserve, his doctrinal and personal boundaries, would return, but at that moment one of my father's great gifts, his love for artists and outcasts, shone through and I loved him.

My father stood up and started gathering items from his bed, his glasses, his Bible, and his socks. "So, David, let's get out of this place. I shouldn't be locked up in here. Your mother needs me and they won't let me see her."

"Dad, she's getting better. Don't worry. You need to get better, too."

His face darkened. "I'm not leaving? You're not here to pick me up? I'm not even sick! You tricked me in here. Even the nurses know that."

"Dad, you're still a little manic. The lithium will kick in soon and you'll see." I knew my visit was over and I stepped toward the door. "Nice to meet you, Franklin," I said, and Dad pushed me out.

A few days later the hospital released him. "We can't hold him any longer against his will. We would have to bring him to court, get an order," they told me. "He'll just tie the judge into knots. I'm sorry, but we have to release him."

"Even when he's sick," I said.

"Even when he's sick. We can't hold him. The trick is to keep him on his medications. He is getting better. Incrementally."

True. The next morning, before I picked him up, Roberta and I cleaned my parents' apartment thoroughly. I threw away the foul foam rubber scraps that had cushioned my mother. I stripped her bed and threw out the sheets. Roberta washed the kitchen floor and emptied the fridge. I took all my father's papers and spider-scrawled notes to a box in the basement. I couldn't close his book on Goya. It seemed wrong so I left it propped on the living room chair, still open to the crucified Christ and my dad's marginalia. I flushed the old pills with dark satisfaction: the antipsychotics and antacids, the nameless pretty capsules, all the herbal cures and the vitamins. I placed his new prescriptions neatly in the empty bathroom cabinet. I took note of their pill counts and dosages.

When I got to the hospital, my father was in high spirits. "I'm glad," he said to the nurse while signing the paperwork, "that we've straightened out this whole mix-up." She didn't reply; she just shuffled his forms and asked him to sign.

"This is for your watch, Richard. Also your wallet and keys. And this one indicates why you were admitted."

"Whoa. Wait a minute," my father said. "Let me look at this." He picked up the sheet and it shook with his lithium tremors. "This isn't right. I'm not signing this. It says I was manic."

"Dad, you were. You still are. You're getting better but you're still not right. Just sign it. And promise that you'll take your meds. Even the Seroquel. Swear it to this nurse or you won't get out." My father looked at the uncomfortable nurse, who stared at me. "Go ahead, Dad."

"All right, fine. If that will make you happy I'll sign it. I'll humor you."

"And the meds?"

"Fine. I'll take them, although I think you should remember your place. I'm your father."

He insisted on seeing my mother straightaway and I drove him directly to the nursing home. He kissed Mom's forehead and her face lit up. She needed him. They prayed quietly until dinner. The nurse brought the tray in and my father took it and spoon-fed my mother. Afterward my father went quiet and Mom's eyes filled with tears. The three of us sat together until the nurse came to dress her for bed.

I drove my dad back to the apartment and watched him take his meds. "I'll get you some food in the morning," I said. "I can't do it now. Okay, Dad? I'll be back around breakfast."

"Oh, Dave, that won't be necessary. I've got the car keys. I'll get something on my way over to Mom's."

"Okay, Dad," I said, too tired to argue about the car. "Good night."

My mother languished in the nursing home through Christmas and on into January. The nurses tried their best for her, but the place worked on her fears. Her paranoia took root and flourished there, among the dying and confused. She couldn't recover there, not fully. She missed my father terribly; she needed him whole. Mom needed him more than level, much more than sane. She needed him honest, strong enough to learn from the crisis.

Instead his hypomania lingered and he became Mom's righteous advocate. He argued with the staff and pasted instructional Post-its all over the room, on the walls, doors, and bathroom mirror: "Remember Vitamin B! Do Not Put Glasses in Drawer!" He clipped articles on the health industry and taped them up for the nurses: tales of inefficiency, bureaucracy, pharmaceutical profits, and nursing home horrors. He observed my mother's physical therapy sessions skeptically and began interfering. I heard the complaints and spoke with him but it did no good. He was finally banned from the room when he brought in a jack-knife and whittled sharp sticks.

I became my mother's health care proxy, filling out forms in the office downstairs while Dad prayed over her bed. He missed her so much and he sat with her faithfully. He came every afternoon and stayed throughout dinner. While he stood watch I cased his apartment, checked his refrigerator, and counted his pills. He was eating pretty well; the pill counts kept dropping, but he stayed pretty high. I used to sit outside in my battered old truck and just punch at the dash. I joined a gym near my mother and pushed its machines till my pain felt simple.

My father contacted one of those swank, condolike clusters offering assisted care to the wealthy. He was excited and brought me right over. I was impressed; it was nice. The sales manager was pleasant and dressed in a pantsuit. The glossy literature explained that a one-time entrance fee was required at the time of acceptance. It was the size of a mortgage.

"As you can see, gentlemen, we do require a financial report. It's our way of making certain Pheasant Ridge is affordable."

"Of course, of course." My father waved it off. "That's understandable in this day and age. That won't be a problem. I have considerable investments in British gold sovereigns and—"

"Right," I said. "Thank you very much. You've given us plenty to consider."

My father could not be dissuaded. He kept up the pressure. He took their tours and studied their waiting list. He had found a way to save Mom. I took the sales team aside and told them the fiscal truth. They stopped answering his calls after that.

My mother was still heavily sedated; she rested in half dreams but I watched the fear move through her face like dark weather. One afternoon my father arrived looking well. He seemed almost focused and he emptied his book bag with purpose: a white sleeve of saltine crackers, one can of tomato juice drink, and *The Book of Common Prayer*, Episcopal. He announced to the nurses, who ignored him by now, that the Eucharist would be celebrated at five p.m. in room 242. All were welcome. No one came but my mother's roommate Alice, age ninety-six. She had to come; she was bedridden. Dad read beautifully from the book, his voice solemn and fearful. He made the sign of the cross over my mother and I tore open the crackers. He made it again and I gave him a coffee cup filled with Christ's blood. I found him a straw. And then I stayed back like an altar boy does. I was too young and too angry for something so holy. I left my parents still praying, got in my derelict truck, and drove home.

Weeks passed and then my father was sane. He acted appropriately and efficiently. He found a new, one-floor apartment that was perfect for Mom. He arranged all the details, worked

out the lease, and stored extra furnishings. He bought new bed-
spreads and blankets. He met all the social workers and signed
up for health aides and meals. He had all of Peniel, all their old
friends, praying for Mom. I helped him hang my mother's paintings and sort her supplies. By the time she returned it was home.
Mom had visibly aged in the five months she was gone, but she
was happy again. She was glad to be home where she belonged,
with Richard, her husband. Now, two years later, my mother is
unsteady at times but rarely needs her walker. My father drives
her to the hairdresser and does all the laundry and tries his best
to cook. They are devoted to each other and God. When I drop
by there is opera and politics and always the Bible. They're
happy, I think.

I know our disease. I deserted my family and ran from it. I denied
it three times and refused it. All that drama may seem pointless
and sad but it taught me. I know the empathy borne of despair; I
know the fluidity of thought, the expansive, even beautiful, mind
that hypomania brings, and I know this is quicksilver and precious and often it's poison. There has always existed a sort of psy-
chic butcher who works the scales of transcendence, who weighs
out the bloody cost of true art. Any list of the great artists who
suffered from manic depression is both impressive and macabre:
Anne Sexton, Percy Bysshe Shelley, Virginia Woolf, Vincent van
Gogh, John Berryman, Paul Gauguin, Robert Schumann, Sylvia
Plath, Arshile Gorky, Herman Melville, Gustav Mahler, Robert
Lowell, Charles Mingus—a list full of asylums and addictions,
depressions and suicides and exquisite beauty.

I know all this, but no one—not me, not the sick or their doctors, their families or priests—will ever understand this sickness, its magic and rot. My brother and I have spent years strung between its two poles and we can't explain it to our sister and wives or demark the distance between heaven and hell, between our father and mother that autumn.

My father's psychosis was murderous. He watched and he prayed while Mom slipped into darkness. He could have phoned the family but he called upon God. He swept away lithium and ascended into the clouds while my mother lay on the floor and watched him from hell. Mom was getting better, much more herself, and Dad felt great, never better. Before that, before he felt great, my father kept his demons at bay with prayer and medicine. After Hamilton, he sutured the great sucking wound made by his long sadness. He cauterized the stumps and buried the parts. He's never spoken of it, at least not to me. Once I asked him if he had lost God during those years and what it was like. He answered with shock and bluster, like such a commonplace loss was unthinkable, impossible. I've asked what bipolar illness has done to him and he waves it away like an inconvenience, one extra errand, one more prescription to fill. I fear he may never forgive himself. He may never forgive our illness.

It's difficult. I take a low dose of lithium nightly. I take an antidepressant for my darkness because prayer isn't enough. My therapist hears confession twice a month, my shrink delivers the host, and I can stand in the woods and see the world spark. Twenty-two years ago I loved my family but I started running. Now my children are growing and I cannot hide. I can't hide this disease or unmake this knowledge or swallow the whim-wham niceties, the euphemisms. Love is not enough. It takes courage to grab my father's demon, my own, or—God help me—my child's and strap it down and stop its mad jig; to sit in a row of white rooms filled with pills and clubbed dreamers and shout: stop smiling, shut up; shut up and stop laughing; you're sitting in hell. Stop preaching; stop weeping. You are a manic-depressive, always. Your life is larger than most, unimaginable. You're blessed; just admit it and take the damn pill.

ACKNOWLEDGMENTS

Thanks to my parents, my brother, and my sister for their courage and the trust they placed in this project. Thanks to Roberta and my children for humoring and supporting me through it. I want to thank Susan Shilliday for use of the cupola, Karen Chapman for her encouragement, and Dori Ostermiller for demanding new chapters. Thanks to Bill Monahan for his certainty; my agent, Byrd Leavell, for his vision; and my editor, Ben Sevier, for his clarity and insight.

David Lovelace is a writer, carpenter, and former owner of The Montague Bookmill, a bookstore near Amherst, Massachusetts. His poetry has been nominated for a Pushcart Prize and *Paterson Literary Review*'s Allen Ginsberg Award. Lovelace lives in western Massachusetts with his wife and children.